Lou,

Best of Luck.

*[signature]*

# THE NASDAQ INVESTOR

# THE NASDAQ INVESTOR

Max Isaacman

**McGraw-Hill**
New York   Chicago   San Francisco
Lisbon   London   Madrid   Mexico City
Milan   New Delhi   San Juan   Seoul
Singapore   Sydney   Toronto

**Library of Congress Cataloging-in-Publication Data**

Isaacman, Max.
    The NASDAQ investor / by Max Isaacman.
        p.   cm.
    ISBN 0-07-136367-X
    1. Nasdaq Stock Market.  2. Stocks—Prices—Databases.  3. Stock exchanges.   I. Title.
    HG4574.2.I8   2001
    332.64'273—dc21                                                          00-048675

## McGraw-Hill

*A Division of The **McGraw-Hill** Companies*

Copyright © 2001 by The McGraw-Hill Companies, Inc. All rights reserved. Printed in the United States of America. Except as permitted under the United States Copyright Act of 1976, no part of this publication may be reproduced or distributed in any form or by any means, or stored in a database or retrieval system, without the prior written permission of the publisher.

1 2 3 4 5 6 7 8 9 0   AGM/AGM   0 9 8 7 6 5 4 3 2 1

ISBN 0-07-136367-X

*This book was set in Times Roman by Matrix Publishing Services.*
*Printed and bound by Quebecor World/Martinsburg.*

This book is not intended to give investment advice or recommendations or even a suggestion to invest in any of the markets. The author and the publisher assume no responsibilities for the investment results by an investor or trader who relies on information in this book. Before investing or trading, a person should consult a trusted investment counselor and work with him or her in accordance with the investor's risk profile.

　　The author may hold securities mentioned in this book. At the present time the author holds shares of CHK, ABT, MDY, MRK, JNJ, XOM, XLK, BIOI, WCOM, and IEV. The author may or may not hold these stocks when this book is published.

McGraw-Hill books are available at special quantity discounts to use as premiums and sales promotions, or for use in corporate training programs. For more information, please write to the Director of Special Sales, Professional Publishing, McGraw-Hill, Two Penn Plaza, New York, NY 10121-2298. Or contact your local bookstore.

This book is printed on acid-free paper.

# CONTENTS

**Introduction** *vii*
**Acknowledgments** *xi*

PART I
## NASDAQ AND THE NEW ECONOMY
1. Understanding the Nasdaq Market  *3*
2. The Nasdaq Explosion  *17*
3. The Internet Economy  *31*

PART II
## INDEXES, STOCKS, AND FUNDS
4. The Index and Exchange Shares  *53*
5. Internet, Technology, and Other Growth Sectors  *66*
6. Top Nasdaq-Weighted Funds  *89*

PART III
## STRATEGIES FOR TRADING ON THE NASDAQ
7. Discipline: The Key to Success for Long-Term and Short-Term Investing  *105*
8. Strategies for the Long-Term Investor  *115*
9. Strategies for the Short-Term Investor  *125*
10. Putting It All Together: Nasdaq and the Overall Portfolio  *139*
11. Behavioral Finance and Sentiment Shifts  *146*

## Part IV
## NASDAQ RESOURCES

Appendix A   Nasdaq Stocks with Low P/E Multiples   *167*
Appendix B   Stocks of the Nasdaq-100 Index (QQQ)   *185*
Appendix C   The Top 50 Cap-Weighted Stocks in the Nasdaq-100 Index   *189*
Appendix D   Nasdaq Stocks That Are in the S&P Indexes   *199*
Appendix E   Helpful Investor Web Sites   *214*
Appendix F   New-Economy Terms   *216*

**Index**   *219*

# INTRODUCTION

## A NEW MARKET TO ASSESS

About 10 years ago there was much discussion on Wall Street regarding the high valuations being put on stocks. The S&P 500 Index was valued at over 20 times earnings; this was a high valuation then, and lately the valuation has been much higher. There was much opining that stocks were too high and could not continue to stay at that lofty level, and were destined to decline.

Over the next year or so stocks continued at what many thought was too high a level. But what kept eating at people on Wall Street and investors and traders at home was that the market kept climbing. Especially strong were technology and health-care stocks, two sectors with much higher P/Es than customary; and money kept pouring into these sectors. I suspect that traders and investors knew that in the final analysis (as well as the first, second, and so on, analysis) the market is always right. Whatever the market says, by doing, is the final word.

The conflict that money managers and market participants had was that to make money they had to invest in sectors such as technology and biotechnology, and it no longer seemed reasonable to justify the price of these sectors with the usual yardsticks, such as P/E ratios and price-to-book ratios.

As the years went on, it became somewhat easier to justify prices in growth sectors. Moore's Law, among other studies, helped investors understand the built-in strength that the new economy kept exhibiting. Understanding the advances in genome research and other activities in the biotechnology area fed the growing conviction of many investors that something very new was afoot in the economy. Also the home prices kept soaring in Silicon Valley, one of the centers for technology, solidifying the notion that something new and real and big was stirring.

## MOORE'S LAW

Moore's Law is covered in Chap. 2 of this book. The law states that the power of technology will keep increasing, while the price for this power will keep decreasing.

With Moore's Law proving to be a reality, it is easier to understand the recent price increases of stocks in the technology sector. Tacking onto this price increase is the realization that perhaps never before have we had this confluence of events: a technological revolution that is industrial revolution sized, and a new type of stock market to trade the stocks, which is the Nasdaq market.

This is a major story. This book covers the issues that investors and traders and just perplexed people want covered.

## NEW VALUATION METHODS

Until the Nasdaq pullback in late 2000 and early 2001, it was estimated that about 20 percent of the Nasdaq market was made up of stocks above 100 times earnings. This is a very large percentage; usually investors are told to shun companies above 20 or so times earnings.

A way to justify buying stocks about 100 times earnings is by considering that valuation, but also looking at other ways to value stocks prices. As covered in this book, a P/E measurement is not the only way that companies are valued. If an investor had only used P/E ratios as a guide to purchase stocks, she or he would have missed out on many very large gainers. Many of the new-economy stocks do not lend themselves to be analyzed by a P/E ratio or other standard way of measurement.

Other ways to value stocks are sprinkled throughout this book. Using new ways of measuring stocks is not a new phenomenon. About 100 years ago, for instance, stocks had to yield more than bonds. Because of the risk of equity investing versus debt investing, investors would not buy stocks with yields that did not surpass bond yields. Stocks started going up in price, with their yields dropping below the yields of bonds. Some investors balked at buying stocks, figuring they would buy when conditions were "right."

Well, those investors who waited for conditions to right themselves, and did not buy stocks, would still be waiting. And they would have missed a subsequent great bull move. Growth stocks have not paid dividends for years, and they would be criticized if they did.

# RISK

No matter what valuation an investor uses, however, it is important when dealing with new valuation methods to remember that the market is a place for risk capital. The money that goes into the market should be funds not needed for a very long time, if ever.

Living through bear markets is no fun, as we are now seeing. Very few investors today, or even money managers, had experienced a market down-leg of any length of time until recently. There are bear market and down-leg strategies in this book. Do not be afraid to use them either as a hedge or as an aggressive trading posture. Bears as well as bulls make money.

As long as the knowledge that an investor's or trader's funds can be lost in the stock market is accepted, there is the element of realism. This element will have to be faced many times when dealing in the markets.

*Max Isaacman*

# ACKNOWLEDGMENTS

Thanks to my wife, Joyce Glick, for putting up with me typing into the late night; also thanks for the support of our family, Jon Edel Isaacman, Carrie Edel Isaacman, and Danielle Kaplan. A thank you to my friends at McGraw-Hill for their help in putting together this book: my publisher, Jeffrey Krames; his assistant, Laura Libretti; and my editor, Ela Aktay.

The following professionals contributed their time and effort, and they deserve acknowledgment:

- Karl Sternberg—Deutsche Asset Management, London
- Tony Denninger—Hewes Communications, Inc., New York City
- Charles W. Proses—Charles W. Proses Accountancy, San Francisco
- Michael Byrum—Rydex OTC Investor
- Garrett Van Wagoner—Van Wagoner Emerging Growth Fund
- Michael Schwartz
- Price Headley—BigTrends.Com
- Joseph Battipaglia, Kevin Caron—Gruntal & Company
- William H. Bales—Janus Venture Fund
- Alan J. Wargaski
- John Jacobs—Nasdaq Stock Market
- Lawrence Sterne—Internet.com
- Steve Bodurtha
- Robert D. Arnott—First Quadrant, Inc.
- Charles Allmon—Growth Stock Outlook
- William Schneider—Warburg Dillon Read
- Christine Nairn—E Offering
- Jonathan Edel Isaacman—Deutsche Securities

Safa Rashtchy

Douglas Patterson—Nasdaq Stock Market

Douglas Coté—Aeltus Investment Management

Robert Janus—Warburg Pincus Asset Management

Chip Bayers—*Wired* magazine

Terrance Odean

Kathleen L. Mitchel—Nasdaq Stock Market

My associates at East/West Securities in San Francisco—Leslie U. Harris, Dr. Charles Chen, Benedict Choi, Helen Lam, Wilson Chow, and Kevin Tam.

# PART I

# NASDAQ AND THE NEW ECONOMY

CHAPTER 1

# UNDERSTANDING THE NASDAQ MARKET

## BEFORE THE NASDAQ

To understand the Nasdaq market, it might be helpful to go back before the Nasdaq market was formed. Before 1971, if stocks were not listed on an exchange such as the New York Stock Exchange (NYSE) or the American Stock Exchange (Amex), they were traded over the counter (OTC). There was no Nasdaq market then. The OTC stocks were traded by dealers, as they are today. A dealer was, and is, a market intermediary who trades as a principal (for her own account) rather than as an agent (trading for others). Often, dealers are market makers; a market maker is a dealer who, on a regular basis, makes bids and offers and is ready to act on either side.

Because they quote bids and offers and stand ready to execute either side, market makers are in a risk position. And because of this risk position, market makers are the guts of the workings of any OTC market. To clear up any confusion: the Nasdaq market is *not* the national OTC market, but it is *an* OTC market.

By posting a bid/ask price, the market maker can lose money if a stock moves far in either direction. If the stock price rises the market maker has to sell his stock, limiting his participation in any rally. He may even have to short stock to meet demand, which means he will borrow stock to sell to buyers; he will have to buy the stock back later to close out his short position. This adds to his risk; if a short stock continues advancing, he will continue to lose on the short side; he will be forced to buy back borrowed stock at higher prices. Alternatively, if the stock price falls, the market maker will lose money on his inventory; the market maker must carry stock in inventory to sell to buyers; this stock will be worth less in market declines.

So why is the market maker making a market? Because most times there is a regular stream of buyers and sellers, buyers who take the stock at the offered price and sellers who sell at the market maker's bid price. The market maker makes her money on the small differences between the bid/asked prices. That difference is called the spread; for example, bid at 15, offered at 15¼. The market maker, if she bought stock at 15 could sell it at 15¼, making ¼.

## Pink Sheets and OTC Stocks

Dealers, before 1971, would circulate quotes on OTC stocks on pink-colored sheets of paper; a thick stack of this paper would be stapled together. These stacks were sent out to brokerage houses for use by brokers to relay quotes to their customers. Because of the pink paper used, the stocks listed were referred to as pink-sheet stocks. It didn't work all that well. I know. I was there. On a quote for stock, there is a bid side, which indicates at what price traders are willing to buy, and an ask side, which indicates the price at which traders will sell. Sometimes I would drop an order on the bid or ask side and not get an execution. So I would call the dealer and have to negotiate directly with him to get a trade-off. The "pinks" just weren't current.

Today the pinks are still published weekly by the National Quotation Bureau. The system is vastly improved; pink sheet stocks are updated daily over computer terminals.

There is also an OTC bulletin board (OTCBB) quote system. This system supplies quotes on stocks to its subscribers; the stocks are listed on a national "bulletin board." The OTCBB supplies quotes on over 6500 securities. Companies often list on the OTCBB to get some seasoning before applying to Nasdaq.

## Up to the Present: Regulation of OTC Stocks
The Securities Exchange Act of 1934 (amended) led to the creation of the National Association of Securities Dealers (NASD) in 1939. The NASD is the parent of the Nasdaq market. The NASD is a self-regulating body, and oversees the trading activity of Nasdaq, OTCBB, and Amex.

NASD set up a separate subsidiary in 1996 to separate the broker/dealer regulatory activities of the NASD from its active operation of the Nasdaq market. Regulation is an important activity for the NASD. The association regulates over 5000 member firms; these include over 50,000 branch offices at which are employed over half a million investment professionals.

The NASD strives to keep an open and public operation. Both the public and the NASD members are represented on the 33-member board of governors of the NASD: in 1999, there were 17 nonmember or public representatives and 16 industry or staff members on the board.

## WHAT IS THE NASDAQ?

There are two markets: the Nasdaq National Market and the Nasdaq Small-Cap Market. They are commonly lumped together and referred to as the Nasdaq market. Companies in the Nasdaq National Market are some of the biggest and best known in the world. Over 4100 securities are listed on the Nasdaq National Market; about 1400 securities are listed on the Nasdaq SmallCap Market. The SmallCap Market lists smaller capitalized companies, with less stringent financial criteria for listing. The SmallCap Nasdaq fulfills two functions for the national market: it allows companies that are small and growing to get some seasoning before moving up into the national market; it allows companies that have lost value to continue getting Nasdaq exposure until they are healthy enough to again move to the national market.

The corporate governance listing standards, however, are the same in either market. Some of the corporate governance standards that Nasdaq companies must meet are: they must have voting rights; certain corporate actions must have shareholder approval; proxies must be solicited; conflicts of interest must be reviewed; there must be a shareholder meeting annually; quorums must be used; there must be an audit committee, and independent directors must account for a majority; there must be a minimum of two independent directors; the companies must make available interim reports and distribute annual reports.

## Competing Market Makers

One of the features distinguishing the Nasdaq market from listed markets is that, like the other OTC markets, the Nasdaq has competing market makers. These market makers are independent dealers; they compete for orders from investors and traders by using Nasdaq's vast electronic trading market; the Nasdaq system uses cutting-edge technology and telecommunications, which allows trading competitors instant information.

Nasdaq's market makers commit their own capital in trading Nasdaq stocks. Nasdaq's market makers must belong to the NASD. Not all NASD member firms work as market makers; some NASD member firms work in areas such as general brokerage or investment banking. There are strict requirements to be a market maker on the Nasdaq:

1. The market maker has special capital requirements. These requirements are generally higher than the requirements for other OTC market makers.
2. The Nasdaq market maker must guarantee to execute each order at the best possible price.
3. The market maker must stand ready to buy and sell each security that she makes markets in.
4. Within 90 seconds, the market maker must publicly report each transaction, including price and volume.

The Nasdaq market maker must register with the NASD to make a market in the stock of a company. The Nasdaq has no limit on the number of market makers that can trade the stock of any one company. In some of the larger Nasdaq-listed companies there are more than 60 market makers. On average, about 10 market makers trade each of the companies listed on the Nasdaq.

Nasdaq believes that having competitive, independent market makers with high capital bases keeps the Nasdaq market liquid enough for both large institutions and the smaller traders.

Unlike most other OTC markets, Nasdaq market makers are required to display investors' limit orders which are better than the market maker's bid or offer; limit orders are orders that name a specific price that investors are willing to pay for or sell stock. For example, the present bid of a market maker may be 15, and an investor is bidding $15\frac{1}{8}$ against the market maker's bid. The market maker must display the 15⅛ limit order even though it is not the market maker's quotes. This rule has the effect of tightening the spread. Also the entire marketplace sees entire spreads and quotes.

### Electronic Communications Networks (ECNs)

To further enhance the liquidity of Nasdaq stocks, Nasdaq allows nine ECNs to operate within the network. ECNs are trading systems set up by broker/dealers; these traders are allowed to match new orders for Nasdaq stocks with orders they have in their own system. Also the ECNs display their quotes, allowing market makers an additional place to get market fills. To be considered for approval to trade within the Nasdaq system, an ECN must meet the following requirements:

1. Be a member of the NASD and be a registered broker/dealer.
2. Receive approval from the Securities & Exchange Commission (SEC) to operate as an alternative trading system (ATS).
3. Agree with the Nasdaq market contractual terms regarding the link of its ATS system into the Nasdaq network.

The network of market makers in the Nasdaq system includes the heaviest capitalized firms around the world. There are about 550 broker/dealers that make markets in Nasdaq stocks. These firms enhance the liquidity of Nasdaq stock trading.

Also regional broker/dealers make markets in Nasdaq stocks. Regional firms make markets in about 400 stocks, a smaller number than the major firms trade in. Additionally, there are firms that act as wholesalers; these firms make markets in about 4500 Nasdaq stocks. Wholesalers primarily deal with brokerage firms that do not make their own markets and with other financial institutions.

Nasdaq quotes go out to terminals in about 60 countries. Because of Nasdaq's state-of-the-art telecommunications networking and the broad market for Nasdaq stocks and the heavy capitalization of the Nasdaq market makers, Nasdaq stocks have deep liquidity.

## Broker/Dealers

A broker/dealer is a firm or individual who is acting as a principal in a securities trade. When acting as a principal, the dealer is at risk; the dealers are buying or selling stock for their own account and may lose money in the transaction. When you, as a customer of a broker who is acting as a dealer, buy or sell stock, you must be made aware that the dealer is trading to you out of his own inventory. You can ask the firm's representative in which capacity the firm is acting: as a principal or broker. The firm will tell you. Also, you will be informed on your trade confirmation.

Most firms operate as both brokers and dealers. Brokers are not at risk in a transaction; they merely charge a commission for facilitating a trade between the customer and a dealer.

So when you buy or sell a Nasdaq stock from a broker/dealer, the broker/dealer may trade out of his own inventory, acting as a dealer. Or the firm may simply go out to the different dealers and find you the best price, acting as a broker.

Usually Nasdaq stocks are more liquid than a pink sheet or OTCBB stock. If your broker is acting as a market maker, you might get a better trade in the stock because market makers profit from "order flow." When a market maker is in the order flow she is a factor in the stock's volume; the more volume a market maker transacts, the more people will come to her to trade. A market maker will try to get a trade completed if an order is anywhere near her quote.

If your broker is not a market maker in the stock, you can always go to another broker, one who is a market maker in the stock.

## Trading Systems for Listed Stocks versus Nasdaq Stocks

There are differences between the Nasdaq and the listed market system. A company will decide which exchange is best for it as far as listing requirements and listing costs. The factors a company considers include the liquidity its stock will receive, the relative prestige of the various markets, and the attention given the company by the exchange once it is listed.

To list on the New York Stock Exchange (NYSE), a company must meet stringent requirements. These requirements include earnings, size of the company represented by market capitalization, number of outstanding shares, and others. The requirements are the most stringent in the world. Once companies are listed on the NYSE, they must continue to maintain minimum standards. In the past, it was assumed that because of the prestige of listing on the New York Stock Exchange, the liquidity of having an NYSE listing, and other factors, the NYSE was the choice place to list.

The Nasdaq market also has listing and maintenance requirements, though not as stringent as the NYSE.

Nasdaq's dealer system has market makers competing for customer orders, with the market makers using their own capital. With the diversity and number of market makers, both large and small investors and traders can usually find a market maker that suits them.

CHAPTER 1   UNDERSTANDING THE NASDAQ MARKET

The Nasdaq way of trading is a dealer system, that is, the dealers following an electronic market, which is shown on computer screens across the world. The market is not located in any one location as are listed exchanges. The New York Stock Exchange (NYSE), for instance, has its trading floor located in New York City.

Nasdaq is an open, *negotiated* market as opposed to a listed market. A negotiated market can have more volatility than a listed market because there is no central person to trade a company's stock; in a negotiated market there is no open outcry of bids and offers as there is in the listed system. Bids and offers and trades flashed simultaneously to over half a million computers around the globe create the volatility in the Nasdaq market.

## *Listed Stocks*

Listed stocks, that is, stocks that trade on exchanges, trade in an *auction* system. In that system one specialist is assigned to match buy and sell orders in an orderly fashion to maintain a continuous market. Unlike negotiated markets, listed market trading revolves around one person, the specialist.

The specialist, when she has to keep an orderly and fair market, acts as a dealer; in this capacity she buys and sells stock for her own account. The specialist also acts as a broker at times; in this capacity the specialist will execute orders for others. Orders can be electronically sent to the specialist or physically given to the specialist by other exchange members.

The specialist raises and lowers her bids and offers to effect changes in the market quote. In her quotes, the specialist has to stay fairly close to the bids and offers coming from others; if she strays too far off the price at which others are willing to trade, she will be away from the flow; then she will have to buy or sell for her own account to make an orderly market.

The specialist makes her money by taking small amounts, if she can, from each trade: a $1/32$ or $1/16$ or $1/8$ of a point. The specialist is risking her own money when trading as a dealer. Think of the trader as an auctioneer, advertising the price at which stock can be bought and sold through her. Through this method she brings buyers and sellers together.

The specialist doesn't participate in every trade done in her stock; but all trades are done at her "location" on the floor. Trades can be made in her stock electronically, with orders matching and executing. She would see the trades completed on her computer screen. Brokers also match orders against her "book." The specialist's book is shown on monitors and the information is public knowledge. Also brokers on the floor walk over to her location and trade the stock among themselves. So the specialist, even though not engaged in every trade, is still cognizant of the order flow in her stock.

There are differences in the ways the OTC and listed markets trade. Which market is better is debatable. They both have advantages and disadvantages. To most investors and traders, which market to trade is not that big a factor. The stock being traded is the overlying factor.

Some observers opine that the specialist system on the NYSE, pulling everybody into one location, has served as a dampening influence on volatility; the dealer-to-dealer market spurs more competition. There are many market markers in the big stocks such as Microsoft, Intel, Cisco Systems, and Oracle. When you have that many competing market markers it makes the market more fragmented, which favors volatility. In fragmented markets there are more ways to play the market, such as buying stock from one dealer and shorting that same stock to another dealer, thereby arbitraging price differences.

Understanding differences between the markets and which orders can be placed in each market may help your investment and trading performance. For example, certain orders, such as stop limit orders, can be placed on listed stocks but not on Nasdaq.

## *The Spread*

The spread is the difference in the bid/asked quote. Different types of spreads can affect trading of Nasdaq stocks.

Market makers post quotes electronically; the quote is the price they will pay for stock and at what price they will sell stock. A quote could be, say, 49 to 49¼. The difference between the bid/asked, ¼ of a point, is known as the *dealer* spread. This spread does not mean that the market maker will make a quarter; the market maker had to buy stock for inventory for use on the sell side; you don't know what he paid for that stock. Also the market maker may be buying stock for several reasons. He may be covering a short, for instance, and may have a loss in the short cover. Also, if he buys stock to go long at 49, he doesn't know the price at which he'll sell the stock. So each market maker has different reasons for his posted quote; because of this, rarely is a market maker the highest bid and lowest offer at the same time.

So a trader or investor will check the bid/asked quotes over the Nasdaq market makers, finding the highest bid at one dealer, the lowest offer at another. Say the highest bid on an issue is 49¹⁄₁₆ and the lowest offer is 49³⁄₁₆. That means the best prices throughout Nasdaq are 49¹⁄₁₆ to 49³⁄₁₆. This spread, ¹⁄₁₆ to ³⁄₁₆, is known as the *inside* spread.

The narrowest spreads are the *actual* spreads paid; this spread is based on completed trades. The spread is calculated by comparing the trade prices vis-à-vis the inside spread at the time the trade was done. This spread shows the difference of the inside spread against finished trades.

## GROWTH OF NASDAQ

The Nasdaq market has experienced spectacular growth for several years. As an example, Nasdaq increased its total trading dollar volume by over 88 percent in 1999 versus 1998. The dollar numbers were $10.8 trillion in 1999 versus $5.8 trillion in 1998. In 1999, Nasdaq transacted 51 percent of the dollar volume of securities traded on the three major markets: the Nasdaq, the NYSE, and the American Stock Exchange.

The Nasdaq market trades more shares a day, at a higher dollar volume, than any other U.S. market. In fact, in terms of dollar volume, Nasdaq became the world's largest stock market in 1999, trading a total of $40 billion worth of shares a day; a Nasdaq record of 1.4 billion shares traded on April 14, 1999.

Nasdaq, for most of the year 2000, averaged about 1.5 billion shares a day, which is quite impressive. Also the number of Nasdaq trades that are fewer than 1000 shares as a percentage of total volume has been growing on Nasdaq. That indicates that a larger number of smaller investors are trading on the Nasdaq market. Serving the small investor are the broker/dealer firms. About 480 broker/dealer firms trade Nasdaq stocks; these firms took over 57,000 positions in 1998.

Tech is not the only sector in which Nasdaq is important. The Nasdaq market dominates the trucking industry: of the top 25 trucking companies in terms of market caps, 23 of them are on Nasdaq. Another industry dominated by Nasdaq is the wine industry: all the public wineries in California are listed on Nasdaq.

The requirements for stocks to list on Nasdaq are generally higher than the standards set in other OTC markets. The Nasdaq market is vast: about 5500 companies trade their stock on Nasdaq, and many of these are household names. The top five U.S. companies in terms of market cap are: Microsoft, Inc., $548 billion; General Electric, $447 billion; Cisco, Inc., $414 billion; Intel Corporation, $360 billion; Exxon/Mobil Group, Inc., $280 billion. Of these top five companies, three are listed on Nasdaq: Microsoft (MSFT), Cisco, Inc. (CSCO), and Intel Corp. (INTC).

### International Growth for Nasdaq

The Nasdaq market continues to grow, also internationally. Nasdaq recently announced a partnership with the Stock Exchange of Hong Kong (SEHK).

The two exchanges are linking up a joint Internet Web service to supply information about their respective markets. The SEHK is the second-largest exchange in Asia; the exchange is the trading center for Hong Kong and China.

Investors will be able to gather prices on Hong Kong and U.S. stocks quickly and easily. Other features make it possible for investors in SEHK stocks to track their portfolios; investors can follow mutual funds, options, and other U.S. equities, in U.S. or Hong Kong currency.

Also Nasdaq established a joint venture with a division of SSI Ltd. of India. The venture will develop market and trading systems for Nasdaq global markets, including systems for Europe and Japan. These systems give European and Japanese investors opportunities to invest in stocks worldwide, including initial public offerings (IPOs).

Nasdaq is courting IPOs around the world. For instance, the first Polish company to go public in the United States went public on Nasdaq; the first Indian company to offer an IPO went public on Nasdaq.

A harbinger of Nasdaq's planned growth was the announcement on May 4, 2000, that the London and Frankfurt stock exchanges planned to merge. Along with that, the merged exchanges planned to forge an alliance with the Nasdaq exchange.

> *European markets are changing, and this change is linking Europe to the U.S. markets and the Nasdaq market. The London and Frankfurt stock exchanges are merging and forming an alliance with Nasdaq.*

These developments are significant as Nasdaq pursues the position of being the world's leading global stock market; this expansion will improve investors' exposure to trading and investing on a global basis.

Better trading capabilities, more information, and a fuller exposure to international securities will broaden an investor's and trader's choices regarding investment opportunities.

## THE NASDAQ COMPOSITE INDEX

As the prices of the securities on the Nasdaq Composite Index rise and fall during the day, they cause either an advance or decline in the index; this is a market cap-weighted index. Market cap is the price of a stock times the amount of its outstanding shares. The market value of each security in the index is calculated throughout the trading day.

**Table 1–1** NASDAQ Industry Breakdown

| Industry | Percent |
| --- | --- |
| Industrials | 56.6 |
| Computer | 14.5 |
| Banking | 14.2 |
| Telecommunications | 3.8 |
| Finance | 3.7 |
| Biotechnology | 3.2 |
| Transportation | 2.3 |
| Insurance | 1.7 |

The Nasdaq Composite Index is a comprehensive barometer containing more stocks than most other indexes. The index contains more than the Russell 2000 Index (2000), Standard & Poor's 500 Index (500 issues), or the Standard & Poor's Mid-Cap Index (400).

Many well-known U.S. companies, especially those companies in the newer growth sectors, are listed on the Nasdaq Composite. The broad range of companies covers the entire span of the U.S. economy. Table 1-1 gives a breakdown of the companies that are listed on the Nasdaq, according to industry.

# GROWTH COMPANIES IN THE NASDAQ

Nasdaq is known for the many growth-oriented technology companies that it lists. Some of the better-known companies include Yahoo! Inc.; Amazon.com, Inc.; Cisco Systems, Inc.; Qualcomm, Inc.; Intel Corporation; Microsoft Corporation; Dell Computer Corporation; and Sun Microsystems.

Because of the dynamic growth of the Nasdaq technology companies, Nasdaq now lists over 659 companies with a market capitalization of over $1 billion; in 1990, there were just 49 companies of this size. Also, the Nasdaq market continues to attract and retain large companies as the companies grow in market value. In 1989, Nasdaq listed about 496 companies with over $100 million in market capitalization; in 1999 that number grew to 2357. The total market capitalization on Nasdaq companies now exceeds $5 trillion—a staggering amount.

Many companies are choosing to go public on the Nasdaq market. A total of 485 companies had their initial public offering (IPO) on Nasdaq. In fact, Nasdaq had 151 IPOs in just the fourth quarter of 1999. This was about 89 percent of the companies going public on one of the three primary U.S. markets.

## Nasdaq-100 Index

The 100 biggest nonfinancial companies listed on the Nasdaq are included in the Nasdaq-100 Index. They have gotten to be the biggest, in terms of market capitalization, by growing fast; so, not surprisingly, this index includes some of the world's fastest-growing companies.

The companies in this index include different industry groups. All the companies have a market capitalization of $500 million or more; each company is trading a minimum average daily trading volume of 100,000 shares.

In March 1999, the Amex began trading QQQ, exchange shares based on the Nasdaq-100. The assets in QQQ rose to a record level of $6 billion by December 1999, an impressive growth. The asset growth is connected to the performance of the Nasdaq-100; as the shares of the underlying companies kept rising, people and institutions poured money into the exchange shares.

Many of the underlying QQQ companies rise in value because they are in growth industries: computer, telecommunications, biotech, semiconductor, and Internet. Because some of these companies are involved in the newer growth industries, such as Internet and computers, these companies are seen as "emerging" companies rather than mature companies. App. B lists the QQQ stocks.

Not all companies in the Nasdaq-100 Index are in what would be called growth industries. There are companies in retailing and other rather staid industries. But all of the companies in the index are fast-growing.

The Nasdaq market is pleased that QQQ has grown substantially. Among other things the growth of QQQ helps Nasdaq make the claim to the investment community that Nasdaq is the market in which to invest. Momentum players, in this momentum market, as well as long-term investors are investing and trading in the Nasdaq market because of the high amount of volatility.

## Non-U.S. Companies in the Nasdaq Index

Many non-U.S. companies trade on the Nasdaq. Some of these are the best-known companies in the world. For example, Fuji Photo Film Co.; Reuters

Holdings PLC.; Global Crossings, Ltd.; Canon, Inc.; and Louis Vuitton trade on Nasdaq. Nasdaq has more foreign stocks listed than the other major exchanges—and the list continues to grow. In 1999, 67 percent of the new non-U.S. stocks that listed chose Nasdaq. In the fourth quarter of 1999, Nasdaq listed 22 new non-U.S. companies.

It is important to understand that stock trading is becoming more worldwide. With easier access to global markets, it is important for an exchange to gain a larger share of foreign securities to be traded in the United States. It is expected that listing foreign securities will be a growing of revenues for U.S. exchanges in the future.

The Internet, as it seeps into and floods all segments of U.S. and worldwide culture, is changing the way business is getting done. The Nasdaq market very well reflects the Internet explosion.

The rising importance of the Internet has affected all the tech stocks. Tech stocks represent a large percentage of the Nasdaq Composite Index, and they represent a full two-thirds of the Nasdaq-100 Index as measured by market cap.

Nontech stocks are also involved in the tech revolution in their respective businesses. Companies that sell steel or cars or boats or other items are starting to use some sort of e-commerce for their marketing. Manufacturing, retailing, and service companies of all sorts will increase their tech exposure in ways that are still developing.

## NASDAQ LISTING REQUIREMENTS

The Nasdaq market has certain criteria that companies must meet to be accepted for listing. The exchange seeks to list companies that have financial staying power, enough stock outstanding to ensure a liquid market, and other requirements.

Included in the initial listing requirements of the Nasdaq national market are:

| | |
|---|---|
| Net tangible assets | $6.0 million |
| Public float (market value) | $8.0 million |
| Public float (shares) | 1.1 million |
| Minimum bid price | $5 |
| Pretax income (in latest fiscal year or of last 3 fiscal years) | $1.0 million |
| Market makers | three |

Included in the initial listing requirements of the Nasdaq small-cap market are:

| | |
|---|---|
| Shareholders (round lots) | 300 |
| Market capitalization | $50 million |
| Public float (shares) | 1 million |
| Market value of public float | $5.0 million |
| Minimum bid price | $4 |
| Market makers | three |

The Nasdaq market is expected to continue adding companies for trading. As the world economies grow and change, Nasdaq will attempt to list the companies contributing to this growth. Many of these companies will be smaller, but are expected to grow in the future.

The Nasdaq market is attempting growth in many ways. One of the areas that holds promise for the future is after-hours trading. The Nasdaq, as well as other markets, has experimented with after-hours trading. So far there seems to be little appetite for trading at other than normal trading hours. This could change, however, in the future. As more trading is done across national borders and more exchanges list stocks of foreign companies, there could be a natural breakdown of what is considered "normal" trading hours. This could lead to trading 24 hours a day in some markets.

This evolution could start soon, leading to more active markets with expanded trading times. Nasdaq is expected to be among the leaders as this develops.

CHAPTER 2

# THE NASDAQ EXPLOSION

## THIRTY-SIX KEY STOCKS

When the S&P 500 Index added Yahoo to its index in 1999, it surprised many people. It was unusual to see a super-high P/E Internet stock, which is appropriately listed on the Nasdaq-100 Index, also listed on the more staid S&P 500. This raises the question of which other Internet/tech/growth stocks are also listed in the other benchmarks, such as the Russell 1000, the Russell 100 Growth, as well as the S&P 500.

This question takes on importance when you consider that the performances of many of the larger money managers are based on these indexes. If there are stocks that have to be bought and held by managers to replicate certain indexes, when the stocks are bought, the managers could bump into each other in their hurry to buy those stocks.

This can run into major money. When giant funds, including index funds, come into the market to benchmark a stock (own the same proportional amount in the index fund as is held in the index: say the index has a 17 percent weight of Microsoft, then a $20 billion fund will have to buy a 17 percent weighting of MSFT—$340 million worth), that stock can be driven upward. This is not a rare occurrence. There are many $20 billion funds out there, as well as active managers, who want to own the stocks that the indexes, against which they are compared, own.

Also, transaction costs are a big factor for money managers. Transaction costs are not just commissions; transaction costs can also be impact, which means how much it costs in terms of market price because the institution moved stocks higher when it had to rush in to buy. Big funds would have to tiptoe into these stocks slowly so as not to move them; maybe take a week to a month to get their position built. Tiptoeing in when a stock is added to an index is hard to do; the funds have *got* to own the shares. And this is where the volatility starts, with managers bidding against each other and themselves.

Douglas Coté at Aeltus Investment Management studied 36 stocks that were heavily weighted in the different indexes. The equal-weight average return for these stocks over most of 1999 was an impressive 172 percent. The problem gets clearer: funds do not have a chance to tiptoe into a stock when those stocks are appreciating 172 percent in a year.

Also, these stocks are not for the faint of heart: according to the study by Coté, the equal-weighted price-earnings multiple (P/E, which is price divided by earnings per share) is a lofty 240 times, so there is no reason for buyers to wait for the P/E to get more reasonable. Considering forward earnings, the P/E is a still very high 126 times. The chart in Fig. 2-1 shows the weight of the 36 stocks in each of the three mentioned indexes as well as the Nasdaq-100. Figure 2-2 shows the 15 stocks of the 36 that have a greater than 1 percent weighting in the Nasdaq-100 Index, with their weighting in the index. These stocks have forecasted high rates of growth. So on a long-term basis, the earnings power of the companies could reduce the risk of holding them. But many big money managers buy them to reduce their risk of underperformance against their index benchmark. The fewer of these stocks a money manager owns, the higher the risk that his performance may lag against his benchmark. The 36 stocks are found among the 50 Nasdaq stocks reviewed in App. C.

> *Thirty-six stocks keep showing up in the major indexes. An investor can research these stocks, pick the ones he or she likes, and fashion his or her own mutual fund.*

CHAPTER 2  THE NASDAQ EXPLOSION    **19**

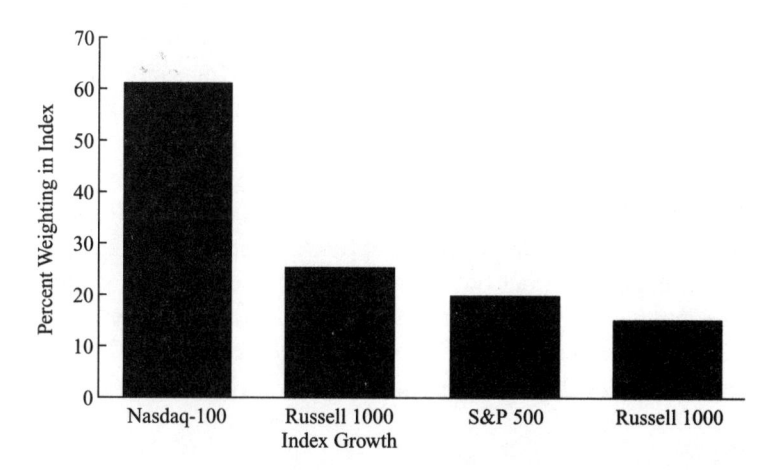

**Figure 2-1** There are 36 stocks in common to the indexes. (*Courtesy of Aeltus Investment Management.*)

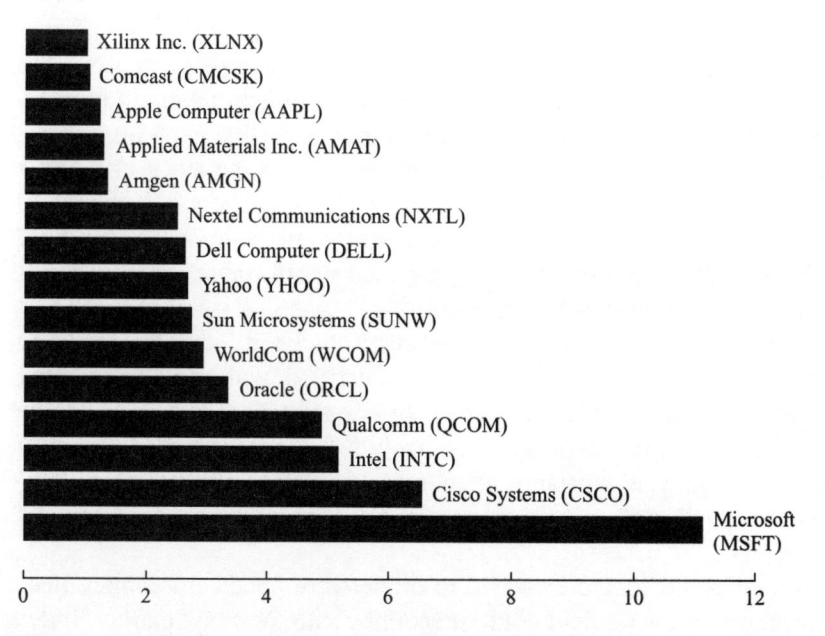

**Figure 2-2** Of the 36 stocks in common to the indexes, 15 of them have a weight greater than 1 percent in the Nasdaq-100.

The factor that could be overlooked by the big money managers is how heavy buying of their index stocks increases their transaction costs. Individual investors, those who buy 500, 1000, 5000 shares, do not have an impact on the price of these stocks; but a buyer, say, of a million shares will, essentially, start bidding against herself. Some of these stocks do not have a large daily trading volume; a million shares to buy could drive many of the "have to own right now for index representation" Nasdaq stocks higher.

Also stampedes can cut both ways: if everybody heads for the exits at the same time, a scenario I'm not suggesting is developing, but could, sellers could be stumbling over themselves and each other in order to get out, driving the prices of these stocks lower.

## Can the Stocks Get Bought Up?

A concern would be whether all the big money managers could complete their stock positions with the stocks needed to match the indexes or the stocks required for enhanced index needs. And with that happening, would the stocks that need to be bought for the indexes drift lower or even collapse?

Before pondering that question further, it should be understood that an enhanced index fund or portfolio is one in which there are stocks held that mirror the stocks in an index; additionally, the fund or portfolio will purchase stocks or synthetically increase holdings of stocks to improve the performance over that of the benchmark index, without materially increasing risk. For example, an enhanced fund might buy calls on an up-moving stock; if the stock continues to go up, the fund calls the stock at a lower price, and perhaps outperforms its index benchmark. There is a change in the risk profile of the fund using this strategy: the amount that the fund paid for the call premium will lessen the fund's performance if the stock it bought options on does not go higher.

As for the previous question of whether stocks in the index could be bought up to a point that demand would be filled, with the stocks going down after demand is filled, it is a set of circumstances that seems to be an oversimplification and probably unlikely to happen. The need for all of the indexes simply is not large enough to keep stocks propped up. Ultimately, the stocks will sell on their own merit, according to earnings and other factors.

As long as stocks are expected to outperform bonds and money market funds, new money might continue coming into the stock market. Index funds have to replicate an index with their newly injected cash, and to this end will go out and buy more stocks. Some nonindex funds have experienced $1 million a day coming into their funds. Some of this cash will be invested in stocks in proportion to the indexes. And as for the enhanced-index funds, the more stocks they buy that are in their benchmark, the easier their job to match the benchmark.

Active managers as well as individual investors do have to be careful, though: these stocks can go down fast. You have to make sure that the growth outlook for the companies is still there.

For instance, in early 2000, Dell Computer Corporation (DELL) recently announced that it would not make its sales and earnings projections; the stock was immediately punished, going down over 20 percent.

Conversely, growth in earnings is rewarded. Intel Corporation (INTC), a company well represented in the list of 36 stocks, announced new products and joint ventures; the stock went up 17 percent.

## A NEW ECONOMY?

Is there a new economy? One that is and will experience unbridled growth for as long as the mind can imagine? Do we throw out the old economic models and say that trees (economically speaking) will now indeed grow to the sky?

There is a new economy that is expanding. But in a certain sense none of this is new. All this growth in the technology sector is a continuum started years ago that is just now being recognized and reflected in technology stock prices.

The coming of the present technology-driven economy was pretty much predicted in 1965, in a theory known as Moore's Law. In that year, Gordon Moore, then employed at Fairchild Semiconductors, wrote an article for *Electronics* magazine. Moore expounded his theory that microchip technology change would remain dynamic indefinitely; changes would create a doubling in microchip computational power every year or so. Later, this time was lengthened to about 18 months. Gordon Moore later founded the Nasdaq listed company, Intel, Inc.

Today it is generally accepted that Moore's theory is accurate. This continuing increase of microchip power is one of the reasons for the drop in the price of PCs. The consumer today can buy a more powerful computer at a lower cost than ever; and this trend continues.

Microchip computational power increasing, however, is not the only reason for low computer costs. There have been technological advances, the popularity of the Internet has spurred consumer demand for computers, and there are marketing considerations and other factors. Computer prices have dropped below the $1000 level on the low end; and the under-$1000 computers are far superior to the high-end computers of years ago.

Also the high-end computer of today is much superior to the best of years ago. All this is a result of the workings of Moore's Law.

Today's technology-led economy has been developing for quite a while. It is hard to imagine that the influence of technology in the U.S. and world economy will peter out: the popularity of the Internet; needed improvements in software to satisfy the demands of new PC usages; the penetration of technology in underdeveloped countries (China, as an example); and many other factors should keep the technology sector changing and growing.

Computers should continue to get cheaper and better. Realistically, computers will sell for over $400—it costs about that to make them today. The new frontiers seem to be in the software sector; software, especially, that is linked to the Internet, should continue to become cheaper and better.

## Evolving Uses for the Internet

It is misleading to brand the present an Internet economy. This is a broader, more technology-driven economy. This economy has developed an infrastructure the capability of which did not exist even a few years back, an infrastructure that connects many millions of customers and suppliers worldwide.

To understand how this infrastructure can impact the future, consider business-to-business (B2B) Internet commerce. A company such as General Motors or Ford, instead of having people get on the phone to order goods and services, can now go on the Internet to connect to suppliers, and lower its overall costs.

The savings can be dramatic. A part that costs General Motors $200 to order, for example, can be purchased for only a few dollars. The few dollars is the cost of the part after negotiating. The $200 would include the time and expense to hire a person for the position of contract negotiator; also there are office expenses, wages, commissions, employment taxes, benefits, the cost of phone calls, and other items when a person is hired to do the job.

As a consequence, General Motors and Ford are building Internet sites that are linked to suppliers; this allows Ford, for instance, to go out into the marketplace and, because of its Internet connectivity, offer to service smaller companies. Ford will act as a middleperson for the smaller companies' supply needs and charge the smaller companies to get them the best deals.

This supplier/customer development is a direct outgrowth of Moore's Law; the productivity of technologically driven interfacing is increasing exponentially but the price of using that technology is decreasing.

An example of how the Internet has changed daily life can be found in how traders use their brokerage accounts. Many of us use the Internet for our personal finances by using an online broker.

You can use an online broker's system, make a trade, and instantaneously receive a report. The broker will furnish full statements. When you sell (or buy to cover a short position) the statement will include the trade details and also your cost basis so that tax records will be complete. An online broker charges about $14 to $25 a trade, less than it costs to trade through a full-service broker who probably does not offer these reporting details.

The service is so complete and the cost so low that even if there is a broker downstairs from your office, if your broker doesn't have online trading you will probably leave that broker. The day of going downstairs, even if your broker is in your building, and "visiting" with your broker is pretty well gone. Because people are so busy, it takes too much time, so you click and the trade is done. It is hard to quantify how much this saves in terms of money.

Because of the Internet, all brokers have become much the same: brokerage trades now are a commodity, a transaction to be done quickly and well. And online brokers do an excellent job at a far less cost than customers previously paid.

So the Internet makes people that much more productive with their time; this is the way that technology is affecting companies like Ford and General Motors similarly.

All sorts of companies are using the Internet for very big capital transactions. For instance, on the Web is a company dealing in railcars. Basically a middleperson, the company offers railcars for lease or the company will lease railcars from suppliers. Now, railcars are seriously large items, and they are being traded on the Internet.

Even in large items the supplier or user can get a better response on the Internet than dealing in the old way. The old way would take a lot of time and expense to determine what buyers and sellers are looking for at any given time. It's hard or impossible to find a wider audience than the Internet for supplier and user to interface globally, and shopping on the Internet has very low cost.

## The New Highway System

The U.S. economy, the most accessible market in the world, is very much involved in the world economy via the Internet; this makes trade opportunities boundless.

One of the reasons that Internet trade has grown explosively is that the start-up costs for a company to link up with the Internet are low, which is a result of technological advances. Internet users are just starting to see how these advances are affecting everyday life. And this technological revolution can be measured in real dollars. Just as you can now trade through an online broker cheaper and better than before, so can companies like General Motors and Ford and the railcar trader use this technology.

When planning a business strategy, the technology component is showing up in about every company's plans. The reality is that businesses in our present economy *have* to leverage through technology. In the prior scenario, for example, General Motors let go of hundreds of sourcing agents and replaced them with a Web site and a few technicians. In fact, the whole exercise was so successful that in February 2000 General Motors, Ford, and Chrysler announced plans to set up the world's largest online marketplace for use by the auto industry. The site would auction off parts, at which the companies would buy the $300 billion of goods they purchase each year.

Demand is worldwide, with all sectors of the globe participating. Gartner Group, a well-known consulting firm, estimates that Europe's B2B Internet trade will soar over the next several years. According to Gartner, the B2B European e-commerce was about $31.8 billion in 1999; it expects this to grow to over $2.3 trillion by 2004. To accomplish this, Europe's growth rate in this area would outstrip even the United States. Some of the biggest European companies are getting involved in B2B, including BMW, British Telecom, KLM, and Swissair.

The Internet could be thought of as today's highway system. When a new system comes along, people try to use it to expand commerce. Years ago, the railroad was built, and that system had an explosive impact on that era's economy. Today, the Internet is facilitating the development of a new world of e-commerce.

If a business does not use that technology, the business cannot lower its cost on a regular basis, but its competition will. A business not using the Internet will have to do more work at higher costs. That will be a problem, especially because technology will continue to grow. The competition will be improving its operation while saving costs; the business not using the Internet will fall further behind.

## BACKGROUND FOR THE NASDAQ EXPLOSION

The brokerage industry went from fixed commissions to negotiated commissions on May 1, 1975. It was thought then by Wall Street that this move would destroy the market. The commissions would be negotiated down, it was feared, making it difficult for brokers to make a living. This fear went unfounded. The market exploded in volume, going from about 20 million shares a day to its present 1 billion shares a day on the NYSE. From an insignificant amount, Nasdaq grew to about 1.5 billion shares a day.

Competitive commissions made a difference for Nasdaq. Nasdaq could now compete with the then dominant market, the NYSE. Also the Nasdaq trading structure, having competitive dealers negotiating with each other regarding prices, lends itself to a negotiated commission world. The Nasdaq system is a sort of "computer-matching orders" system. If it didn't exist today, it would probably have to have been created.

The next event to impact Nasdaq was in 1984. In that year the SEC granted Nasdaq exemption from the "blue-sky laws." Blue-sky laws are regulations passed by various states to protect investors. These laws require sellers of securities to register said securities, disclosing financial details so that buyers can be fully informed. Before 1984, only the ASE and the NYSE were exempt from these laws. Not being exempt was a problem for Nasdaq. Nasdaq had to go through a whole extra procedure to offer shares for sale on an IPO or secondary offering; this extra procedure took time and necessitated additional costs.

Partly as a result of rule changes, Nasdaq has grown, and in 1994 passed the NYSE in annual share volume. In 1999, Nasdaq passed the NYSE in dollar volume. In fact, Nasdaq accounted for 54 percent of the dollar volume and 56 percent of the share volume of the domestic equity trades in the United States.

As another sign of growth, 2 years ago Nasdaq listed companies that comprised about 18 percent of the market cap of the U.S. economy; today that number is 30 percent.

## Explosive Growth in the Size of the Nasdaq

The stocks on Nasdaq which receive much attention from both traders and investors are the new-economy tech stocks, issues such as technology, biotechnology, semiconductors, computer software, the Internet, and those involved in e-commerce, telecommunications, and some health-care stocks. Many of these companies are on Nasdaq because the companies had their IPOs on Nasdaq and, rather than taking the traditional route of going on to the NYSE when they got large, they stayed in the Nasdaq system.

This factor has allowed Nasdaq to develop into a legitimate national stock market. From a competitive standpoint, Nasdaq must have features to compel companies to stay with it rather than leave for another exchange.

Nasdaq must continue to attract as many IPOs as possible. The advent of the Internet has dramatically helped Nasdaq.

The architecture of the Nasdaq trading system is identical to the architecture of the World Wide Web. In a technical way—the manner in which traders are hooked together by computers, forming a Web of competing traders and market makers—Nasdaq resembles the Web. Or, put another way, Nasdaq could be considered the largest *intranet* in the world. Nasdaq is very innovative and just beginning to put its electronic trading skin around the corners of the world.

## Nonstop World Trading

Nasdaq is spreading over the globe. Nasdaq started Nasdaq Japan, which is a sort of clone of the U.S. Nasdaq system and Nasdaq Europe. It formed an alliance with Hong Kong that includes dual listings (listing stocks on more than one major exchange—as an example, a company could be listed on the Hang Seng, the major Hong Kong market, and also the Hong Kong Nasdaq market). Nasdaq is speaking with officials from other countries, such as Australia, regarding setting up a Nasdaq market.

These developments are leading to 24-hour-a-day trading in Nasdaq markets around the world and trading in the regular trading hours in each country. This arrangement will allow Nasdaq to essentially pass the "book." A book is a record kept by a specialist of buy and sell orders; specialists once kept a notebook for these purposes. The specialist is not a part of the Nasdaq system, and the notebook has mostly become electronic and open, but the expression lingers on.

An example of what Nasdaq envisions follows: One day there could be trading in Japan; as Japan's morning turns into late afternoon and the trading day expires, trading would start on the Nasdaq market in the morning in Europe; and as in Europe the morning turns into afternoon, trading would start on Nasdaq in the United States.

This development will allow the Nasdaq market to not be open 24-hours a day in any one country. The Nasdaq market will be trading in a country during that country's regular market hours. An investor or trader could trade in those Nasdaq markets around the world. For some markets a trader would have to get up very early or stay up very late at night to trade, however.

## Money Flows into the Tech Sector

The large tech and Internet stocks have grown in sales and earnings and market price. Some investment professionals such as banks, mutual funds, and money managers have shunned the group, saying that the group is too speculative. The professionals not invested in the group over the last few years have not had nearly the returns that they could have. The tech and Internet and other new economy stocks have proved to be stellar market performers, leaving most other industry sectors behind. For the first several years of this bull market, the institutions could get away with staying in value stocks. But as the tech stocks continued strong, the institutions have been increasingly under pressure for higher performance.

As a result, many investors and traders and investment professionals took money out of value market sectors, nicknamed the "bricks-and-mortar" sectors, and put funds into the stocks of the new economy. The beneficiary of this shift was mostly the larger tech, Nasdaq-type stocks. That money shift pushed the prices of tech stocks even higher.

At the other end of the market, the small-cap and mid-cap stocks were ignored; later these stocks picked up volume and appreciated. The attractive valuations of the smaller companies in comparison to the larger companies have attracted institutional and retail investors and traders. This development is reflected in the performance of the different markets: the Nasdaq indexes have risen sharply over the last few years, even though these indexes have suffered setbacks from time to time.

Another indicator of tech-stock influence is that the DJIA added two Nasdaq stocks; this is the first time a Nasdaq stock was added to this benchmark. There is speculation that because these two companies, Microsoft and Intel, were added to the DJIA, they may list on the NYSE. That however doesn't seem likely. But one trend will probably continue: more companies from Nasdaq will be added to the DJIA.

## The Importance of E-commerce

The bricks-and-mortar companies are beginning to see that e-commerce is important. The major companies have begun spinning off dot-com companies. Many of these dot-com companies track subsidiaries of the major companies. As these dot-com companies are spun off, many are listed on Nasdaq, even if the parent is listed on the NYSE.

For instance, Barnes&Noble.com was recently listed on Nasdaq, as well as American Greetings.com. Both of these companies are spin-offs from parent companies that are listed on the NYSE. There will probably be more dot-com companies, adding to Nasdaq's explosive growth.

## THE NYSE ADVANCE/DECLINE LINE

The risk of the Nasdaq market has caused dislocations in some of the old market measurement tools. One of those tools is the NYSE Advance/

Decline line. The NYSE Advance/Decline line (A/D line) is a measurement that shows the number of stocks advancing and number declining. All the stocks listed on the NYSE are used in the calculation. There is no market capitalization or other factor: the statistics merely show the number of stocks going up, and those going down. If more stocks advance than decline, the A/D line is considered bullish; more declining stocks than advancing signify a bearish trend. This is one of the oldest and most closely watched of the market indicators, going back about 100 years. Often the A/D line is calculated on a 30-day average or 45-day average, as a means to measure the undistorted market direction. Many traders buy and sell according to the direction of the market as predicted by this indicator.

There are times when the indicator hasn't worked very well. The Nasdaq market would be climbing, yet the A/D line shows overall NYSE market deterioration. Market savants have offered up reasons why.

They note the fact that 25 percent of the issues on the NYSE are preferred stocks, not common stocks. Preferred stocks tend to act more like bonds than stocks, reacting more to interest rates than any other factor. Therefore, if interest rates change dramatically during the day, the preferreds will react, skewing the A/D line. For example, the bond market can go down and the stock market up, so followers of the A/D will not receive a pure equity read.

Another problem with the A/D line is that the NYSE doesn't have the wide market capitalization superiority to Nasdaq than it previously had. Therefore, the A/D line does not conclusively represent the U.S. stock markets.

## THE NYSE RULE 500 AND ITS IMPLICATIONS

Another change this is affecting the NYSE and Nasdaq relationship is the loosening of the NYSE Rule 500. The NYSE had Rule 500 since the 1930s, and it was recently modified. Until this modification, the rule specified that a company listed on the exchange had to go through certain procedures to voluntarily delist from the NYSE. The delisting company was required to conduct a vote of the shareholders; two-thirds of the voting shareholders would have to vote to delist; if 10 percent of the voting shareholders objected, the company could not delist.

Many large companies, such as Coca-Cola or IBM, that had listed before Nasdaq came into prominence, had no choice but to list on the NYSE; there was no other major market on which to list. Then after Nasdaq became a true national market, the listed companies were faced with a delisting process if they wanted to leave the NYSE.

Conversely, there are no requirements to leave Nasdaq. A Nasdaq company can send the exchange a letter stating that it was leaving, and it goes. Nasdaq has a history of being an inclusive market, including any company that meets its requirements. Nasdaq believes that it is a service organization, providing a place for companies to have their stock traded; if a company doesn't want that service, that company is free to move.

The NYSE procedures resemble more of an exclusive club. To trade on the floor of the NYSE, one has to purchase a "seat." Not with Nasdaq. If a member meets its requirements, she can sign up, pay a fee, and become a dealer. This lack of exclusivity of the Nasdaq, a sort of democratization of the market, lends itself very well to today's Internet milieu.

The NYSE has loosened Rule 500. The exchange has done away with the shareholder's vote. The rule today compels a company that wishes to delist to conduct a vote of that company's audit committee. Once the audit committee votes for delisting, then the board must vote. If the board approves delisting, the company must write the top 35 shareholders and disclose its intention to delist. The 35 shareholders are given at least 20 business days to approve the delisting.

This loosening allows the NYSE to be more directly competitive with Nasdaq to list quality companies, because it is now easier for those companies to delist later if they wish.

## THE LOWER-COST NASDAQ

In the bricks-and-mortar world, the more customers that are added, the more infrastructure that must be added, at least initially, which is an additional cost. This translates into initial decreasing returns to scale.

In the e-world it is the other way around in that there are increasing returns to scale: the more people there are in the network, the more people who are involved, the bigger the system gets; and there are just incremental costs to add customers. Nasdaq has an e-commerce cost model. For Nasdaq to admit another stock for trading, it simply places its name on the screen.

On the NYSE, however, to add stocks for trading, the NYSE may have to add equipment on the exchange floor; even though orders are electronically sent to the floor, the orders are still manually executed. Also if the NYSE adds a number of stocks, a new trading location might be necessary.

There is a cost differential between the two exchanges. A large company will generally pay more to list on the NYSE than on Nasdaq.

## The Word Games

Over a period of time, words have developed that favor the NYSE trading system. The use of semantics emphasizes the exclusivity of the NYSE. Not that stocks can't and don't go down, no matter how exclusive the exchange that the stocks are traded on.

One such example: the NYSE uses the term "specialist," which is the one person who trades a designated stock. The term is an invention of the NYSE; in legal filings this person is labeled "designated dealer." In comparison, Nasdaq is a multiple dealer market; the term *dealer* seems inferior to *specialist*. Dealer conjures up visions of used-car dealers or a dealer in a casino—not that these are not honorable professions, just that specialist sound more, well, *special*, similar to having a doctor's specialty.

Another term that seems prejudicial is "over the counter," and how this term compares to "listed." Over the counter sounds akin to under the counter—a bit suspect. But these terms are rather old, and as we go into the Internet age, we will see the vocabulary change. The verbal comparisons between the two exchanges should become less meaningful as the terms die out over time.

# CHAPTER 3

# THE INTERNET ECONOMY

## A PARADIGM SHIFT FOR TRADERS

From a trader's perspective, particularly momentum traders, when the Nasdaq market was climbing, there was a reasoning that Nasdaq stocks were going up because they had been going up. That is how momentum traders think and trade. The axiom "The trend is your friend" in a market up-leg had worked. A trader's philosophy spread out into the mainstream, causing a hyperactive element in the market.

Also, momentum investing has broadened. Not only is stock price considered, but also momentum investing and trading has grown to encompass buying stocks that have earnings momentum. This would include stocks that are growing faster than the comparables in their industry or buying in sectors whose comparables are growing faster than other sectors. As long as the earnings keep growing, momentum stocks perform. When earnings disappoint, the disappointing stock get dumped: the momentum investors head for the exits simultaneously.

We have seen growth stocks receive much attention in the past. When companies such as Tyco International and Gillette were growth stocks, they would trade actively with high amounts of volatility. The stocks are now more mature and do not normally trade as ferociously.

> *"Don't fight the tape"* is an ancient Wall Street axiom that has received attention by traders in this long-running bull market. Traders have bought stocks when they broke up and shorted when they broke down, and the volatility of the market has accentuated both the up and down swings.

There seems to have been a gradual shift toward the general public having more of a trading philosophy, and these people are sensitive to earnings and price momentum. When the Nasdaq Composite Index outperformed the older indexes, such as the DJIA or the S&P 500, the performance prompted traders to go to the Nasdaq.

Nasdaq is a younger exchange with good credentials, having had listed companies such as Microsoft and Intel and Cisco. These companies, and others like them, are instrumental in driving Nasdaq's growth, and they are companies from the fastest growing part of the U.S. economy. These companies, with their success, have become the business model for a plethora of start-up companies.

The types of companies traded on the Nasdaq, plus the type of market it is, with dealers competing against each other, have sparked public interest. Also traders often follow a theory that Nasdaq will go up when an upleg is in force.

## New Market Participants and Technology

There is a new universe of people involved in the market. This accounts for the increase in volume and the increase in media attention, which, in turn, leads to more people and dollars getting involved in the market.

Many people now in the market were not in the market 5 years ago; many were not even in the market 2 or 3 years ago. These people do not adhere to the same valuation models of earlier investors; they don't have the same fears of earlier investors; they don't use benchmarks that were developed, say, 30 years ago; these people simply do not have the market memory that older market participants possess and, therefore, they are more prone to throw caution to the wind. An aggressive strategy paid off for several years, aided by a bull market.

The popularity of participating in the market has spread out into the public mainstream. Recently, on the cover of *The New York Times Magazine* section, there were pictures of day traders; this is unheard of in recent history. Brokerage trading offices have opened up that cater to people who believe they can make a living day-trading the market. A daunting task, in my view.

Technology may be the most important factor in the recent growth of the number of market participants. Technology has made it possible for people to access the markets directly, using online brokers, and has made trading so much easier, more efficient, and less costly.

Technology has made following the market, via the Internet, very easy: the coverage of company developments is much better; the access to an analyst's and portfolio manager's opinions is much more open; the regulatory oversight has given people more confidence that the markets are essentially honest; the globalization of markets has given people more choices; and the dual listing of securities has created more competition. Besides, people have made serious money in this long bull market, attracting even more participants.

## Self-Reliant Investors

The public has been made responsible for its own financial well-being. Admonitions from politicians and financial pundits advising not to "count on Social Security for your future" has been heard and accepted by the general population. As a consequence, more and more people are turning to their own investing activities to secure their futures. People are now managing their own portfolios; this could be in individual accounts or tax-sheltered plans such as a 401(k), IRA, Roth IRA, Defined Benefit Plan, or others.

Also the United States is on the verge of huge transfers of wealth from the parents of the baby-boom generation to the baby-boomers themselves. The numbers vary, but a total number of $14 trillion in transfers over the next decade seems reasonable. This money transfer is going to younger people with younger ideas and attitudes. The people are well educated, less risk-adverse, and willing to cash in bonds and like instruments to buy stocks and mutual funds.

## Will the Shakeouts Hurt Nasdaq's Long-Term Prospects?

Nasdaq, with its trading system attuned to technological advances to constantly improve its trading system, and also continuing to add tech stocks to trade, should benefit from the secular growth of the participation of investors and traders in the equity markets.

Of course we have seen good shakeouts—declines of 50 percent or so—on the Nasdaq market and don't know if more are coming or when. Market forecasting is a dicey business, at best.

Although the Nasdaq market had declines, it still has good momentum on the basis of years of gains. Shakeouts can hurt individual traders who are not well-capitalized traders; those traders on margin might be swept away in a deep correction; day traders could take some deep losses and give up.

Many of the day traders are trading on margin, a financial arrangement that in a severe correction could lend to their being wiped out. Trading on margin means that you are borrowing money to purchase stocks. Brokerage firms, subject to federal regulations, can lend money to securities traders. The ongoing fears of the officers at the Federal Reserve Board, which regulates the nation's money supply, is that people might borrow money against their credit cards, or borrow from other sources to play the stock market. On shakeouts, these people can get hurt and forced out of the market.

With the large amounts of cash available today, even after a market dip, much of that cash finds its way back into what has worked for years, which is stocks. Especially attractive are stocks that have had good momentum, such as Nasdaq technology securities; these probably will stay high up on institutional and retail BUY lists.

Also, cash could flood in from Europe. There is much cash stuffed in savings accounts and short-term bonds, which could come into the market. Skeptics, both professional and retail traders, who missed some of the upward move in the market and were reluctant to chase the previously high prices, often come into the market. It might take a few price breaks, but at some point there is plenty of cash available to buy stocks.

The U.S. government is stating that with the current surplus, less debt will be needed, and the government will not be selling much in the way of bonds. In fact, the government will buy back some bonds that it issued. This creates a supply/demand equilibrium that is new to the stock market; the money that would have gone into bonds might go into stocks. If the economy stays strong and (relative) peace in the world continues, people might pour more into what has worked: tech stocks.

A hint of the Nasdaq's equanimity to bad news is that the market has not been destroyed by the increase in oil prices, which have risen from $10 to $30 a barrel in late 1999 through late 2000. In the past, a major raw material component such as oil tripling in price would have caused anxiety among investors leading to a total collapse of the markets.

## New Ways of Looking at Things

Many historical economic and market assumptions are being challenged. The graduates of top schools are being hired by major money managers such as Fidelity Investments and given the charge of valuing new economy stocks. And the new managers look at stocks in new ways.

Also the stocks they are looking at are changing in the new tech milieu. As an example, only a few years ago investors could buy American Telephone and Telegraph (T) and hold it through good and bad markets. But T has changed. From that one company many companies have developed: T has spun off countless "Baby Bells," Lucent, and other companies. Analysts have to decipher the value of T and its spin-offs.

Also today's trends have to be considered from a global perspective. The telecom industry, for example, now operates globally. There have been consolidations and spin-offs in the group with many of the new entities operating across international borders.

This global rotation has benefited the U.S. and world stock markets. The worldwide traders follow the U.S. telecom and Internet stocks daily. Activity on these stocks in the United States stimulates traders in Tokyo and Hong Kong to trade stocks in these groups in their own markets.

## THE INTERNET AGE IS JUST STARTING

There are investors, including professionals, who believe that the Internet and related e-commerce is a phase and will not last. From Europe, there are opinions that the Internet rage is just another American excess and will flame out. Many European periodicals have panned U.S. technology stocks, saying that declines will lead to further declines.

There are analysts who advise portfolio managers and investment institutions such as banks and mutual funds, who are concerned that perhaps the Internet and e-commerce is a fad, one that will fade. Although there are plenty of signs that there is a fundamental shift in the economy because of the Internet, there are many people discounting that conclusion. The skeptics say that whenever hype such as the Internet comes along, the claim that it will be huge is nonsense, and the opinion that a paradigm shift will develop is wishful thinking.

The fact is that there are many companies coming up with novel, interesting solutions to everyday problems using the Net, and these solutions are producing substantial revenues. These revenues, in turn, are adding to a company's earnings. But for companies to create more profits, the companies have to build up scale.

There is real value being created for people and businesses using the Internet, and there is no going back to the days before the Internet. We are actually embarking on a time of even *more* rapid changes; the Internet will find more uses and become more important in the consumer area.

## New Applications for the Internet

The personal computer is a key to the spread of the Internet. As the number of homes that have computers grows, so does the importance of the Internet. It has been estimated that 35 percent of the homes in the United States have access to the Internet. Fifty percent of the homes wired to the Internet is thought to be a critical threshold. At 50 percent there will be massive growth in Internet traffic and usage.

There are opinions that the number of homes with PCs is not the only important number for Internet growth. The thinking is that PCs are just one method to access the Internet, and maybe in the future there will be more important methods. Up to now the Internet has been followed mostly by people in the investment and technology industry and used by the more technologically savvy people. There are opinions that for the Internet to gain wide adoption it has to go beyond being accessed only by PCs and go to the average person wherever he or she is.

The Internet must go to the average person's living room or to his or her kitchen. Perhaps an Internet hookup will be installed on her refrigerator or in other places or forms.

The Internet will evolve by helping people and saving them money. This situation is similar to the PC, which did not really take off until programs were introduced to help people. For instance, Quicken, a program to help with accounting and tax reporting, was sold as easy-to-use software to the public. With Quicken, users prepared their taxes, prepared bills, and used the program in other ways. The new software made these tasks seem less onerous. Many showed their children how to use the software—it was that easy to use.

Quicken, and other everyday applications made for average people to use, was a key for the growth in the number of PCs. Then the Quicken scenario developed to where a person, in addition to preparing her bills, can now pay bills directly using the Internet. Also a person can bank using the Internet and save the time and trouble of going to a bank branch office or ATM.

Just as Quicken showed a new practical way to operate, this has been true for the Internet also. The Internet did not grow because of the entertainment it offered, or even using the e-commerce in old ways. The Internet grew because the average person could do things differently and more efficiently.

The Internet has barely begun to scratch the surface of potential uses. Advances could be dramatic, with unforeseen consumer conveniences flooding the market.

## The Perfect Market: The Internet

With the Internet, for the first time ever, consumers can transact in a perfect market. The opportunities for buying and selling goods and services are available to everyone around the globe at the click of a mouse. Prices are competitive on a worldwide basis, forcing prices lower, and there are little or no transaction costs.

This was never possible before. A perfect market such as this appeared only as an economist's dream or in a textbook example of how a market should work. This perfect market is at the heart of the evolution of the Internet.

This doesn't diminish the other facets of the Internet. People can go into a chat room to discuss politics or movies or stocks, which is a fun, informative, and perhaps profitable thing to do; exchanging e-mail has become a necessity as a mode of communication; bringing up weather forecasts in the areas in which a person is about to travel is an important convenience. But the driving force of the Internet evolution is commerce and the way people and businesses can interact for profit.

### The Perfect Auction

An example of evolving Internet commerce is the activity of the company GOTO.COM (GOTO). People go to the site to buy goods or services. For instance, a person types in WALKMAN. In response, every business that is selling Walkmans lists their product offerings. This is a tremendous venue for small businesses that want to build up volume and will work on skinny margins. The buyer will make a bid on a product, for instance, $50. Another person out there, watching the screen somewhere in the world, decides that a Walkman is a good buy at that price, and bids higher, say, $51. And the auction is on. In this way, the worldwide perfect market is now functioning.

Another company that creates perfect markets in this way is eBay (EBAY). EBAY creates an online auction where consumers bid for goods and services. None of the value that EBAY and GOTO and other similar companies create could be done without the Internet.

## MAKING SENSE OF A NEW ECONOMY

With the markets favoring technology stocks, which are selling at high valuations, one can question the market's wisdom; deciding that the market is incorrect is a line of reasoning that never made anybody any money and is costly if done too often. The stock markets over the last hundred years or so would usually go up for a year or two, and then pull back. Here we are with some markets around the globe being up 4 or 5 years. Many think that we're due for a correction, and that the risks are too high to buy tech stocks.

Traditional valuation yardsticks such as price/earnings ratios (P/Es), especially in tech stocks, show shockingly high multiples; but P/Es and other traditional yardsticks may not be as valid today as they were previously. The reason it is not fair to use such old yardsticks is because old yardsticks assume a number of things: They assume that the growth rate of earnings is unchanged; they assume that capital usage is unchanged; they assume that accounting distortions are the same over time.

The issue of P/E multiples speaks to the fact that technology stocks are not the same as the old bricks-and-mortar stocks of the past and perhaps should not be valued in the same way. On a relative basis the P/E correlation between tech stocks and the nontech sector is the same today as it was in the past.

For example, IBM's P/E versus the P/E for steel companies had a similar correlation in the past as it does today. Steel companies in the past were about 10 times earnings; at that same time, computer stocks, such as IBM, were 60 times earnings. That would be similar to today's correlation, wherein many steel companies are 20 times earnings and many computer stocks sell at 120 times earnings.

If earnings growth is considered, it is obvious that there is a dislocation between what the stock market has done and what the economy has delivered. The stock market has become less and less reflective of the underlying economy.

Specifically, although tech stocks make up a large part of most stock indexes, they are not that large proportionally to gross domestic product (GDP). Also the pharmaceutical industry is not that large a proportion of GDP, although pharmaceuticals make up a disproportionately large part of the market indexes. If you take the dreary, old-economy capital goods sectors, they are a smaller proportion of the stock market but they are a large proportion of GDP. So there is a serious dislocation between the stock market and the economy.

The earnings difference between the tech sector and the rest of the market has been growing. Going back about 15 years, the tech sector had about 1 percent more earnings per share (EPS) growth than the rest of the equity market; back 5 years or so, the EPS of the tech stocks grew to be about 10 percent better than the balance of the market; just 2 years ago the premium of tech over nontech EPS was about 15 percent. So the EPS difference of the two sectors, the tech and nontech, has been accelerating.

On the accounting distortions issue, there are opinions that as we move to a knowledge-based economy we should be using a different accounting system. A knowledge-based economy has a critical component, namely research and development (R&D). There are many up-front costs attached to developing software; there are also many up-front costs attached to developing a drug. Many of these costs get expensed against the P&L in the earlier years of a product's development, and these costs depress earnings. And yet, these developments are a company's capital, that is, its intellectual property is the future of a tech or drug company.

As a result, many think that modern accounting is inadequate to deal with the complexities of a knowledge-based economy. These accounting distortions would seem to make a P/E ratio even less useful than the ratio was in the past in valuing companies of the new economy.

A reason that the P/E might be less useful is because the ratio says nothing about how much capital has been invested in order to generate earnings. In other words, a company that has $1 billion in capital and generates $10 million in earnings is a lot less attractive than a company that has $100 million in capital and generates $10 million in earnings. And this greater capital usage is generally occurring in the new-economy companies. This is because the new-economy companies, such as the Internet, software, and computer service companies, do not have the capital requirements that bricks-and-mortar companies have. So the P/E might really be less useful from the point of view of a knowledge-based, less capital-intensive economy.

Some analysts prefer cashflow return on investment as a more appropriate yardstick for tech companies; it is a way to look at stock prices as a multiple of future cashflows. Cashflows are much less easily distorted, and cashflows allow like to be compared with like. Capital usage can also be better ascertained using this method.

Also cashflow return on investment takes into account the factor of inflation. Using cashflows shows a real return on invested capital. Rather than looking at today's P/E earnings, which express a capital base built up years ago, an investor can consider cashflows, which show a company's real return. A P/E might give a false impression of how successful these older companies are.

## TECH COMPANIES OF YESTERYEAR

There are differences between today's tech companies and those of the 1960s. One difference is that the companies of yesteryear were very capital intensive. IBM was a huge manufacturer. And not only was it a manufacturer, but it leased out equipment. To manufacture and lease out this equipment, IBM used an enormous amount of capital. Today, being capital consumptive is not the model; Microsoft and the other tech giants do not operate that way.

Another difference is that previously, success of tech companies spelled success for corporate America. When IBM did well it was selling many computers, and the people buying the computers were becoming more productive. Efficiencies were incorporated into the manufacturing process, and everybody benefited.

Not so today. Today's companies are much more cannibalistic. For example, if Amazon.com does well, does that mean that Barnes & Noble will also be successful? Hardly. Today's Internet economy is winner take all. So successful companies, because their success may mean that the competition will fail, arguably should command a higher multiple than successful companies have commanded in the past.

### The Worldwide Internet Shock

The U.K. market is experiencing this Internet-related savaging of the marketplace with resultant shrinking profit margins, as much as is the United States. The return on equity of the companies in the U.K. stock market is as high or higher than it is in the United States. But this return is being lowered by the emergence of the Internet. This is happening in all businesses. For example, the Internet is destroying prices on High Street. High Street is a major shopping area in the United Kingdom.

This price savaging will probably continue. For example, the United Kingdom is ahead of all other countries in the field of interactive television. A good number of people in the United Kingdom will be able to interact over the TV, just as those people use a PC today. By the end of 2000, about 5 million households in the United Kingdom will have interactive TV. By 2003, about 15 million households will have it. This increases the price transparency of goods and services throughout the country.

Because of this growing price transparency, margins in car prices are easy to find. As an example, people in the United Kingdom can see how much cheaper cars sell for on the continent. Companies are being set up to buy cars on the continent for U.K. consumers. The companies charge 500 quid or so to buy a car for a consumer. Consumers have slowed their purchases of cars in Britain, and there has been a plunge in car prices.

As a corollary to the transparency in consumer items, the goods price inflation in the United Kingdom is minus 4 percent. The United Kingdom has the lowest rate of inflation of any European country. The question arises as to whether consumers are the recipients of the dollars generated by the shrinking of the profit margins? In many cases the answer is yes. It seems that there is a secular trend down in profits as a percentage of gross domestic product (GDP), much as the secular trend was up in prior years. If this is the case, the worldwide markets will have trouble making much headway except where there is solid earnings growth.

## P/E Ratio and the Internet Stocks

As a tool the P/E is not misleading when measuring a bricks-and-mortar company, but is not as effective when measuring an Internet company. The companies have different backgrounds.

In the old economy, companies grew gradually day-to-day, building their revenue stream and developing earnings. By the time a company had, say, $20 million in revenues, the company would be profitable and ready to go public. All of that process has been compressed for the new-economy companies. The statement that "Internet companies do not make money" is a generalization. Some Internet companies are doing what old-economy companies have done, just faster.

In the past, an Internet company could have generated revenues of $200,000 one quarter, then $900,000 the next quarter, then $2.5 million the following quarter. When a company grows revenues in this way, it has to spend money much faster than if it grew at a slower pace. Internet companies have historically spent money and grown at a fast clip because the Internet was growing fast. It was important to take advantage when opportunity occurred and spend money to gain market share, otherwise the opportunity might have been gone.

Another reason why Internet companies burnt money like timber recently is because the time was still the period of "land grab." This was especially true in the e-commerce to consumers area. Internet companies want to have as many consumers, or, in the Internet vernacular, "eyeballs," as possible. For this, a company may have to spend a lot in order to gain the critical mass necessary to survive and flourish.

For example, suppose a company has a Web site and attracts 1.5 million visitors. The company may have to spend $20 million to $30 million to attract 5 million visitors. But if that company has to spend another $50 million to attract 12 to 15 million visitors, the company would possess a huge critical mass that could bring a lot of advertising to the site. Vendors will pay to advertise on a highly visited site. A common axiom is that advertising basically follows eyeballs, or where eyeballs go, money will follow.

So companies have to spend sums of money to get the attention of people and create a critical mass. Companies involved with the Internet have to move at warp speed. To garner their critical mass. Corporate development is not more expensive on the Internet; it is just that the pace of everything, including spending money to grow, is incredibly fast.

But since the crash of the Internet companies in late 2000, the ability of these companies to raise money has been seriously curtailed. Internet companies are being forced to rethink financing their "land-grab" strategy.

### Unwise Spending

There are companies, however, that do spend money foolishly. The milieu in which the Internet companies are operating has been so competitive that some companies think that even if the company is not attracting people to the site, spending is still acceptable.

For instance, a company could have only $20 million in revenues, yet it spends $60 million to create those revenues. Spending that $20 million in itself is not bad if the company will grow revenues to $40 million or $60 million over the next year or so. But not all companies are growing that fast. When investing in this group, it is important to do the due diligence to ferret out the companies that will grow; this is no easy task.

In the past, even the slow-growth companies spent loosely, which was due to the huge pools of money available to the Internet group. The venture capitalists had deep pockets available for a deal they liked. Also the investment bankers, eager to bring IPOs and secondary offerings, were a source of money. The public, which had made much money in the Internet and technology group, would buy the offerings, sometimes without checking each company's merits. This money pool, however, has dried up since many companies have not become profitable.

Some companies do reach critical mass and generate sizeable revenues and earnings. Yahoo! Inc. (YHOO) is such an example. And the reason Yahoo and like companies have become profitable is that they were in early.

It is possible that Yahoo can become more profitable than Microsoft, Inc. (MSFT) on a relative basis. Microsoft has always been thought of as one of the most profitable companies in the world because of its use of the Internet model of spending money to grow sales and earnings rapidly.

The model of the Internet business is that there are very low costs of operation, especially on content-driven sites. Yahoo is such a site. Yahoo's sales to earnings margins have been very wide, possibly over 50 percent. Margins are a very important element, and one that investors need to watch closely.

## UNDERLYING VALUE OF INTERNET COMPANIES

One of the reasons investors bought an Internet stocks is because of their "take-out value." This is a company's buy-out value, which is the amount a company would receive if it were taken over by another company.

Being taken over is a good way for a stockholder to receive cash on his investment. Dividends could be another way to receive a return, but the possibility of receiving dividends is remote, because no Internet company is expected to pay a dividend of any meaning. Even if a company increased its earnings dramatically, it would plow earnings back into expansion, not benefiting the investor on a shorter-term basis.

What, then, would make an Internet stock go up? One factor is the expectation of growth; the expectation that earnings growth would drive the value of the company higher in the marketplace has made investors buy Internet stocks. And this is what many Internet-related companies have sometimes delivered: substantial growth.

Often earnings estimates from analysts have been lower than Internet stocks have delivered. But if an investor is paying 100 times earnings for an Internet stock, the investor is paying for substantial upside potential in earnings. To buy a stock at 100 times earnings is a risky proposition. If the company meets only estimated earnings, it is often a disappointment, and this has caused many of these stocks to decline. Investors are paying on expectations of even faster growth than the companies anticipate. As long as the Internet companies would deliver, they could command these high valuations.

Investors are also getting more discriminating and are perusing the business models of Internet companies. The gulf is wide between the "haves" and "have-nots" of company earnings in this group—the haves being those companies with high operating margins, the have-nots being the companies that do not have big margins or maybe even earnings. Mostly the have-nots are companies that sell something over the Internet and attract customers because of the convenience of shopping at the click of a mouse. But unless the site has an auction, the consumer's price for that merchandise will not be much lower than buying that merchandise in a store. Also the operating margins of the Internet companies selling the merchandise will not be that wide.

Selling a camera for under $20, for instance, won't make much sense for an Internet company if the camera costs $19.50. The Internet company needs to garner a wider profit margin.

On the other hand, Yahoo, the giant Internet portal, and Infospace.com (INSP), should do well. INSP is a content infrastructure company in the wireless area. Wireless is another area of growth for the Internet sector. Infospace has wide margins, and could become a force in the Internet if the company's earnings grow. Also Go2Net, Inc. (GNET) should grow. The company is a combination of several kinds of Web sites and syndicates the content of other companies. GNET also has very high margins. Digital Impact, Inc. (DIGI), an e-marketing services company, is another high-margined company with a business model that allows for substantial growth. There are other companies like these, which have business models that may continue to grow their earnings.

## Advertising on the Internet

Perhaps the expectation of how well advertising would do on the Internet was too high. Banner ads, that is, ads that appear on the various Web sites, did have a high "click-through rate" when they initially appeared. Click-through rate is the frequency with which visitors to the site click on the banners, allowing the banners to take the visitors to a message or destination. It is now suspected that banner ads had a high click-through rate because they were novelties. Visitors would click on them just to see them work. As the novelty wore off, the numbers of click-throughs dropped.

Banner ads will remain part of e-marketing campaigns. Sponsorships, that is, links from one site to another, will also remain tools. Direct mail, which is an extremely large advertising tool for Internet commerce ventures, will continue to be used. Although it has been predicted that advertising saturation would yield too little in the way of results, advertising is still highly regarded.

## Megamergers

Large mergers, such as the Time Warner Corp. merger with AOL announced on January 10, 2000, are harbingers of the continuing huge flows of capital going into the Internet. This merger indicates that the Internet is the future for media growth. Time Warner was the biggest media company in the world, but had trouble competing with the largest Web provider, AOL. To supply the AOL huge customer base with Time Warner products, Time Warner agreed to the merger.

There are usually gains for the entire industry when megamergers occur. Often, combined companies can affect cost savings, develop innovative advances, and create positive synergies for the combined new company.

This is not lost on the stock market. Often with megamergers there are enthusiastic buyers of the stock. Skeptics of a merger can short the stock, and arbitragers can try to make money on the stock movement of a merger. Arbitragers will go long or short depending on the price differentials of the stock of the merging companies and lock in their profit by taking an offsetting long or short position.

Because of the media coverage of a megadeal and the concomitant large volume of stock trading attached to the coverage, megamergers are events that impact the companies involved and their industry in often a lasting way.

This merger could prove to be a watershed event, with other megadeals being struck between media and Internet companies. Yahoo had been reported to be speaking with The News Corporation, the holding company for the Rupert Murdoch media empire. The two were reported to be discussing ways of joining forces to compete with AOL/Time Warner.

## The Hidden but Vast Internet Infrastructure

The Internet is undergoing a dramatic buildup of infrastructure to service the Internet companies.

Cisco Systems (CSCO) is a company directly involved with building the infrastructure that allows Internet companies to operate. Another sector developing infrastructure for the Internet is optical networking. A company active in this area is JDS Uniphase (JDSU). The optical networking companies are developing a wealth of applications for the broadband, both for the business and consumer users.

Broadband can be thought of as an Internet pipeline that allows the flows of the Internet system into an office or home. Broadband modems come with different power applications. When users experience the more powerful broadband modems, the experience is that of using a fire hose instead of a garden hose. When utilizing a source that delivers more broadband, users can apply video, video conferencing, and other more complex applications.

> Many analysts opine that we are in the "bottom of the first inning" as far as Internet growth is concerned. If this is true, the need for infrastructure is also just starting.

More powerful broadband is delivered with wider broadband suppliers. And with wider bandwidth, the Internet can be accessed much faster. Many users are frustrated with the slowness of accessing the Internet, particularly those working on their computers at home where the equipment may not be that effective. To be more effective it must be possible to download a Web page instantly.

Infrastructure buildup is important to improve the Internet process. Delivering more broadband is one factor to implement. Another factor in upgrading the Internet infrastructure is the buildout of the Web sites. The buildout of Web sites includes adding software and improving the software tools.

Data growth on the Internet is growing tremendously, perhaps 25 to 30 percent each quarter, and this pace is expected to continue. This growth requires a continual buildup in infrastructure, and items such as routers and switchers will be added to handle the data.

As for optics, Sycamore Networks, Inc. (SCMR) is a company that is very active in this area. SCMR markets optical networking products that enable network service providers to enhance and upgrade existing fiber-optic networks; this upgrading will create more bandwidth. One of the technological advances in fiber optics employs electrical impulses, which opens up tremendous capacity through a fiber.

Telecom service providers, Internet servicer providers, and cable operators all need to keep upgrading to keep up with demand. It is imperative to grow capacity quickly because the Internet is slowing due to heavy traffic. The Internet cannot handle all the traffic it is now experiencing, let alone that planned for the future.

## Wireless Internet

Many new companies are contributing to the recent wave of Internet efficiencies. E-Tek Dynamics (ETEK) and Corning Incorporated (GLW) are companies involved in the optics sector.

Wireless Internet has become an important growth niche. This technology will eventually enable users to access the Internet through a handheld telephone. Whether you want to trade stocks, receive weather forecasts, or find a restaurant in which to dine, the means to accomplish this will be at your fingertips. Whether driving or strolling, you can check your e-mail, or do a number of other tasks. Wireless data Internet access is widely used in Europe and Japan. The United States is behind these countries.

Another growth area is in the area of wireless application protocol (WAP). This allows functions such as a person taking the browser on the Internet and fitting it onto her phone screen. This function presently operates at a slow pace but, over time, a company such as Qualcomm, Inc., will supply chips that will enable faster access.

## The Internet Jungle

A lion has a better chance of surviving in the jungle than a smaller animal. A large, strong lion has a better chance than a thin, weak lion. This is pretty much the law of the jungle. In business, usually the stronger a company, the better chance it has to grow: success begets success. This is very true when it comes to Internet companies.

This truism helps explain why some companies have low valuations and some have high valuations. But in the Internet jungle most stocks have a low valuation and a very few have high valuations. Many investors are of the opinion that every dot-com company is commanding a high valuation, and that almost all of these dot-com companies are overpriced. Company valuations are calculated by multiplying the number of outstanding shares by the market price.

A report by Michael Mauboussin, the chief investment strategist at Credit Suisse First Boston (CFSB), along with his colleagues, Alexander Schay and Stephan Kawaja, published a study on Internet valuations and their implications.

The strategy team found that, in fact, Internet stocks might be reasonably valued, comparatively with each other, when the group is analyzed as a whole. The team found that the top 5 percent online companies comprised about 50 percent of the group's total market capitalization. About 90 percent of the group's capitalization was accounted for by the top 50 percent of the companies. Also, the average size of the online companies is about $500 million. This number is misleading because of the large number of companies, and the dominance of a few large companies. The median value, that is, the number at which half the companies are below the median and half are above, is $53 million. That is a very small number, indicating that a few companies are worth very much and many are worth very little. Another finding of the CSFB study is that the bigger companies, in terms of market cap, received the most traffic in a disproportionately high amount.

**Table 3-1** Percentage Volume by User

| % sites | All sites, % | Adult sites, % | Educational sites, % |
|---|---|---|---|
| 0.1 | 32.36 | 1.4 | 2.81 |
| 1 | 55.63 | 15.83 | 23.76 |
| 5 | 74.81 | 41.75 | 59.50 |
| 10 | 82.26 | 59.29 | 74.48 |
| 50 | 94.92 | 90.76 | 96.88 |

SOURCE: Lada A. Ademic and Berand A. Huberman, "The Nature of Markets in the World Wide Web," *Quarterly Journal of Electronic Commerce,* 1(2000) pp. 5–12.

Table 3-1 shows that the top 119 sites, which represent 0.1 percent of all sites, received 32.36 percent of users visiting the Internet; the top 1 percent of the sites received 55.63 percent of the users coming to the Internet. Also, the chart shows that the top 50 percent of the sites captured almost 95 percent of the traffic on all Web sites.

The conclusion is clear: After the bigger sites handle most of the traffic, there is very little traffic for the smaller sites to service. If 50 percent of the sites take all but 5 percent of Internet traffic, many of the remaining sites will have little or no traffic. And traffic is what it takes to achieve profitability.

Just like the lion in the jungle, the bigger one gets on the Internet, the study shows, the better one's survival chances. And the smaller one is, the lower the chances of survival. The Internet, it is clear, is a winner-takes-all proposition.

## Internet Valuations

If the bigger get bigger and the smaller companies languish and fail, it follows that larger companies with more traffic should be valued higher, which they are. The CFSB study concludes that for valuations to be accurate, Internet companies should be valued against other Internet companies, and not against bricks-and-mortar companies. When done this way, the valuations do not seem so sky-high.

It is doubtful that the tendency of the stronger getting stronger will change. The larger and well-known sites have brand names that will be hard for smaller sites to overcome. As large amounts of money are invested to advertise and promote new names, the public is being swamped by dotcom names that are easily forgotten. For instance, people are left wondering if the name they wanted to remember was pets.com or petsetc.com or pet.com.

The problem with building a brand name is further appreciated when it is understood that an online firm has only a Web address to distinguish it. Without a brand name the firm must spend freely to link up with search companies so that its site can be referred to and visited. But sites that already have a name also link to other sites, therefore attracting more visitors and getting even more popular. Many factors on the Web favor the strong, well-known names.

## PRICED LIKE AN OPTION

It has been suggested that Internet stocks, especially those of the smaller-cap variety, more closely resemble stock options than stocks. A stock option gives the buyer the right to buy a stock at a price, called the "strike price," through a certain date, called the "expiration date." For this the option buyer pays a price, called a "premium." A stock option is time-sensitive; if the stock does not trade above the strike price at the expiration date, the option will expire worthless.

Small Internet stocks may or may not make it, and they only have so long to stay alive. The deep pockets behind the small Internet company, the management and/or bankers of that company, will give the company just so long—usually 2 or 3 years—to start making money. If the company doesn't make money the backers will give up and not fund the company anymore, and the company will "go away," which is a nice way of saying close down.

For investors, purchasing stocks in these companies are gambles, which are more akin to buying options than buying stocks. A buyer in a small company must understand that the company has only so long to make it. Like an option, the stock will be virtually worthless if the company does not start making money and the backers give up.

This time factor view highlights the riskiness an investor has when buying into this group; with this risk comes the extreme leverage, which could lead to substantial profits if the company succeeds.

# PART II

# INDEXES, STOCKS, AND FUNDS

# CHAPTER 4

# THE INDEX AND EXCHANGE SHARES

## THE EVOLUTION OF THE NASDAQ-100 EXCHANGE SHARES—SYMBOL QQQ

Back in 1997, the strategists at the Nasdaq exchange explored the possibilities of new products. They considered everything such as sector allocation models, international market exposure, and Internet exposure. One of the findings was the possibility of developing an investor's tool and, to this end, Nasdaq might develop an exchange-traded fund based on the Nasdaq-100 Index.

At that time there was a mutual fund tracking the Nasdaq-100 and an option on the Nasdaq-100. But there wasn't much activity on these or any other derivative product based on Nasdaq, although the strategists thought there could be much demand for such a product. So in 1998, Nasdaq commenced a process of developing an exchange-traded fund on the Nasdaq-100. It was thought that the product would be an excellent tool to extend the Nasdaq brand to investors and traders.

Nasdaq is different from the other index sponsors because it is also a stock market. Because of this, Nasdaq has an added relationship with the companies listed on its index; the companies listed in the Nasdaq index are also listed on its exchange. Nasdaq figured it could also solidify its relationship with companies listed on the Nasdaq-100 Index. Companies such as Cisco Systems, Intel, Inc., and Dell Computers, Inc., are listed on the Nasdaq exchange and are also included in its index.

Also Nasdaq wished to create an investment vehicle for investment bankers and brokers to allow those groups a vehicle to participate in the broad performance of the Nasdaq exchange. The Nasdaq strategists developed the exchange share in 1998, and listed it under the symbol QQQ. At about the same time, Nasdaq merged with the Amex. Amex probably trades more exchange share than any other exchange.

QQQ was launched on March 10, 1999, with the first trade at 102¼. The value of QQQ increased: on March 3, 2000, QQQ traded at about 220, on a presplit basis. On the first day of trading, QQQ had an asset base of about $15 million. As orders came in during the first trading day, the asset base grew to where, by the end of the day, the asset base was $250 million. The assets have grown dramatically since then. By March 3, 2000, the asset base of QQQ was $9.3 billion. QQQ trades about 16 million shares a day, making it the most actively traded security in terms of volume on the Amex.

## Internet, Technology, and Growth Stocks

Internet stocks are not driving QQQ because most of the Internet stocks have not been around long enough to be in QQQ. The driver of QQQ is technology stocks. Major companies in QQQ include Microsoft, MCI WorldCom, Inc., and Qualcomm, Inc., all important technology companies. It is clear that over the last few years, the Internet has become important to these companies, as well as to many other QQQ companies. Most major technology companies on QQQ are involved in building the backbone of the Internet. The routers of Cisco Systems and the Internet Explorer from Microsoft, for example, are important products for the Internet.

An advantage of QQQ is that it covers a variety of sectors. There are nontech companies as well as high-tech companies in QQQ. Computer hardware, software, telecommunications, and biotech companies have been stellar performers for the index in the past.

### How Will QQQ Perform in the Future?

QQQ will perform well if the Nasdaq-100 companies comprising the index grow their earnings. Nasdaq is the home of new companies, new industries, and new sectors. The companies that will build the economy of the future should end up going public and list on the Nasdaq. Nasdaq believes it is the capital engine for new companies.

The Nasdaq-100 Index is exactly what it describes: it is comprised of the 100 largest nonfinancial companies on the Nasdaq exchange. Therefore, the index is an ongoing selector of growing companies. Nasdaq reranks the companies in the index each December. Those companies that are not growing are dropped, because their market capitalizations have not kept pace. Those companies that have grown are added to the index.

For instance, if a biotech company has grown to one of the 100 largest companies, it is added to the index. If in a year a telecom stock or an Internet stock or a stock of any other industry does better than one of the stocks in the index, that stock is added.

Nasdaq is home to all of these new technologies, as well as old economy companies. All companies are moving at different rates of speed, but because the Nasdaq-100 Index is limited to the number of stocks in the index, the process continues to pick the growing companies.

During the year, if a company falls out of the Nasdaq-100 Index because of a merger, it will be replaced. The company is replaced by the next largest 100 company. The replacement company will be a growth company by the very fact that it has grown large enough to be in the index.

Recent IPOs will rarely be included in QQQ. A criterion of QQQ is that a company has to be listed on an exchange for 2 years before it can make the index.

If a company has been listed on another exchange, the period of time that the company was listed on the other exchange is counted for the 2-year time requirement. Also if a company has grown sufficiently in a year after its IPO to be among the top 25 companies on the Nasdaq exchange the stock is admitted to the index.

## The Nasdaq Model

Nasdaq has grown up in this age of technology, along with many of the companies that trade on its exchange. As far as the Internet is concerned, the exchange is involved in having Internet-related stocks trading on the exchange and in the Nasdaq-100 Index. Every business has an Internet strategy. The Internet may be the focus of a company, or helpful in how a company conducts its business, but the Internet is as indispensable to a company today as is the telephone. Nasdaq's type of market blends in well with the workings of the Internet.

For about 30 years Nasdaq has experienced the value of networking computers. The Nasdaq market is the largest private intramarket in the world. The private network set up by MCI WorldCom for the Nasdaq market links together all the securities firms that trade inside the Nasdaq market system. As measured by MCI Worldwide, the Nasdaq system is the largest private computer network in existence.

### Nasdaq 100—A Cap-Weighted Index

The Dow Jones Industrial Average is a price-weighted benchmark. A price-weighted index moves differently than a market cap-weighted index. The underlying stocks in a price-weighted index are weighted by their price. The higher the price of the stocks, the greater their percentage impact on the index. In a price-weighted index a $30 stock is worth twice as much as a $15 stock. If the $30 stock represents a $2 million company and the $15 stock represents a $2 billion company, the $30 stock, in this example, would have the heavier impact. The $30 stock would have more impact even though the $15 stock represents a company with a much bigger market cap.

A market cap-weighted index takes into consideration the size of the company when calculating the values of the index price. The Nasdaq-100 is a market cap-weighted index. Most indexes today are market cap or modified market cap indexes. Market cap appears to be a better way to value indexes, because that type of index takes each company's size into consideration. Technically QQQ is not an index, but a tracking stock mirroring the Nasdaq-100 Index.

### QQQ Has Split

QQQ sells in 100-share increments. A minimum order of 100 shares of QQQ at 220, its presplit price, would cost about $22,000. Many investors wanted to invest in QQQ, but could not afford this minimum purchase.

On March 20, 2000, QQQ split 2 for 1. Nasdaq thinks that pricing QQQ back to its original price range of about $100 a share put QQQ within reach of more retail investors.

No change in value or adjustment in the index resulted as a consequence of this split; the only change was the price per share of QQQ. QQQ has fallen to about $60 a share. Now a minimum 100 shares will cost about $6000.

## Internet HOLDRs—Symbol HHH

Merrill Lynch created and marketed an Internet basket of stocks entitled Internet HLDRs. The basket is structured as exchange shares, and trades on the Amex under the symbol HHH. Through handling individual accounts, Merrill noticed investor concerns regarding the volatility of the markets, especially regarding the Internet stocks. Merrill wanted to address the expanding opportunity in equity markets globally, but also the increasing volatility of equities.

It is difficult for any investor to be an expert stock picker, especially in each and every sector of the market around the world that represents an opportunity. So Merrill Lynch put together a tradable basket of stocks, which offers diversification in this volatile sector.

The difference between the HOLDRs and most other exchange share classes is that with HOLDRs investors actually own the underlying stocks. Investors can take delivery of the stocks that they are holding in the HOLDRs baskets.

Among the stocks in HHH is Exodus Communications (EXDS), which is in the business of Web hosting services. Also in the basket are stocks such as Amazon.com (AMZN) and Priceline.com (PCLN), which are more consumer-oriented issues.

Investors and traders interested in participating in Internet stocks can pick their own issues and put together their own portfolios. But by buying HOLDRs, a lot of the work of getting exposure to a wide range of Internet stocks has already been done. If you wish to tender your HOLDRs for the underlying stock, your broker can assist you in this transaction. Table 4-1 lists stocks comprising HHH.

**Table 4-1** Stocks Comprising HHH

| Name and symbol | Name and symbol |
| --- | --- |
| America Online, Inc. (AOL) | E*Trade Group, Inc. (EGRP) |
| Yahoo!, Inc. (YHOO) | Double Click, Inc. (DCLK) |
| Amazon.com, Inc. (AMZN) | Ameritrade Holding Corp. (AMTD) |
| eBay, Inc. (EBAY) | Lycos, Inc. (LCOS) |
| At Home Corp. (ATHM) | CNET, Inc. (CNET) |
| Priceline.com, Inc. (PCLN) | PSINet, Inc. (PSIX) |
| CMGI, Inc. (CMGI) | Network Associates, Inc. (NETA) |
| Inktomi Corp. (INKT) | EarthLink Network, Inc. (ELNK) |
| Real Networks, Inc. (RNWK) | Go2Net, Inc. (GNET) |
| Exodus Communications Inc. (EXDS) | |

SOURCE: Courtesy of freeEDGAR.com.

## INTERNET-RELATED INDEXES

Internet-related indexes are important because they gauge investors' sentiment on the Internet group at a given time. The indexes can move for a number of reasons: good or bad news emanating from the industry, such as the amount of traffic on the Net, profitability of companies that are Net-related, new developments, or other factors.

Investors' sentiment as related to Internet developments often impacts the prices of the stock in the group. Not all stocks will follow negative or positive sentiments, but it is often foolish, and costly, to back group sentiment.

Another reason to peruse indexes such as an Internet index is because invariably there are key companies that show up in many of the indexes of a sector. This is no mistake, as each group has key companies that are bellwethers for the group.

Instead of buying an index you could research a few of the more representative stocks and buy these stocks. This may add to your risk, choosing less stocks, but may also add to your profit.

### The *Wired* Magazine Index

The Wired Index, put out by *Wired* magazine, is not strictly an Internet index. The Index contains a variety of companies. The idea for the Wired Index started being developed in 1998. *Wired* magazine had been reporting on the new economy since the magazine was founded, and the editors decided to develop a list of 40 companies that best represented the new economy. The editors wanted to create a sort of "updated" Dow Jones Industrial Average.

Some of the guidelines used by the editors were that a selected company had to be operating globally; would prosper in the new economy; would have demonstrated innovation; would have the need to use information in its business everyday; would have to be knowledge-based; would use technology as an integral daily part of the company's business; and would have demonstrated an adherence to its long-term strategic goals.

The editors at *Wired* magazine revise the index every year, taking into account the growth of the companies on the index. They replace companies that have been merged off of the index, and also consider the other included companies in relationship to the general economic outlook.

Wired wants the list to be as representative as possible, over as many industries as possible, as long as editors believe these companies and industries are going to be a key to global economic growth.

The telecommunications industry is represented in the index. The industry representation includes telecom technology suppliers such as Lucent Technologies, Inc. (LU), as well as companies that own bandwidth, such as MCI WorldCom (WCOM) and Qwest Communications International, Inc. (Q). Also included are companies such as Cisco Systems (CSCO), which is a supplier to the bandwidth companies.

Represented are the semiconductor and computer hardware industries. Intel, Inc., and Dell Computers are included in this group. Information services companies are also included. Two examples are Reuters Group PLC (RTQ), which is a global information company known for supplying financial information but which also supplies news, and America Online, Inc. (AOL). Software companies are represented, with Microsoft, Inc. (MSFT) being one of the represented companies. Yahoo! Inc. (YHOO) and Walt Disney, Inc. (DIS), are included in the Wired Index.

There are companies included which are part of the old economy. Nucor (NUE) is a steel company but is using technology and new production techniques and, therefore, using knowledge in an interesting way.

### Managing the Wired Magazine Index

The editors believe that technology and information management is paramount in their assessment of various companies and is the key to the Wired portfolio. The index includes companies that supply information and entertainment software. Companies such as this are not weighted as heavily in a traditional Dow Jones Industrial Average type of portfolio.

The editors that manage the Wired Index are a rather loose-knit group and not a formal committee. The editors also consult with analysts at investment banks who are experts on the new economy.

Many times the companies included in the index are discovered by the writers or editors researching the company for the magazine. Sometimes a writer will suggest a company to the editors for inclusion, or in covering a company the magazine might decide a company should be included.

The managers realize that the stocks they include in the index are very volatile, and that this volatility will probably continue. But they also believe that the development of the new economy has barely begun and that there are several decades of growth left in the new economy. See Table 4-2 for a listing of Wired Index stocks.

Because of *Wired* magazine's business, which is reporting on trends and difficult-to-see new developments in the technological field, including Internet activity, the index developed by the magazine is important to consider. The Wired Index seeks to pick out and use those companies that are

**Table 4-2** Wired Index

| Symbol | Name | Current price level | Last 52-week stock price High | Last 52-week stock price Low |
|---|---|---|---|---|
| ACXM | Acxiom Corporation | $35.812 | $ 45.75 | $16.75 |
| AFFX | Affymetrix, Inc. | $71.250 | $163.50 | $42.31 |
| AOL | America Online, Inc. | $38.280 | $95.81 | $34.48 |
| AIG | American Int'l. Group, Inc. | $96.810 | $103.75 | $52.37 |
| AMR | AMR Corporation | $35.930 | $70.00 | $26.00 |
| AMAT | Applied Materials | $38.625 | $115.00 | $34.12 |
| CWP | Cable and Wireless Plc. | $40.312 | $75.25 | $34.50 |
| SCH | Charles Schwab Corp. | $28.562 | $44.75 | $21.33 |
| CSCO | Cisco Systems, Inc. | $41.500 | $82.00 | $35.15 |
| DCX | DaimlerChrysler AG | $40.380 | $78.68 | $37.75 |
| DELL | Dell Computer | $18.375 | $59.68 | $16.25 |
| EMC | EMC Corporation | $68.250 | $104.93 | $41.65 |
| ENE | Enron Corp. | $81.187 | $90.75 | $35.12 |
| FDX | FedEx Corporation | $38.530 | $49.85 | $30.56 |
| FDC | First Data Corporation | $49.375 | $57.68 | $37.00 |
| GSTRF | Globalstar Telecommunications | $1.000 | $53.75 | $1.00 |
| INCY | Incyte Pharmaceuticals | $24.000 | $144.53 | $14.12 |
| INTC | Intel Corporation | $32.937 | $75.81 | $31.25 |
| LU | Lucent Technologies, Inc. | $13.625 | $84.18 | $12.18 |
| MAR | Marriott Int'l., Inc. (new) | $39.687 | $43.50 | $26.12 |
| WCOM | MCI WorldCom, Inc. | $13.875 | $56.08 | $13.50 |
| MSFT | Microsoft Corporation | $46.430 | $119.93 | $40.25 |

CHAPTER 4  THE INDEX AND EXCHANGE SHARES

**Table 4-2** (*Continued*)

| Symbol | Name | Current price level | Last 52-week stock price High | Last 52-week stock price Low |
|---|---|---|---|---|
| NWS | News Corporation Limited | $31.250 | $67.00 | $30.87 |
| NOK | Nokia Corporation | $43.687 | $62.50 | $27.62 |
| NUE | Nucor Corporation | $38.250 | $57.43 | $29.50 |
| PMTC | Parametric Technology | $12.937 | $35.93 | $7.37 |
| PSFT | Peoplesoft Incorporated | $34.750 | $50.00 | $12.00 |
| RTRSY | Reuters Group Plc. | $103.250 | $157.25 | $64.87 |
| SLB | Schlumberger Ltd. | $76.500 | $88.87 | $52.68 |
| SBH | Smithkline Beecham | $61.875 | $72.18 | $52.50 |
| SNE | Sony Corporation | $69.500 | $157.37 | $67.00 |
| STT | State Street Corporation | $121.990 | $136.80 | $62.43 |
| SUNW | Sun Microsystems, Inc. | $31.875 | $64.65 | $25.12 |
| TMO | Thermo Electron Corp. | $29.200 | $31.24 | $13.68 |
| WMT | Wal-Mart Stores, Inc. | $52.500 | $70.25 | $41.43 |
| DIS | Walt Disney Company | $26.437 | $43.87 | $26.00 |
| WIND | Wind River Systems, Inc. | $35.562 | $66.12 | $25.37 |
| YHOO | Yahoo! Inc. | $29.562 | $250.06 | $25.06 |

Copyright 1994–2000 Wired Digital, Inc. All Rights Reserved.

active in the new economy. These businesses are chosen for their understanding and use of technology in their operating strategy. By necessity this means developing and using cutting-edge tools.

An investor interested in being apprised of companies that are innovative in the use of technology in their everyday activities should look at the names in this index to stay up to date. Also an investor could look to the index to find companies to invest in, perhaps constructing a basket of stocks from the index for her own portfolio.

## The Internet.com Index: The Isdex Index

The general purpose of the Isdex Index is to track the Internet economy. The staff at Internet.com keeps track of all the Internet stocks, basically starting from their pre-IPO stage through the time they become mature public companies. Every Internet stock is placed into one of the 12 sectors that Internet.com has devised as the Internet universe. The number of stocks change, and at the present time there are 321 companies that are Internet companies as defined by Isdex. Internet.com requires that a company must have over 50 percent of its revenues from Internet-related activities in order to be classified as an Internet company.

Internet.com categorizes the 321 companies by sectors. Some of the sectors are e-tailers, e-commerce enablers, financial services, Internet service providers, and bandwidth supply companies. Out of the 321 companies, Internet.com places 50 stocks into the Isdex Index.

Inter.com uses the larger, more actively traded companies in its attempt to capture the Internet economy. The Isdex Index represents about 66 percent of the market capitalization of public Internet companies. The market value of the stock universe used by Isdex is about $1.6 trillion; this is a huge pool of pure Internet companies. The index has a requirement that no one company can account for more than 10 percent of the index. Because of this, three stocks were capped out at 10 percent and were held at a lesser number of shares than their importance indicated. The index is posted on the Kansas City Board of Trade Web site.

On March 1, 2000, the index closed above 1000 for the first time ever. The Isdex started trading in June 1996 at 100, so the index at that time was up about 900 percent since its inception. In 1999, the index was up 155 percent. The year 2000 was a rough one for Internet stocks, and the index had returned −24 percent by October 2000.

Overall, the index has performed comparatively well. America Online and Yahoo! are two of the stocks capped at 10 percent. These stocks did poorly in 2000, so capping these companies at 10 percent helped the overall performance of the index.

### Choosing Isdex Stocks

It takes some work to screen out a universe of stocks to arrive at 321 Internet stocks, and then to filter these down to 50. Internet.com works

CHAPTER 4   THE INDEX AND EXCHANGE SHARES                                63

**Table 4-3** ISDEX®—The Internet Stock Index®

| Company | Stock symbol | Business |
|---|---|---|
| Aether Systems, Inc. | AETH | Wireless and mobile data service provider |
| Allaire Corp. | ALLR | Performance software |
| Ariba | ARBA | E-commerce/procurement solutions |
| @Home | ATHM | Cable Internet services |
| 24/7 Media, Inc. | TFSM | Ad network |
| Amazon | AMZN | E-tailer of books, music, video |
| Ameritrade Holding Corp. | AMTD | Internet trading provider |
| America Online, Inc. | AOL | Consumer online services |
| Broadcom | BRCM | Broadband chips |
| Broadvision | BVSN | Web marketing software |
| CheckPoint Software | CHKP | Web security software |
| Cisco | CSCO | Leading Internet routing firm |
| CMG Info | CMGI | Internet venture firm |
| CNET | CNET | Web and cable content |
| DoubleClick | DCLK | Web advertising |
| E*Trade | EGRP | Web stock trades |
| Earthlink, Inc. | ELNK | Internet services provider |
| eBay | EBAY | Leading personal auction service |
| eToys Inc. | ETYS | Internet toy retailer |
| Exodus | EXDS | Web hosting data centers |
| GoTo.com | GOTO | Navigation services |
| WebMD Corp. | HLTH | Leading health-care Web service |
| Homestore.com.Inc. | HOMS | Online home products, services, information |
| i2 Technologies | ITWO | Supply chain management |
| Infospace.com | INSP | Navigation services |
| Inktomi | INKT | Network caching, search wholesaler |

**Table 4-3** (*Continued*)

| Company | Stock symbol | Business |
|---|---|---|
| Internet Security Systems, Inc. | ISSX | Security software |
| Juniper Networks | JNPR | Faster Internet infrastructure |
| Liberate Technologies | LBRT | Software provider |
| MarchFirst, Inc. | MRCH | E-business services |
| Net2Phone, Inc. | NTOP | Internet phone service provider |
| Openwave Systems, Inc. | OPWV | Wireless phone software provider |
| Portal Software Inc. | PRSF | Domain name registrar |
| priceline.com Inc. | PCLN | E-commerce buying service |
| PSINet | PSIX | Internet services provider |
| RealNetworks | RNWK | Internet streaming media software |
| RSA Security | RSAS | Internet security software |
| Scient Corp. | SCNT | eBusiness Systems Innovator |
| S1 Corporation | SONE | Web banking software |
| Sportsline.com, Inc. | SPLN | Web-based sports news |
| StarMedia Network, Inc. | STRM | Leading Web guide for Latin America |
| Sycamore Networks, Inc. | SCMR | Optical networking |
| Terra Networks, S.A. | TRRA | Spanish ISP |
| Tibco Software, Inc. | TIBX | Software provider |
| TicketMaster-CitySearch | TMCS | Leading local city guide |
| Verisign | VRSN | Web Digital ID issuer |
| VerticalNet | VERT | Vertical community services |
| Vignette | VIGN | Performance software |
| Wireless Facilities, Inc. | WFII | Global leader in telecommunications outsourcing |
| Yahoo! | YHOO | Navigation services |

fastidiously to accomplish this feat. Internet.com started following the industry in 1996, so it has a good working knowledge of the group. It watches all the IPOs, looking for stocks that will fit into the index. The index rarely purchases a new issue or recent issue because the index does not know the trading characteristics of the issue. Some IPOs trade furiously at first and appear to be liquid, but it is not until trading settles down and the stocks trade for awhile that one can ascertain that the stocks are in fact liquid.

After screening the stocks of the Internet sector, Internet.com considers market capitalizations and trading patterns of the different issues. Inter.com wants its Isdex Index to be representative of the Internet industry, not a hot stock index. Market cap, trading volume, shares outstanding, and size of the company as measured by revenues, are the most important criteria for the index. Growth and future prospects are also considered. Sometimes the managers have to make judgment calls, buying one stock rather than another on a gut feel. But rarely does the gut call come into play. The managers are trying to reflect the Internet economy rather than making a guess on the future of Internet stocks in the marketplace. Internet.com follows company stock developments closely, and every quarter it rebalances the index.

### Participating in the Isdex Index

People can participate in the Isdex Index in two ways. For the adventuresome there are futures and options on futures traded on the Kansas City Board of Trade Exchange. For less adventuresome investors there is a mutual fund, the Guinness Flight Inter.com Index Fund. The symbol is GFINX. It is a no-load fund that tracks the index. Information can be gathered by visiting the Guinness Flight US Mutual Funds Homepage. See Table 4-3 for a listing and description of Isdex Internet stock index companies.

# CHAPTER 5

# INTERNET, TECHNOLOGY, AND OTHER GROWTH SECTORS

## COMPONENT PARTS OF THE INTERNET

The Internet can be broken down into four parts. There are the infrastructure piece, service piece, content piece, and commerce piece; these parts put together build the Internet. Usually, when people think of Internet companies, they think of Amazon.com (AMZN), eBay (EBAY), and Yahoo! Inc, (YHOO). These are content and commerce companies. People think of these companies because they are the most prevalent in the lives of general consumers.

However, when the Internet is pulled apart, it can be seen that the value pools are in areas across the Internet spectrum. The different component parts are linked together in a value chain, which could be from being an electron in a content part to being part of a service that can be used by consumers. When an investor understands these components, he or she might see that there are many ways to invest in the Internet; there may be better places to invest than just in the known names.

## Valuing Explosive Growth

The growth rate in the technology group at times has been very extreme. Before the Internet explosion, it was rare to see a group of companies growing this quickly. Some analysts say that investment valuation is a nonlinear type of issue with this sort of growth. There are opinions that P/Es reflect only the present underlying earnings performance. This is relevant when there are normal growth rates of 15 to 20 percent. When growth rates become nonlinear, and in the case of Internet companies, explode on the upside, some think that P/Es don't really work well as valuation tools. A solution could be to use other valuations such as growth rate to P/E ratios, which tend to normalize a stock's growth and earnings factors. But once growth rates go beyond 30 percent or so, a ratio such as this may not work effectively either. How to value these new-economy stocks continues to be a problem.

Recognizing that the driver for companies to grow is revenue growth, some analysts are using revenue growth more as their major quantitative barometer. Other analysts are using stock price to sales (P/S) as a yardstick. The thinking here is that you can manipulate earnings somewhat, but sales you cannot; therefore, sales is a more accurate measurement.

A measurement gaining in usage is the price-to-earnings growth ratio, referred to as the PEG ratio. This ratio allows analysts to view a company's price and earnings in comparison to its growth.

The mathematical expression of the PEG ratio can be calculated by comparing the price and earnings to the growth expected by using these factors as numerators and denominators. For instance, if a company has a P/E of 10 times and is expected to grow at 10 percent a year, the PEG ratio is 1.0. Interpreting this calculation, the lower the PEG ratio, the better. A fair PEG ratio value would be 1.0. If a company has a P/E of 20 times and is expected to grow at 10 percent a year, the PEG ratio is 2.0 times, which is a high ratio; a PEG ratio of 0.5 times would imply that a company is selling at a low ratio, roughly at half of its real value. The use of the PEG ratio is expected to grow, especially in the faster-growing new-economy stocks.

In an attempt to use relevant analysis, some analysts have turned to revenue multiples. But the Internet industry is so new that other analysts think this is a weak approach. Those who question the high prices in the Internet group in relation to most valuation methods, and conclude that the group was in a bubble pricewise, have to be seriously considered.

But the industry is considered by many analysts to be in its infancy. Not many analysts will argue that the growth for the Internet industry is topping out for all times.

## The Day Trader's Effect

Many Internet stocks have a small float of outstanding shares. And against this small float there have been legions of day traders, clicking on and trading the volatile Internet group for small moves. The stocks of the smaller Internet companies sometimes traded up and down on big volume. Many of these trades were not made on the basis of fundamental valuation. These were trades from day traders who were going with the momentum, either up or down, for small profits.

A long- or short-term trader can take advantage of the excess volatility caused by point and click day traders. Because of the "buzz" during the trading day, stocks move quickly and a trader can get whipsawed out of a good position.

One strategy so as not to get whipsawed is to avoid placing stop orders during the day. With a stop order, when the stock reaches a certain price, the order becomes a market order to buy or sell a stock. Stop orders are usually used to protect a profit or limit a loss. If a trader is short, she can use a stop order to limit her loss against the stock going higher; if she is long stock, she can limit her downside risk by selling at a certain lower price and taking her loss.

Instead of entering stop orders during the day, a trader could place her stop orders after the close, at the end of the day. This could cut down on a trader getting stopped out before a stock reverses itself during the trading day.

A trader can also take advantage of excess volatility by standing back and looking at a longer-term chart before making her buys and sells. These charts, such as monthly or yearly charts, give a longer-term perspective of the trading characteristics of a stock. This often allows a trader to better time her purchases and sales.

The excess volatility caused by the point-and-click traders seems to be mostly centered in the technology, biotechnology, and telecommunications area—the new-economy stocks. Many of the more conventional sectors, such as finance or consumer staples, have not experienced nearly the excess volatility of the new-economy stocks.

## Infrastructure Pieces

There is a wireless transport component, which includes companies that are engaged in connectivity functions. Companies involved in hardware, routers, and hubs, would fit into this category.

Emerging kinds of service companies are developing on the Internet. First there are the Internet service providers (ISPs); included in this group are personal and commercial versions. Then there are companies such as Exodus Communications, Inc. (EXDS), that facilitate the hosting of these Web pages. A newer category, which is attracting much interest, is the application service providers (ASPs). ASPs function similarly to time-sharing arrangements for bandwidths. Bandwidth has become relatively abundant lately, and the ASPs offer to rent bandwidth when more is needed by a user.

So the Internet is very expansive, and there is much more happening behind the scenes than consumers can easily see. It is expected that the next big leg of growth will occur in the infrastructure of the Internet.

## Core Internet Companies

Amazon.com, Yahoo! Inc., Akamai Technologies, Inc. (AKAM), and CMGI, Inc. (CMGI), are all key players in the Internet universe. Another key company is Network Solutions, Inc. (NSOL). This company owned the brands for dot-com. The company controlled brands such as dot-edu, dot-org, and dot-go. Network Solutions was a quasi-governmental agency for many years, and as the Internet grew, it was able to acquire these brands. The company owns the phone book that connects the Internet addresses. The addresses are technically known as the GCPIP address. The address gives the actual name of the Web page, called the URL, which stands for Uniform Resource Locator.

An example of how this cyber-addressing works is to suppose that you go to a telephone book and cannot remember somebody's phone number, but do remember the person's name. So you look up the number and make the call. The same thing is true for a cyber-address. You go to your computer. You can't remember a person's Web page, but you do know the person works at, say, Prudential Securities. So you type Prudential Securities into your link to the Web.

When you type that name in, the name goes to the Network Solutions database. The database locates the TCPIP address, which is usually a number and letters on the Internet. The database refers you to the correct Web page address.

Network Solutions registers every domain name. The company has a virtual monopoly on the Web telephone book itself, which is called the Registry. The company is in the process of losing its monopoly as the registrar for the Web. Still, NSOL, because of its situation as a registrar to the Internet world, is in an advantageous position to know what type of commerce is developing on the Net. The first place a company goes when they sign onto the Net, is to register their name. This could benefit NSOL as it makes investments in other companies or plans its own corporate strategy.

CMGI, Inc., also is in a position to invest in other companies wisely on the Net. The company reviews over 1000 business plans a month. Through the flood of plans it receives, the company has an extraordinary opportunity to view new-product developments on the Net. CMGI can leverage this insight to the over 70 companies that make up its loosely knit conglomerate.

CMGI, down sharply from its highs, had benefited from the substantial premiums paid for Internet conglomerates. This is a recent development. Back in the 1960s, conglomerates, that is, diverse companies that are knit together within a corporate structure to fit a unified whole, sold at premiums. A conglomerate's market value as a single entity was valued higher than if its individual parts were sold separately. It was believed that efficiencies of scale justified the companies' selling for more as a package. But for the last 20 years or so conglomerates have sold at a discount at the marketplace. When conglomerates were related to the Internet, they had again commanded a premium. For this reason, many companies connected to the Internet are forming their own venture subsidiaries. The subsidiaries go out and put together a stable of Internet start-ups.

Amazon.com (AMZN) is another highly visible Internet player. The consumer space on the Internet, which is called B2C, or business to consumer, is fundamentally breaking down. Many of the business models in this sector are just not working.

> *An open question is whether the e-tailing models of building traffic at any cost will ever work. Many investors have lost their patience. They will not tolerate companies following this model, and they will continue avoiding the group.*

The Internet is creating an extremely competitive pricing environment. Many consumer-type companies have started selling goods at cost. For instance, Egghead.com, an online seller of computer products, has gross margins on some of its products of only 1.5 percent. And this is before they deduct some SG&A items, which are additional costs.

The business models of these companies calculate that the companies may not make money for their goods and services for a while. But Internet companies expect to make money on advertising such as banner ads, for which advertisers will pay the Web site to show. The Internet companies are trying to use e-tailing business to build traffic, and plan to monetize this expected traffic in certain ways.

Amazon.com has some of these problems. Some of the products it sells, such as electronics, are being sold at close to cost. However, AMZN gives such superior customer service, offers such a breadth of products, and has so many product lines that have wider profit margins, that the company is unique in its consumer space.

For instance, Amazon.com receives about a 25 percent gross margin for the books it sells. It receives this wide margin because it completely dominates that consumer space. The company has been successful in getting customers back to reuse its services by offering many extras, such as commentaries on books.

Yahoo! Inc. (YHOO), however, has a business plan that has worked fairly well. Yahoo does not produce its content. The company is an aggregator and distributor of content. It has been successful in gathering eyeballs and monetizing those large numbers of visitors. Yahoo, through its brand name, has created a sense of a continual presence of Yahoo in people's lives. The price pressure on Yahoo stock is due to the recent linkup between AOL and Time Warner, Inc. There is speculation that Yahoo will have to integrate vertically with a large-content multimedia company to expand its presence. Yahoo has been having discussions with others about strategic alliances.

## Internet Companies That Have Broad Analyst Coverage*

**Amazon.com (AMZN)**—Sales, $1.680 million; 1-year sales growth, 168.8 percent. Reputedly the largest bookstore in the world, the company offers millions of books. It also offers many other products such as pet supplies and drugs.

**Yahoo! Inc. (YHOO)**—Sales, $588 million; 1-year sales growth, 189.5 percent. This is one of the largest of the Internet portals. The company draws more than 43 million visitors to its site each month. The site has about 3800 advertisers.

**Excite@Home (ATHM)**—Sales, $48 million; 1-year sales growth, 602.1 percent. This is a better-known portal and Internet access company. Its features include content, e-mail, and search services; one of its services offers free Internet access.

**Akamai Technologies, Inc. (AKAM)**—Sales, $4 million; 1-year sales growth, 3900 percent. As a service provider, Akamai fills the needs of

---
*Source: Hoover's Online.

commerce companies and content providers. The company covers the globe ensuring that content is available.

**CMGI (CMGI)**—Sales, $175 million; 1-year sales growth, 92 percent. The company is a network of diverse and interconnected companies involved in Internet business. It has a large cash position and billions of dollars of marketable securities.

**Network Solutions, Inc. (NSOL)**—Sales, $26 million; 1-year sales growth 135.6 percent. This is a registrar of Internet addresses. It offers many services including a dot-com directory, Web site maintenance, and dot-com promotions.

**Lycos, Inc. (LCOS)**—Sales, $291 million; 1-year sales growth, 114.8 percent. This is a portal that has grown in use to serve other needs of its visitors. It is one of the most visited hubs on the Internet, reaching one out of two Web users.

**Prodigy Communications Corporation (PRGY)**—Sales, $189 million; 1-year sales growth, 38.9 percent. This is a national Internet service provider, with a subscriber base of about 1.2 million subscribers.

**InfoSpace.com, Inc. (INSP)**—Sales, $36.8 million; 1-year sales growth 291.5 percent. The company is a leading provider of infrastructure services for consumers, merchants, and wireless devices. Its services are distributed through portals and affinity sites.

# BIOTECHNOLOGY
## Background of the Second Revolution
The present biotech wave is seen as the second coming of the biotech revolution. Its origins are back in the 1980s. Companies like Amgen, Inc. (AMGN), and Chiron Corp. (CHIR) were using some very specific technologies to come up with pharmacological solutions to problems. What these companies needed was a great amount of capital to fund a significant amount of research and development (R&D) to complete their research. The companies wanted to get their products into clinical testing and then to the Federal Drug Administration (FDA). The FDA would then test their products before giving or refusing approval for these products to be offered to the public.

During the 1980s the market values of these companies waxed and waned as the success and failures of their products were announced. There were many casualties of those times, but also some very big successes.

Amgen was and is a notable success. Also Biogen, Inc. (BGEN), and

Chiron were and are successes. In the past these companies would target certain products; they were attempting to get a product commercialized as soon as possible because they knew that time and money would run out quickly. The companies set up milestones, dates when they would get their products in front of the FDA to be approved for the public. The companies knew they might not be able to raise more capital and go forward if the dates weren't made.

## The Present Revolution

In the 1990s, and continuing into 2000, a number of companies are taking on even more ambitious projects, including mapping out the human genome, which may unlock many solutions for health issues. Although the timing of the conclusion of these projects is very much in question, the niche has become a hot market segment. Genomics is that part of research that deals with the study of the entire genetic structure of an organism, in this case, humans. Genomics firms have been making a great deal of headway in laying out the map of human genes. Genomics is involved in cancer research, wound healing, neurological disorders, and many other areas.

Dealing with human genomics is a three-part process. First, the DNA evidence has to be unraveled to identify the proteins; second, the compounds that are going to be used for efficacy have to be identified; and, third, the compounds have to be examined to see how each compound works with the other compounds and what chemical reactions the compounds cause in other compounds and separately. This process entails years of basic research that has to be done before new products can be introduced.

There is a newer tier of big-valuation companies, which would include Affymetrix (AFFX), and Human Genomic Sciences (HGSI). These companies are given valuations on the basis of an open-ended promise of opportunity. It is still too early to see how soon companies such as these can ferret through all their data to find useful products. Also at question is the value of the royalties from their products.

The same high-risk and reward profile of biotech companies exists today as in the past, but the efforts of the companies are even more ambitious. The projects are more ambitious because technology has enabled companies to process data quicker. Today's biotech companies are relying more on computer "bits and bytes" to do more of the laboratory analysis, instead of leaving analysis in the hands of trained clinicians.

Also this bull market, lasting about 20 years, has made it easy to raise money to pursue grander projects. The easy money the bull market has created has made it possible to launch a significant number of start-up biotech companies. These new companies are going after even more esoteric projects. But these companies will soon face the same daunting responsibility: come up with real product revenues to create a flow of earnings with which to reward investors in the company.

The market valuation of many biotech companies is extremely high. A number of the top Nasdaq biotech companies are relatively new, with little revenue; but these companies are working on among the most esoteric projects in the biotech field.

Waiting in the wings for the fruits of these small, development-stage companies are the large, global pharmaceutical companies. The large companies also have biotechnology experience. In a merger or takeover, the global companies can offer money for R&D, personnel, technology experience, and worldwide manufacturing and distribution capabilities. These larger companies can step in and complete the work of the small companies. The valuation of the smaller company would be absorbed into the larger company's valuation after a takeover, justifying the huge multiples paid by the larger company for the smaller company.

The stock market, before its recent pullback, was presently infatuated with the products of biotechnology. So this second wave of biotech sentiment was occurring in a supercharged, liquidity-driven market that believes technological innovation will accelerate the success of these small biotech companies in terms of getting viable product to market.

All of this potential success still remains to be seen. In studying human genomics, for example, more combinations and matchings of compounds to proteins can be processed. But clinical testing has to support whether there is an express relationship of high efficacy and successful application. The next step is presenting the case to the FDA and getting their approval. And there is still the challenge of bringing the product to market and being successful at marketing the product.

## A Cooling-Off Period

When the Nasdaq market corrected, investors started to discriminate among different types of biotech companies. Companies with products growing in the market that place at 20 to 30 percent or more a year have been placed in one category, and those companies still burning cash and attempting to get products out are in another category.

As with Internet companies, valuations exploded in this group and have retraced, but there still remains the promise of future products and earnings. Risks, of course, are still present.

## Biotechnology Companies That Have Broad Analyst Coverage

**Amgen (AMGN)**—Sales, $3.204 billion; 1-year sales growth, 21.3 percent. The company manufactures and markets products for the production of blood cells, neurobiology, and other health-care areas. Amgen spends one-quarter of its sales on R&D.

**Chiron Corporation (CHIR)**—Sales, $762 million; 1-year sales growth, 3.5 percent. Chiron concentrates on the areas of vaccines, blood testing, and biopharmaceuticals. It develops products to prevent and treat sicknesses such as AIDS, cancer, cardiovascular disease, and hepatitis.

**Biogen, Inc. (BGEN)**—Sales, $794 million; 1-year sales growth, 42.5 percent. Biogen develops and markets biopharmaceuticals to treat many ailments, including multiple sclerosis. Other drugs in the developmental stage include products for autoimmune diseases and heart failure.

**Affymetrix, Inc. (AFFX)**—Sales, $96 million; 1-year sales growth, 86.3 percent. The company's GeneChip system, along with other products, develops the area of complex genetic information. It makes a number of products such as fluidics stations and probe arrays.

**Human Genome Sciences, Inc. (HGSI)**—Sales, $24 million; 1-year sales growth, −17.2 percent. The company researches genes of microorganisms such as bacteria, fungi, and viruses. It also develops drugs based on human genes; a few of its candidates for approval are in the testing phase.

**Gilead Sciences, Inc. (GILD)**—Sales, $169 million; 1-year sales growth, 418.4 percent. Gilead has some major products almost ready for the market: Tamiflu, a treatment for flu; VISTIDE, an AIDS-related viral eye infection treatment. It has other treatments in development, dealing with diseases caused by cancer.

**BioSource, International, Inc. (BIOI)**—Sales, $29.3 million; 1-year sales growth, 33.8 percent. The company develops and produces test kits used in biomedical research. Its products include more than 1700 immunological and molecular biological products used in the diagnoses of cancer, aging, and other conditions.

**Invitrogen Corporation (IVGN)**—Sales, $68 million; 1-year sales growth, 117.5 percent. Invitrogen makes kits that speed up the analysis for molecular biologists and other scientists. The processes addressed are gene cloning, expression, and analysis. The company markets about 250 different types of kits.

**Genzyme Corporation (GENZ)**—Sales, $635.4 million; 1-year sales growth, −7.7 percent. Its main products are Cerazyme and Ceredase; these products are enzymes that are deficient in Gaucher's disease. The company acquires other companies that fit into its development of biochemical products.

**Incyte Pharmaceuticals, Inc. (INCY)**—Sales, $157 million; 1-year sales growth, 16.5 percent. The company has a database of information regarding human, animal, plant, and microorganism genes. Among other things, it provides DNA cloning services and DNA screening.

**Cell Genesys, Inc. (CEGE)**—Sales, $33 million; 1-year sales growth, 39.4 percent. The company develops gene-modification technologies to treat diseases. Its projects include gene therapy research and testing a cancer vaccine. It also has a licensing program in gene-activation technology.

**Cephalon, Inc. (CEPH)**—Sales, $44 million; one-year sales growth, 186 percent. The company is working on a treatment for Lou Gehrig's disease. It markets a drug for sleep disorder, Provigil. It also owns an application for Alzheimer's disease and is working on products on treating cancer.

## TECHNOLOGY

In the past, technology was developed for the big corporations. Whoever could manage the data, controlled the data. This model has been blown apart. Today, data access is easy to buy and use. The market for technology is no longer comprised of just large corporations. The market now is small businesses, groups, and individuals.

Today's world is remarkably different than it was 5 years ago as far as information availability and ease of transporting are concerned. Even a few years ago technology was not nearly so pervasive. Probably the Internet is a reason for the advances, but not the only reason.

Businesses are now compelled to spend heavily on technology. They must preserve their market advantages and access new markets as quickly as they can. Also each business must improve its cost structures, cutting costs and increasing productivity. For this, technology, including the Internet, is necessary.

As for consumers, they now have a host of new computer products that have enlivened the consumption model for the United States. Many parts of the world are underserved regarding access to these new computer products. These parts of the world will be exploited with technology products, especially as the Internet makes new inroads.

## The New Product Cycle

The cycle for the companies that have created the new economy services has been extended, because these services are now in worldwide demand. This has happened because of technology-driven demand and is a rare phenomenon.

For example, the U.S. automobile, in the past, was something desired by consumers all over the world. But because of price and the need for maintenance centers, only consumers in the United States and Europe, and to a lesser extent Japan, could realistically purchase them. Other areas, for instance, Latin America, could not in a meaningful way become a major U.S. automobile consumer. Also, a region such as Southeast Asia could not suddenly become a major consumer of U.S. cars.

But the story of today's PC is something that, perhaps, has never been seen before. The price of the PC keeps falling, making it available to a large pool of consumers. The PC has unique features: it offers access to world news, through e-mail, communication around the world, and a connection to distributors worldwide of consumer products.

Moore's Law seems to ensure further development of technology around the globe. The price of the PC keeps dropping while the power of its features keeps increasing.

## Technology Companies That Have Broad Analyst Coverage

**Microsoft, Inc. (MSFT)**—Sales, $22.956 billion; 1-year sales increase, 16.3 percent. This is the world's leading software company. Its products include the Windows operating system, the Internet Explorer Browser, and a software suite including Excel, Word, and other programs.

**Intel Corporation (INTC)**—Sales, $29.389 billion; 1-year sales increase, 11.9 percent. This is the leading chipmaker, garnering a market share of 80 percent of the microprocessor market. The company's chips are also used for communications, industrial equipment, and the military.

**Cisco Systems, Inc. (CSCO)**—Sales, $18.928 billion; 1-year sales increase, 55.7 percent. The company controls over three-quarters of the market for products that power the Internet and link networks; the products include routers and switches. The company is diversifying into consumer products.

**Dell Computer Corp. (DELL)**—Sales, $25.625 billion; 1-year sales increase, 38.5 percent. Dell is the leader in selling computers directly to the consumer. It sells hardware and markets third-party software and peripherals; Dell also sells network servers and other products.

**Oracle Corporation (ORCL)**—Sales, $10.130 billion; 1-year sales increase, 14.8 percent. The company is the leader in data management software development; its database software runs on everything from notebooks to mainframes. Its sales have spurted recently.

**Adobe, Inc. (ADBE)**—Sales, $1.015 billion; 1-year sales increase, 13.5 percent. The company developed and markets the Acrobat Reader, a product used to display portable document format on the Web. It also markets print technology to OEMs and develops other software products.

**Applied Materials, Inc. (AMAT)**—Sales, $4.859 billion; 1-year sales increase, 20.2 percent. The company is the leader in manufacturing semiconductor wafer fabrication equipment. Some of its customers are Advanced Micro Devices, Intel, Lucent, and Motorola.

**Tellabs, Inc. (TLAB)**—Sales, $2.319 billion; 1-year sales growth, 39.7 percent. This leading communication company makes, markets, and services voice equipment worldwide. It produces high-bit digital subscriber lines, T-coders, and other products.

**Sun Microsystems, Inc. (SUNW)**—Sales, $15.721 billion; 1-year sales growth, 19.8 percent. The company is the leader in making UNIX-based workstation computer storage devices and servers. Its JAVA system is a programming language that can create software on any type of computer.

**3COM Corporation (COMS)**—Sales, $4.333 billion; 1-year sales growth, −24.9 percent. This leading company produces many products, including routers for Ethernet, adapters, and hubs. Its systems products include LAN switches and network servers; its sales are mostly in the area of network adapters and network servers.

**Novellus Systems, Inc. (NVLS)**—Sales, $592 million; 1-year sales growth, 14.2 percent. Novellus produces semiconductor production equipment, including physical vapor deposition (PVD) systems, and other products. Twenty of the largest semiconductor manufacturers use Novellus products.

**PeopleSoft, Inc. (PSFT)**—Sales, $1.429 billion; 1-year sales growth, 8.8 percent. This company is a leader in applications that manage business operations across computer networks. It also develops industry-specific software including applications for the utility and insurance markets.

**KLA-Tencor Corporation (KLAC)**—Sales, $1.498 million; 1-year sales growth, 77.8 percent. The company is a producer of tools that identify semiconductor defects during manufacturing. The company's systems monitor and analyze chips during many of the manufacturing stages.

**Nextel Communications, Inc. (NXTL)**—Sales $3.326 billion; 1-year sales growth, 80.1 percent. It provides paging services to business users, mobile phone service, and two-way radio dispatch, all through a handset. The company is developing Internet access to its handset operation.

**BMCS Software (BMCS)**—Sales, $1.719 billion; 1-year sales growth, 31.9 percent. The company has over 350 software products that enhance database performance and gauge and eliminate bottlenecks from computer systems. It is enlarging its e-business management area.

**Parametric Technology Corporation (PMTC)**—Sales, $928 million; 1-year sales growth, 37.6 percent. It is a leader in manufacturing mechanical computer-aided design, manufacturing, and engineering software. About 50 percent of the company's sales come from training, consulting, and other services.

**Andrew Corporation (ANDW)**—Sales, $791 million; 1-year sales growth, −7.2 percent. More than half of the company's sales are in coaxial cable and related products. It also makes base station, earth station, and mobile antennas and antenna towers.

**Autodesk, Inc. (ADSK)**—Sales, $820 million; 1-year sales growth, 10.8 percent. The company is a leader in supplying computer-aided design (CAD) automation software. It also develops design software for multimedia and home improvement. About 45 percent of sales are outside North America.

**Apple Computer, Inc. (APPL)**—Sales, $6.134 billion; 1-year sales growth, 3.2 percent. The company's products include the MacOS operating systems, the iMac, the portable iBook, and other products. It is focusing on low-cost computers and services for the Web.

## PHARMACEUTICALS

New products can take as long as 10 years or so to develop, and after the product is developed, more years are invested to launch the new product. Viagra from Pfizer is a good example. The product is now in the $1 billion sales category; this is from zero in sales a couple of years ago. Developments such as Viagra cost major dollars.

There are companies involved with the generic applications of already outstanding products. The companies are adopting medications whose patents have expired and are manufacturing similar products under a generic name. Generic products come to market quicker than products that have to be developed from scratch. Because of the quicker development of generic products, these products can have a dramatic effect on sales and earnings.

## Cost Savings through Generic Products

It costs less for manufacturers to produce generic products, so the manufacturers can sell generic products for a much lower price to consumers. Generic producers, whether it is green beans or aspirin or frozen potatoes, are far less costly to produce without the marketing costs and the development brand-name expenses.

Included in the pharmaceutical group are those companies that produce generic products. As a start-up, a generic drug producer can, in a short period of time, become very profitable because the development and other costs are absent.

The generic companies sell products with a high gross margin. Also, pharmaceutical products are usually small, because they consist mostly of pills and capsules. These small-sized products can be distributed widely and at a low cost, further adding to profitability.

Investors are mostly interested in those companies that will ramp up their revenues substantially and quickly. Investors can perhaps accomplish this by taking the time to research the R&D pipeline of the major pharmaceutical companies; investors can also check the patent expiration dates of the existing products on the market. They can check on those companies that are applying for generic licenses to produce patented drugs that are about to lose their patent.

Once a drug is patented, it is protected from any other company producing it for 17 years. Then the patent expires. If the company holding the patent reformulates the formula and proves that, essentially, the formula is "new," then the company can receive an extension of the patent.

A slowdown on the global growth of pharmaceuticals seems unlikely. Part of the reason is that there are new diseases that have to be addressed, such as AIDS. Also older diseases are reappearing, such as hepatitis-B and tuberculosis.

## Past Performance of Pharmaceuticals

The past performance of pharmaceuticals as compared to the other S&P sectors is very high. The group's performance is less than that of technology, however. The argument could be made that modern pharmaceuticals are technology based.

The human genomics projects, which have been undertaken by many biotech and pharmaceutical companies, use advanced computer technologies to gather information. The companies use technology-aided technicians to analyze the information.

## Pharmaceutical Companies That Have Broad Analyst Coverage

**King Pharmaceuticals (KG)**—Sales $348 million; 1-year sales increase, 113 percent. Through its subsidiary, Monarch Pharmaceutical, the company manufactures and sells generic and brand-name drugs. Some of its brands are Anusol, Cortisporin, and Viroptic.

**Andrx Corporation (ADRX)**—Sales, $476 million; 1-year sales increase, 92.6 percent. The company makes time-released generic versions of brand-name drugs; one among many of the company's products is Cardizem, which is used in the treatment of hypertension and angina.

**Jones Pharma, Inc. (JMED)**—Sales, $132 million; 1-year sales increase, 28.1 percent. It makes and sells specialty pharmaceutical products. The products include Tapazole, a thyroid-disorder drug, and Thrombin-JMI, for controlling blood loss during surgery.

**Millennium Pharmaceuticals, Inc. (MLNM)**—Sales, $183 million; 1-year sales growth, 37.4 percent. The company explores the genetic basis of a disease in order to stop it. It has alliances with leaders such as Hoffmann-LaRoche, Eli Lilly, and others. Among its findings is the genetic makeup of tumors.

**Dura Pharmaceuticals, Inc. (DURA)**—Sales, $301 million; sales growth over the last year, 51.3 percent. The company makes and sells prescription pharmaceuticals to treat allergies. It also is developing Spiros, a pulmonary dry powder drug-delivery system that does not require forceful inhalation. Some 400 sales reps market its products.

**Kos Pharmaceuticals, Inc. (KOSP)**—Sales, $36 million; 1-year sales growth, 179.2 percent. The company develops drugs to treat chronic cardiovascular and respiratory diseases. The company also has agreements for the development of products used to treat angina pectoris, hypertension, and other diseases.

**IDEC Pharmaceuticals Corporation (IDPH)**—Sales, $118 million; 1-year sales growth, 35.6 percent. This company develops treatments for cancer, autoimmune diseases, and other diseases. It also has several anticancer drugs nearing approval, with other drugs in the pipeline awaiting approval.

**Isis Pharmaceuticals, Inc. (ISIP)**—Sales, $33 million; 1-year sales growth, −13.5 percent. It has developed drugs that target disease-causing proteins before they are produced. Also it is engaged in clinical trials for the treatment of psoriasis, arthritis, and other diseases.

**Crescendo Pharmaceuticals Corporation (CNDO)**—Sales, $2.4 million; 1-year sales growth, 2300 percent. This development stage company is researching into a number of drug candidates. It is paying Alza to develop treatments for prostate cancer, attention deficit disorder, and other diseases.

# TELECOMMUNICATIONS

Many of the telecom companies act more as enabling solutions providers. Some of the high-growth, interesting companies in this sector are Qwest Communications, Intl. (Q), Windstar Communications (WCII), IDT Corp. (IDTC), and Advanced Radio Telecom (ARTT).

Europe is seeing the first major telecommunications companies in its history. Europe is much like the United States was in the 1980s, with companies such as MCI WorldCom (WCOM) coming into the area.

Today's telecom industry started in 1984, when the United States broke up the AT&T monopoly. The Bell Operating System was broken up into the regional companies, which were dubbed "Baby Bells." The breakup separated long-distance and local services. It created long-distance competitors to the old AT&T, which allowed long-distance companies such as MCI WorldCom to emerge. The Baby Bells continued to have an operating monopoly in their regional areas. The Bell System breakup created seven Regional Bell Operating Systems through mergers; through continued mergers, this number has been reduced to four systems.

In 1996, the Telecom Deregulation Act was passed. This act deregulated the regional companies. Long-distance companies were now allowed to provide local services. The Deregulation Act included a 14-point checklist. When a regional Bell system proves that it has met the 14 points on the list, it is be allowed to offer long-distance services. The points on this checklist attest that the system is allowing full competition in its region.

Recently there was a flurry of activity in the U.S. regional systems.

Many companies in the system are seeking to vertically integrate and also offer more services in their regions. This rush to merge that the regional systems are exhibiting can be understood when considering the economics of the telecommunications industry, including its link to the Internet. The profit from building the infrastructure and operating the infrastructure and selling and marketing and maintaining customers compels the telecom companies to maintain and expand their customers and sell their customers more product. After a customer is sold one service, a large margin is added by offering that customer a number of services. This is referred to as selling customers "bundled services."

The deregulation that happened in the United States in 1984 was experienced in Europe in 1988. In 1988, the countries of the European Community had to fully deregulate their markets.

## The Telecommunication Link to the Internet

The Internet facilitates the movement of data traffic. Data can be comprised of numbers, characters, images, or other methods of recording, in a method that is received by a person or inputted directly into a computer. If stored directly into a computer, the data can be processed at once or at a later date. The data are carried over the pipes that the telecommunications companies have built. Originally these pipes were built to carry voice traffic, and this voice traffic was analogue. As the Internet evolved, the growth in demand for capacity on these pipes was being driven by data traffic, and the means of transmitting this traffic has become digital.

Analogue refers to transmitting via wavelengths. There can be much interference using analogue transmitting. Digital is much more easily transmitted and more dependable; digital is transferred as a discrete signal or a circuit designed to handle such signals.

Presently the Internet is spawning huge amounts of traffic. Consider, people are only going to spend a certain amount of time speaking on the phone. But the amount of data traffic on the Internet is huge. The pipes that transmit data were originally built to operate as telecom networks or voice networks; they are not big enough to handle the vast amounts of Internet traffic.

The amount of data carried by the Internet is virtually infinite. First of all, people send e-mails to each other; next, people start surfing the Web. The Web has text pages, graphics, and video, which are all very data intensive. In addition, people then have their computers speaking to each other at night, while those people are asleep. The Net keeps driving the demand for capacity and for services.

## Moore's Law Again

The newer companies, such as Qwest and MCI WorldCom, have the advantage of being able to build networks specifically designed to handle the new information environment. Qwest started building an original network in 1995. The network was designed to handle data traffic, which has an insatiable demand for bandwidth. Qwest and other newer companies have been able to use the most modern equipment to build efficient equipment for the new types of networks.

Conversely, older companies such as AT&T probably would have been better off building networks from scratch, but they couldn't. They had existing infrastructure and they have been, basically, retrofitting the old system. Fixing up old systems has turned out to be inefficient in terms of service and cost.

It is harder to adapt old systems than to build new systems, which goes back to Moore's Law. This time we are adopting the law to the growth of the use of bandwidth. Consistent with Moore's Law, as time passes, the cost to manufacture new equipment is reduced significantly, and the new equipment contains much greater capacity than its older counterparts.

> *Moore's Law continues to function as the technology industry grows and develops. The price of technology products declines, whereas the quality and power of these products improve. This indicates continued growth as far as we can see.*

Europe is decidedly ahead of the United States in the development of wireless communications because, in the past, the European companies decided on one standard under which to operate. This is entitled the Global Standard for Mobile (GSM).

In the United States, on the other hand, the manufacturers decided that they wanted to keep their technology proprietary and, therefore, adopted no standard. So U.S. companies developed their own products, which made it harder and more expensive to build out many networks.

Wireless is much more prevalent in Europe than in the states as a result. Wireless, in Europe, is referred to as "mobile." In Europe there is much more usage of mobile phones and mobile phones are convenient to use. One travels from country to country and the phone connection remains in your pocket. Your phone number remains the same no matter where you travel. Also, people in Europe use messaging over mobile phones. Probably Europe will be ahead of the United States in terms of gaining access to the Internet over mobile phones.

## Telecommunications Companies That Have Broad Analyst Coverage

**MCI WorldCom (WCOM)**—Sales, $37.120 billion; 1-year sales increase, 110 percent. This is the second-largest U.S. long-distance company, offering a full range of services. The company also operates in international telecommunications and Internet markets in over 65 countries.

**NTL, Inc. (NTLI)**—Sales, $1.584 million; 1-year sales increase, 112 percent. This company is the third-largest cable TV operator. It also offers wholesale Internet access for independent service providers, leased lines, frame relay, and other corporate data services.

**McLeod USA (MCLD)**—Sales, $908 million; 1-year sales increase, 50.4 percent. This competitive local exchange carrier provides telecommunication services, including Internet access. It also owns over 9400 miles of fiber-optic cable and 27 Public Communications Services licenses.

**Aspect Communications Corporation (ASPT)**—Sales, $489 million; 1-year sales growth, −4.5 percent. This company is a leading supplier of equipment and customer software. Its plans are to specialize in software. Among its customers are E*Trade and DaimlerChrysler.

**ADC Telecommunications, Inc. (ADCT)**—Sales, $1.926 billion; 1-year sales growth, 39.7 percent. The company manufactures systems that increase the rate at which voice, data, and video signals are transmitted. Regional Bell systems are customers. The company is entering the wireless and international markets.

**Primus Telecommunications Group, Inc. (PRTL)**—Sales, $832 million; 1-year sales growth, 97.5 percent. The company has 1.7 million customers, directly and through reseller agreements. It has a network with about 20 switches. It also provides long-distance and international calling services around the world.

**Star Telecommunications, Inc. (STRX)**—Sales, $1.061 million; 1-year sales growth, 78.3 percent. The company operates gateway-switching facilities in Los Angeles, Miami, and other cities. It owns interests in 17 undersea digital fiber-optic cables, including the fiber-optic network of Qwest.

**Metro One Telecommunications, Inc. (MTON)**—Sales, $77 million; 1-year sales growth, 72.5 percent. The company offers directory assistance for the wireless telecom industry. Its customers include AT&T Wireless, Sprint PCS, and Vodafone. Over 100 million requests for directory assistance are received each year.

## NON-NASDAQ STOCKS THAT TRADE LIKE NASDAQ STOCKS

Some listed stocks trade like Nasdaq stocks in that they are very volatile and active. The origins of many of these companies predated the emergence of the Nasdaq market. Nasdaq was not there, so the companies grew, listed, and stayed on the NYSE. Hewlett-Packard, Inc. (HWP), for instance, predates Nasdaq and has always traded on the NYSE. Lucent Technologies (LU) is a spin-off from AT&T Corp. (T), and T has always traded on the NYSE. LU went directly to the NYSE. Some companies have grown and switched to a listed market. America Online (AOL) once traded under the symbol AMER on Nasdaq.

The management of a company will switch from one exchange to another to take advantage of the best opportunity for trading its stock.

### Growing Company Caps and Market Volume

Bull markets are almost always accompanied with rising volume, and the present bull is no exception. One reason is that many first-time investors are coming into the market, causing a rise in the pool of investment funds. With the rising pool of investment funds often comes an increase in volatility. With more money and the market advancing, bull markets often spur an increase in the size of company market caps.

For instance, Lucent went public early in 2000. The company has a billion shares outstanding, a very large amount for a new company. The company, although it is fairly new, is one of the largest companies held by the public. It takes a very large, liquid market to absorb a company of this size.

The size of the valuations of U.S. companies is staggering. In fact, there are companies whose capitalizations are bigger than the gross domestic product of some countries. Of the top 10 economic entities in the world today, 3 of them are U.S. companies. The largest are General Electric, Microsoft, and Cisco Systems.

A listed company that is similar to a Nasdaq company is Comdisco (CDO). The company has been trading for many years. But it is forward thinking. The company recently announced that it is spinning off some units to get involved in Internet activities.

Another listed company with similar trading aspects of a Nasdaq company is America Online (AOL). AOL will have a tremendous amount of cost savings through its merger with Time Warner, just considering its sales and marketing and the distribution of its software. For example, AOL is putting AOL "50" software on all the CDs that Time Warner is publishing. Time Warner publishes entertainment products from Warner Brothers Music.

Eventually there will be a broad distribution of music digitally. AOL now has one of the best digital music players in the business. What they plan is to package the CD along with a digital player, with its 50 browser and installation software. Anyone who is listening to a CD will receive these other AOL products. And because music is easy to track demographically, this marketing activity will provide a platform to market other products. Eventually many entertainment products can be distributed over the Internet using AOL marketing tools.

## Actively Traded Listed Stocks That Have Broad Analyst Coverage

**Motorola, Inc. (MOT)**—Sales, $30.931 billion; increase in sales over 1 year, 5.2 percent. About 40 percent of sales are made up of cellular products. The company provides wireless telecommunication services to developing nations. About half its sales are from outside the United States.

**Lucent Technologies, Inc. (LU)**—Sales, $38.303 billion; increase in sales over 1 year, 27.1 percent. This is the leading company in North America in manufacturing telecom equipment and software. It also manufactures integrated circuits and telecommunication power systems.

**Genentech, Inc. (DNA)**—Sales, $1.421 billion; increase in sales over 1 year, 23.5 percent. This is one of the largest biotech companies on the globe; the Swiss company Roche Holdings owns over 80 percent of DNA. Most of Genentech's sales are from eight biotech products.

**Korn-Ferry, International (KFY)**—Sales, $500 million; increase in sales over 1 year, 34.2 percent. This is the top recruiting firm in the world. It has over 70 offices in 40 countries. The company's FutureSted service matches applicants to jobs through the Internet.

**LSI Logic Corporation (LSI)**—Sales, $2.089 billion; increase in sales over 1 year, 40.2 percent. The company develops and manufactures integrated circuits. Its design process utilizes an extensive library of building blocks. Customers include manufacturers in the computer and other industries.

**AT&T Corporation (T)**—Sales, $62.391 billion; increase in sales over 1 year, 17.2 percent. This is the leading telecom company in the United States, serving about 90 million customers. It offers long-distance, wireless phone service and Internet access. It also has a global telecom services venture.

**AFLAC, Inc. (AFL)**—Sales, $8.640 billion; increase in sales over 1 year, 21.6 percent. The company sells supplemental medical insurance policies that cover special conditions, primarily cancer; it is the largest in the United States. In Japan, it is the leading cancer-expense insurance company.

**American International Group (AIG)**—Sales, $32.529 billion; increase in sales over 1 year, 22 percent. This is one of the largest insurance firms in the world. The company also has a financial services division involved in trading, currency hedging, and aircraft leasing.

**Automatic Data Processing (AUD)**—Sales, $6.288 billion; increase in sales over 1 year, 13.5 percent. This is the biggest payroll and tax filing processor in the world. Also it provides security transactions processing for brokerage firms. It offers a number of Web-based services.

**Avery Dennison (AVY)**—Sales, $3.768 billion; increase in sales over 1 year, 8.9 percent. This is a leader in manufacturing adhesive labels used in packaging, mailers, and other items. The company also makes papers, films, and foils, coated with adhesives. It operates about 200 facilities.

**General Electric (GE)**—Sales, $110.832 billion; increase in sales over 1 year, 11 percent. The company operates in a number of industries, including home appliances, lighting, and electric distribution equipment. GE Capital, its financial services division, is one of the largest in the country.

# CHAPTER 6

# TOP NASDAQ-WEIGHTED FUNDS

An investor or trader may want to purchase funds rather than select his own stocks. Or the trader may want to set up his own portfolio. In setting up your own portfolio, it is often helpful to know the stocks that the professionals have bought and those which the professionals have sold; this information can be instructive as to which issues or types of issues you should consider in fashioning your portfolio.

In this and the following chapters is given, as well as the stock issues, the methodology and strategic thinking which has gone into the stock selections and overall portfolio strategy. It should be helpful to understand what professional managers are looking for in the issues they buy and those they sell in constructing their overall investment strategies.

The funds used here are the faster-moving and more aggressive growth funds. These funds are heavily laden with Nasdaq stocks, since many stock choices in these types of funds are laden with stocks of the new economy, which are the faster-growing stock sectors.

Nasdaq heavily weighted funds go in and out of favor, usually according to general market sentiment. Often a fund is not even in the rankings one year, then climbs to the top of the rankings another year, when its stock group is in favor.

Knowing when to be in these funds, their types of stocks, and when to avoid them is of paramount importance.

## RS EMERGING GROWTH FUND (RSEGX)

This fund has performed very well, and it is heavy with Nasdaq stocks. The fund's performance had an increase of 75.14 percent in the fourth quarter of 1999, outperforming its benchmarks, The Russell 2000 Growth Index and the S&P 500 Index. Its return in 1999 was a hefty 182.51 percent. The fund has done well because of its small-cap stocks and technology exposure. The chart in Fig. 6-1 shows its historic return.

As of late 2000, the fund was down 9.46 percent for the year. This is not a bad performance considering the market sell-off in these types of stocks.

### Stocks and Sectors

The fund's largest 10 holdings and sector weightings follow in Fig. 6-2. Technology is by far its largest sector holding, although the fund does have

**Results of a Hypothetical $10,000 Investment as of June 30, 2000 (if invested on 11/30/87)**

| | Year-to-Date Total Return | One-Year Total Return | Five-Year Average Annual Return | Ten-Year Average Annual Return | Total Return Since Inception | Average Annual Return Since Inception |
|---|---|---|---|---|---|---|
| Emerging Growth Fund | 6.25% | 100.98% | 44.98% | 27.12% | 2614.63% | 29.98% |

**Performance Update**

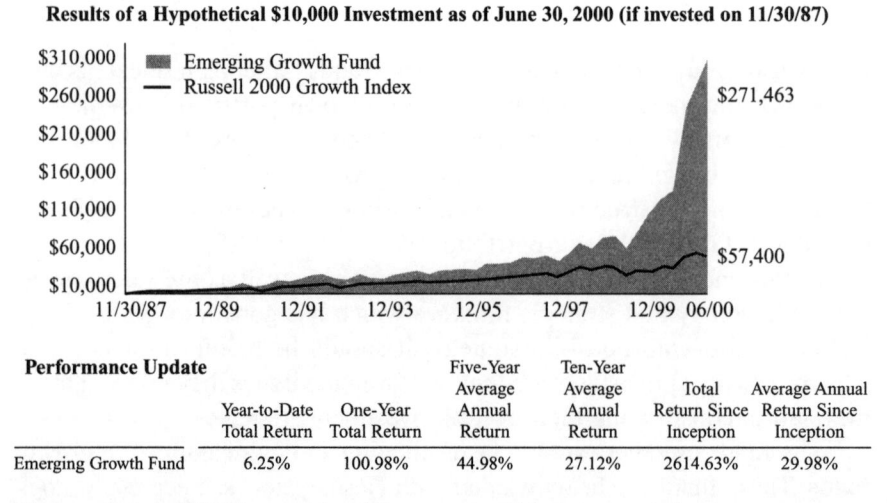

**Figure 6-1** RSEGX growth. (*Courtesy of Morningstar, Inc.*)

## Assets Under Management as of June 30, 2000: $5.66 billion

### Asset Allocation

- Consumer Specialty Retail 1.1%
- Financial Services 1.5%
- Commercial Services 1.9%
- Media 3.2%
- Short-Term Investments 5.4%
- Network Systems & Products 5.6%
- Other & Other Assets 6.5%
- Computer Hardware & Components 9.2%
- Medical/Health-care/Biotech 9.5%
- Telecommunication Equipment & Services 15.1%
- Computer Software & Services 20.2%
- Internet Commerce & Services 20.8%

### Top Ten Holdings as of June 30, 2000

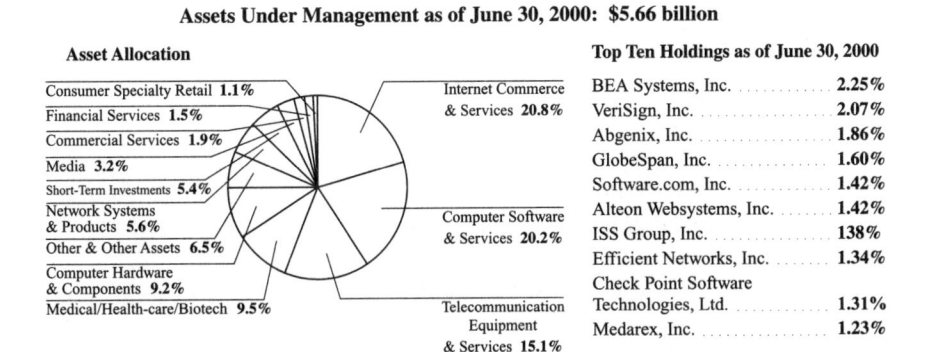

| Company | % |
|---|---|
| BEA Systems, Inc. | 2.25% |
| VeriSign, Inc. | 2.07% |
| Abgenix, Inc. | 1.86% |
| GlobeSpan, Inc. | 1.60% |
| Software.com, Inc. | 1.42% |
| Alteon Websystems, Inc. | 1.42% |
| ISS Group, Inc. | 138% |
| Efficient Networks, Inc. | 1.34% |
| Check Point Software Technologies, Ltd. | 1.31% |
| Medarex, Inc. | 1.23% |

**Figure 6-2** RSEGX top ten holdings and sector weightings. (*Courtesy of Morningstar, Inc.*)

representation in other areas. Notice that there are no big names here; the company has done well with its small-cap investments.

The goal of the fund, managed by Jim Callinan, is to find promising companies that are in an early stage of development. The fund wants to buy companies that can deliver sales and earnings growth of 20 percent a year or more. Also the fund wants companies whose products have a proprietary advantage over their competitors. The fund buys small-cap companies that can eventually grow into major companies. Managers of the fund attempt to buy promising companies before the rest of Wall Street, and certainly before Main Street, discovers them. The managers consider themselves bottom-up investors, which mean that they concentrate on companies rather than industries.

The fund is driven by fundamental research. The RSEGX managers are active managers, meaning that they conduct financial analysis, go to the companies and meet with management (considered kicking the tires), and research the company's industry and its competition.

The portfolio managers consider selling when one or a combination of things happen: if a company starts to lose its competitive edge over the competition; when the managers think that a stock is overvalued; if a company starts missing its numbers and changes its strategic objectives; and if a company's business fundamentals change, whether it is an industry or company situation.

## Investment Aspects of the Fund

The fund has about half its assets in technology; about 25 percent of those assets are invested in Internet-related stocks. Its investments are spread throughout the Internet sector, ranging from retail to entertainment. The technology portion of the Internet holdings is spread into two areas: services, which includes companies that run Web sites and hosts transactions; and software, which includes companies that provide value-added service for Web sites.

RSEGF has about $3.58 billion under management. The fund holds about 250 companies in its portfolio. One would think that because of its size the fund would find it impossible to locate enough small-cap opportunities. But it has five analysts dedicated to ferreting out new companies in the emerging growth areas. The analysts have been able to find companies that are growing as fast or even faster than those companies in its present holdings.

## Investing for the Future

RSEGF plans to continue with what has been successful for them in the past: looking for companies that will grow 20 percent or better in the emerging growth industries. These industries RSEGF focuses on include software, technology, retail, and health care. The managers are also looking into the satellite industry. The managers think that because all but the biggest of the media investors have been scared off because of the size needed to fund this industry, there are investment opportunities. Some companies that have done well in this group are EchoStar (DISH) and General Motors, Class H (GMH).

The fund continued its commitment to the small-cap arenas in the year 2000. By small-cap the fund means stocks in the $2 to $3 billion capitalization range. RSEGF thought that just as there were in 1999, there would be a group of Internet stocks in 2000 that would be 5- and 10-baggers.

## JANUS VENTURE FUND—JAVTX

The fund, managed by William Bales, is invested mostly in small-cap stocks. Janus manages over $6 billion in its groups of funds, with most of the money in the small-cap sector, making Janus a major player in that sector. Janus is one of the top five firms in terms of the amount of money managed by the sponsor of a fund family in a small-cap area. Janus Venture is one of the firm's funds. The Janus Venture Fund is about $3.5 billion in assets, making it by far the largest fund in the Janus family of funds.

Janus attempts to find the best companies in an industry. Because of the size of its investment capital, the Janus funds often become the largest shareholder in the companies in which it invests. Because of this size, Janus cannot actively trade stocks; the management team does its fundamental research and determines which companies are the best in an industry and makes its bets, ending up owning a sizeable portion of those companies it selects.

Most of the competitors of Janus have much less capital to invest. Often these competitors have somewhere in the range of $300 million to $500 million to employ in the market. The competition generally can trade in and out of the small caps easier than Janus, because the competitors deal in small amounts of stock. Figure 6-3 shows the fund's performance, which at times has been quite impressive. At other times, when the type of stocks it invests in has been out of favor, the fund has suffered.

## The Success of Janus Venture

Some of JAVTX's success is that the fund has been in the right market sector. Its strategy of owning good technology companies, and owning them in large size, has worked well during this bull market.

In the strong market of late 1999 and early 2000, almost any company that had a viable plan attempted to go public. Janus has always been shown

**Growth of $10,000**
— Fund: Janus Venture
— Category: Small Growth
----- Index: S&P 500

**Annual Returns**

| | 1997 | 1998 | 1999 | 10-00 |
|---|---|---|---|---|
| Fund: | 12.6% | 23.2% | 140.7% | −32.3% |

**Figure 6-3** Performance of Janus Venture fund. (*Courtesy of Morningstar, Inc.*)

a large number of deals to buy on an IPO. The managers at Janus peruse large numbers of new offerings to find companies that it thinks has merit. Janus thinks that many companies it looks at, although the companies may be successful in their IPOs, are going public a little early. Janus passes on companies such as these. The companies Janus likes, it buys, big.

Janus keeps to an internal rule of not owning more than 15 percent of a company. This is for liquidity reasons; if Janus owns a lot more, perhaps 25 or 35 percent of the float, and the company releases bad news, getting out of the stock would be difficult. Even a 15 percent portion is significant, but workable. If JAVTX changes its mind and wants out of a 15 percent position, the fund managers think it is possible to liquidate without upsetting the stock's trading pattern.

Once JAVTX has made its bet and bought into a company, no matter who initiated the buy, one of the analysts or Will Bales, the portfolio manager, the fund managers stay close to the company's developments.

Because of its large size, JAVTX will get its phone calls returned from the companies it is invested in. The fund calls the management of companies in which it holds stock a minimum of once a month. For some of its bigger holdings, the fund will call management once a week. The fund will query management about how things are going: what the company is seeing in the company's industry. Perhaps an IPO is coming to market in the company's industry. How will this impact the company held by JAVTX?

Also the JAVTX managers will go to see the companies in which it holds stock at least once a year. JAVTX, additionally, meets management at the various conferences it attends; the JAVTX managers will sit down for a half hour or so with company management or join them at dinner or lunch.

It is not the intent of JAVTX to trade the stocks in the fund on a daily basis. But in this warp-speed, volatile market world, especially in the small-cap sector, the only way to keep up with trends in the industries and how these trends impact the held companies is to stay in constant contact with the companies. Also constant contact allows the fund managers to ascertain any change in "body language" from the companies they hold.

Financial spreadsheets and other data are internally created by JAVTX on the companies in which it has larger positions. The fund makes its own predictions of the amount of earnings its companies will generate. This is important because there is a game on the Street: Stocks will go up more if their earnings exceed the Street's expectations; conversely, stocks will get hammered if they don't meet expectations. There have been plenty of stocks that have gone down 30 to 50 percent because they were "a penny light," meaning they were short of projections by 1 cent. Therefore, the manage-

| Total number of stock holdings | 164 | Turnover % | 104 |
| Total number of bond holdings | 0 | Yield % | 0.00 |
| % Assets in top 10 holdings | 22.85 | | |

**Top 25 Holdings**

| Name of Holding | Sector | P/E | YTD Return % | % Net Assets |
|---|---|---|---|---|
| ⊕ Globix | Technology | --- | −85.31 | 4.12 |
| ⊕ SDL | Technology | --- | 116.06 | 3.22 |
| ⊖ VerticalNet | Services | --- | −83.08 | 2.84 |
| ⊖ Enzon | Health | --- | 44.09 | 2.05 |
| Alpha Inds | Technology | 46.01 | 33.26 | 2.04 |
| ⊕ TMP Worldwide | Services | 234.26 | −10.92 | 1.84 |
| Verio | Technology | --- | --- | 1.84 |
| ⊕ Informatica | Technology | --- | 55.58 | 1.76 |
| ✹ 724 Solutions | Technology | --- | --- | 1.61 |
| ⊕ Liberate Tech | Technology | --- | −88.91 | 1.53 |
| Adelphia Bus Solutions A | Services | --- | −89.52 | 1.51 |
| QLT Phototherapeutics | Health | --- | −22.77 | 1.42 |
| ⊕ Radio One | Services | --- | −66.17 | 1.40 |
| ⊖ Navisite | Technology | --- | −90.25 | 1.39 |
| ⊕ Keynote Sys | Technology | --- | −68.31 | 1.28 |
| SFX Entrtnmt Cl A | Services | --- | --- | 1.26 |
| Viatel | Services | --- | −90.68 | 1.22 |
| ⊕ Broadbase Software | Technology | --- | −85.22 | 1.20 |
| ⊕ Citadel Comms | Services | --- | −82.66 | 1.20 |
| ⊕ Rare Medium Grp | Services | --- | −88.64 | 1.17 |
| AppNet | Technology | --- | --- | 1.15 |
| ATMI | Technology | 14.00 | −48.77 | 1.12 |
| ⊕ ACTV | Technology | --- | −85.91 | 1.09 |
| ⊕ Winstar Comms | Services | --- | −62.13 | 1.05 |
| ⊕ Valassis Comms | Services | 11.62 | −31.80 | 1.03 |

⊕ ⊖ Indicates an increase or decrease in holding since last portfolio
✹ Indicates a new holding since last portfolio

Data through 03-31-00
YTD Data through 11-24-00

**Figure 6-4** JAVTX top 25 holdings. (*Courtesy of Morningstar, Inc.*)

ment of companies tries to keep Street analysts' expectations low, so the company can beat the estimates.

The managers of JAVTX think they have to do their own number crunching to calculate how much their companies will earn, not rely on what the Street analysts think the companies will earn. And the only way to do that is to have access to the companies. JAVTX will walk company management through the fund's assumptions to ascertain what the real numbers will be.

JAVTX thinks that many of the technology companies that JAVTX buys for its portfolio possess new, highly conceptual technology. The sales and earnings of this type of company are hard to estimate, especially when looking out over the longer term, say, 4 years or so. So JAVTX gathers input from the companies themselves, but also checks with the companies' competition, their suppliers, other experts in the industry in which the companies operate, and anywhere else the fund can garner information to make its judgments.

Figure 6-4 shows the fund's top 25 holdings. These are not your household names; rather they are aggressive growth stocks. Many of the stocks are newer companies and operate in new-economy industries.

## RYDEX OTC INVESTOR—RYOCX

This structured index fund is set up with the performance of the Nasdaq-100 Index as its benchmark. The fund is not a pure index fund, that is, it is not set up to have the same exact stocks in the same proportion that are found in the benchmark index.

On a daily basis the fund managers compare the fund portfolio to the index. The managers make sure that the risk in the fund will not stray far from the risk in the benchmark. The managers are not trying to figure out what the markets are about to do; they are not picking stocks to buy or sell; they are not raising cash. What they are doing is making sure that RYOCX at least matches the return of the Nasdaq-100 Index and, ideally, beats the index incrementally.

To match the index return, the managers fashion and hold an optimized basket; this basket of stocks is a subset of the Nasdaq-100 Index. This optimized portfolio is crafted so that it will return as closely as possible the same performance as the index. To this end, RYOCX may or may not have the same number of stocks that appear in the Nasdaq-100 Index. The funds have been operating since February 1994. Over that time, the fund has had a low of 65 stocks in the fund at a given time, to as high as 98 stocks. Its benchmark contains 100 stocks.

The number of stocks will vary because of the weightings by the manager of the index stocks. Because of the recent volatility in the market, the managers are staying close to weighting the shares held by the fund to the same proportion as that held by the index. The fund, even when it does not own the same stocks in proportion to the index, still has a tight performance correlation to the index; the fund estimates its correlation stays at about 0.99 percent to the index.

## Factors for Correlation

To correlate the fund to the index, the fund breaks down the risks associated with the stocks in the index and makes sure that the fund has essentially the same risk and reward market exposure as the index.

The most obvious way to correlate the fund with the index is to match industry exposure. The Nasdaq-100 Index has exposure to technology, biotechnology, telecommunications, and other sectors. The goal of the fund is to have the same index industry exposure, but the fund does not have to own every individual stock to accomplish this.

Another factor considered in optimizing is market capitalization. Momentum is also weighed; the fund wants to hold stocks that move similarly to the movement of stocks in the index.

## Optimizing to the Index

In indexing, a fund could employ a generic one-dimensional approach of buying the stocks of an index and holding the stocks. Because the fund will match the index, the only factor on which the fund can fixate is lowering operating costs. Put another way, if a fund purely and simply indexes, whatever the fund charges the fund will lose to the index. If a fund charges 25 basis points (BP), for example, the fund every year will underperform to that expense ratio; in this case the fund will underperform by 25 BP.

The Rydex OTC Investor fund is an optimized fund and tries to overcome its expenses by adding value and outperforming the index. The fund looks at all the factors that it thinks is affecting the index. The managers work as the market changes to keep the fund replicating or slightly beating the Nasdaq-100. As markets change, and this index is certainly about change, the managers will change their industry allocations and security weightings.

Every stock in the index has a correlation to the other stocks in the index. The managers must continually study the factors driving the index

**Growth of $10,000**
— Fund: Rydex OTC Inv
— Category: Large Growth
----- Index: S&P 500

**Annual Returns**

| | 1997 | 1998 | 1999 | 10-00 |
|---|---|---|---|---|
| Fund: | 21.9% | 86.6% | 100.6% | −12.3% |

**Figure 6-5** RYOCX performance and top 25 holdings. (*Courtesy of Morningstar, Inc.*)

and make sure that they purchase stocks in combinations that leave the fund neutral from a risk standpoint.

The managers think that technology is becoming a more important part of the U.S. economy and that the Nasdaq-100 is a very accurate barometer of the overall economy. Technology makes up about 70 percent of the Nasdaq-100 Index and of the RYOCX as well. The managers believe that as long as earnings keep materializing from that sector the index and fund should continue to be strong. Figure 6-5 shows the performance of RYOCX and its top 25 holdings.

## VAN WAGONER EMERGING GROWTH—VWEGX

Van Wagoner buys emerging growth companies in this fund. By this, Van Wagoner means companies that are young, ambitious, and performing in fast-growing areas, primarily in the technology and technology services area. The fund also looks for companies in the health-care and, to a lesser extent, consumer-type sectors.

Van Wagoner wants to buy companies that have a unique product or service that allows the companies to grow at a more rapid rate than the other companies in its field. The fund also wants its companies to possess some sort of defensible business position. The fund prefers companies with

| | | | | |
|---|---|---|---|---|
| Total number of stock holdings | 91 | Turnover % | | 385 |
| Total number of bond holdings | 2 | Yield % | | 0.00 |
| % Assets in top 10 holdings | 38.84 | | | |

**Top 25 Holdings**

| Name of Holding | Sector | P/E | YTD Return % | % Net Assets |
|---|---|---|---|---|
| ⊖ Cisco Sys | Technology | 128.51 | −1.63 | 6.59 |
| ⊖ Microsoft | Technology | 41.14 | −40.10 | 5.14 |
| ⊕ Intel | Technology | 29.39 | 6.89 | 4.59 |
| ⊖ Oracle | Technology | 22.13 | −13.89 | 4.35 |
| ⊕ JDS Uniphase | Technology | --- | −18.17 | 3.95 |
| ⊖ Sun Microsystems | Technology | 68.45 | 9.60 | 3.79 |
| ⊖ Qualcomm | Technology | 100.60 | −52.02 | 3.01 |
| ⊖ Veritas Software | Technology | --- | 5.72 | 2.74 |
| ⊕ Siebel Sys | Technology | 261.93 | 105.80 | 2.55 |
| ✻ Juniper Net | Technology | 472.77 | 133.60 | 2.13 |
| ⊖ Nextel Comms Cl A | Services | --- | −32.36 | 2.05 |
| ⊖ Network Appliance | Technology | 273.37 | 51.39 | 1.98 |
| ⊕ CIENA | Technology | 511.25 | 255.65 | 1.95 |
| ⊖ I2 Tech | Technology | --- | 15.90 | 1.87 |
| ⊕ Gemstar–TV Guide Intl | Services | --- | −34.91 | 1.76 |
| ⊖ PMC Sierra | Technology | 236.33 | 41.52 | 1.76 |
| ⊖ VeriSign | Technology | --- | −51.16 | 1.75 |
| ⊖ Xilinx | Technology | 26.18 | 24.95 | 1.75 |
| ⊖ Amgen | Health | 58.99 | 9.99 | 1.57 |
| ⊖ Maxim Integrated Products | Technology | 59.60 | 23.77 | 1.50 |
| ⊖ WorldCom | Services | 9.58 | −70.20 | 1.48 |
| ⊖ Applied Micro Circuits | Technology | 244.68 | 80.74 | 1.42 |
| ⊖ Immunex | Health | 183.86 | 12.33 | 1.41 |
| ⊖ Global Crossing | Services | --- | −67.75 | 1.39 |
| ⊖ Dell Comp | Technology | 32.50 | −52.21 | 1.38 |

⊕ ⊖ Indicates an increase or decrease in holding since last portfolio
✻ Indicates a new holding since last portfolio

Data through 09-30-00
YTD Data through 11-24-00

**Figure 6-5** *Continued*

experienced management teams, believing that experienced management teams are important to guide companies through tough economic times. Van Wagoner is looking for long-term growing companies, not just companies that produce good numbers for a few quarters.

## A Narrow Niche Field

This fund occupies a fairly narrow niche in the high-growth, highly volatile equity area. The companies in the VWEGX portfolio are growing rapidly in sales, usually from quarter to quarter. These companies are usually subject to major swings in sentiment and market price; the stocks are in or out of fashion, depending on market sentiment.

In 1999, for example, the fund was among the top funds in the United States. In 1997 the fund was out of fashion and off the top fund lists. Through late October 2000, even in a weak market for emerging growth stocks, the fund was up over 27 percent. A glance at the performance chart in Fig. 6-6 shows just how in and out the fund has been.

The company considers a narrow focus of stocks. There are about 4500 companies on Nasdaq, and there are companies on the other OTC markets and more companies in the listed markets. Within this large number, Van Wagoner focuses on only about 300 stocks. Also, larger-capitalized companies are absent from the Van Wagoner list. Microsoft or Intel or similar

**Growth of $10,000**
— Fund: Van Wagoner Emerging Growth
— Category: Mid-Cap Growth
----- Index: S&P 500

**Annual Returns**

|  | 1997 | 1998 | 1999 | 10-00 |
|---|---|---|---|---|
| Fund: | −20.0% | 8.0% | 291.2% | 21.3% |

**Figure 6-6** VWEGX performance and top 25 holdings. (*Courtesy of Morningstar, Inc.*)

| Total number of stock holdings | 166 | Turnover % | 353 |
| Total number of bond holdings | 0 | Yield % | 0.00 |
| % Assets in top 10 holdings | 31.41 | | |

**Top 25 Holdings**

| | Name of Holding | Sector | P/E | YTD Return % | % Net Assets |
|---|---|---|---|---|---|
| ✸ | Storagenetworks Cl B (restr) | --- | --- | --- | 7.32 |
| ✸ | Ariba | Technology | --- | −11.56 | 5.85 |
| ✸ | Cobalt Networks Cl C (restr) | --- | --- | --- | 3.04 |
| | Interwoven 144A | Technology | --- | --- | 2.69 |
| ✸ | Netro | Technology | --- | −71.57 | 2.55 |
| ⊕ | SDL | Technology | --- | 116.06 | 2.40 |
| ⊕ | TranSwitch | Technology | 88.57 | 50.13 | 1.97 |
| ⊕ | Broadcom Cl A | Technology | 244.01 | −14.00 | 1.96 |
| ⊕ | Brocade Comm Sys | Technology | 505.17 | 114.05 | 1.83 |
| ✸ | Natural Microsystems | Technology | --- | −6.55 | 1.80 |
| ⊕ | JDS Uniphase | Technology | --- | −18.17 | 1.58 |
| ⊕ | Juniper Net | Technology | 472.77 | 133.60 | 1.56 |
| ✸ | Copper Mountain Net (restr) | --- | --- | --- | 1.43 |
| ⊕ | IntraNet Solutions | Technology | --- | 30.74 | 1.42 |
| ⊖ | E-Tek Dynamics | Technology | --- | --- | 1.41 |
| ⊕ | GlobeSpan | Technology | --- | 112.19 | 1.32 |
| ⊕ | Exar | Technology | 45.70 | 75.80 | 1.20 |
| ⊕ | Turnstone Sys | Technology | --- | --- | 1.20 |
| ⊕ | Efficient Netwks | Technology | --- | −52.21 | 1.18 |
| ✸ | NVIDIA | Technology | 53.74 | 145.00 | 1.12 |
| ✸ | Virata | Technology | --- | 56.48 | 1.09 |
| ⊕ | Network Appliance | Technology | 273.37 | 51.39 | 1.08 |
| ⊕ | Photon Dynamics | Industrial | --- | −25.81 | 1.07 |
| ⊕ | Art Tech Grp | Technology | 23.37 | −42.63 | 0.97 |
| | Onhealth Net | Services | --- | --- | 0.97 |

⊕ ⊖ Indicates an increase or decrease in holding since last portfolio
✸ Indicates a new holding since last portfolio

Data through 06-30-00
YTD Data through 11-24-00

**Figure 6-6** *Continued*

companies are not considered because Van Wagoner is focusing on the smaller issues.

## Fast-Growing Stocks

In the past, VWEGX estimated that the stocks in its portfolio were growing at a rate of over 20 percent a year. This growth estimate has been increased, with some issues in the fund growing at rates of over 100 percent a year.

The fund has been successful in finding many high-growth companies to buy in the technology sector. In fact, the fund is finding stocks that have promise for the longer term than it ever has. Part of this is due to the Internet and the growth it has spawned in that industry.

The fund estimates that Internet technology provides information on a global basis and expects to continue its growth. The effects of this Internet revolution will spread into the way business is conducted worldwide, and also will affect culture and society around the globe.

The fund knows the risks involved in operating in a small niche sector. Van Wagoner thinks that many of the dot-com companies involved in retailing and other generic merchandising methods will fail. But these are not the types of stock that the funds invest in.

Rather than retailing, VWEGX buys the stocks of companies that are solving business problems in the software area or the telecommunications area or other faster-growth sector. Barring a recession, which would cut into corporate spending plans, VWEGX expects that growth will continue in the companies in which it invests.

# PART III

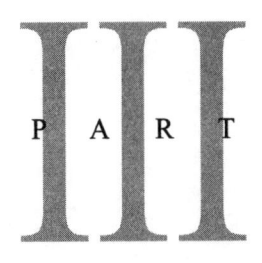

# STRATEGIES FOR TRADING ON THE NASDAQ

# CHAPTER 7

# DISCIPLINE: THE KEY TO SUCCESS FOR LONG-TERM AND SHORT-TERM INVESTING

## WHY ARE YOU INVESTING? TRADING?

The first thing you must resolve in your investment planning is what your objectives are in investing or trading in the market. Equally important is the amount of capital you have to achieve your goals. I put objectives in the plural: You probably have more than one reason to be in the market, and each reason must be apportioned the amount of capital you plan to commit to each reason. For example, perhaps 25 percent of your capital will be very aggressive and will be invested in Internet start-ups. This portion of funds is considered risk capital, and this commitment should be undertaken only with capital that you can afford to lose; you may lose all of it.

The markets are volatile because of many factors, including the faster sales and earnings growth of the new-economy stocks; the large influx of risk capital coming into the market; the proliferation of day traders because of, among other reasons, the ease and efficiency and low cost of on-line trading.

Much has been made of applying discipline to market activities. Very little has been explored regarding what is meant by discipline and how to apply it.

> *Arguably, the most important factor in investing is for the investor to know herself. With the risks and stresses associated with investing for rewards in the markets, she should at least have the comfort that she understands these factors and accepts them.*

Discipline should probably start, not with the investment strategy employed to reach investment goals, but with the investor herself. Whether a person is day trading in the billions of dollars through a private hedge fund, or is placing a trade in her portfolio for $5000 once a year or so, she must face her limitations, goals, resources, emotional makeup, and many other factors, all dealing with her and her ability to handle risk. The stock market is risk capital and this fact, in this long-running bull market, seems to have been at times forgotten. Funds put into the market are at risk, and before a dollar is placed into the market, the investor or trader must understand herself, and know something about her risk profile.

Once this is understood, all kinds of strategies can be pursued. What is important to accomplish is to invest or trade with as little emotional confusion and strain as possible, because in the best of market situations the pressure is always there and must be addressed. The discipline is to do the work to understand how one feels about dealing with risk. Then investing can be done in a clearer way.

## Strategies to Consider: Averaging Down and Up

This strategy is used to lower your average cost when you buy a stock. Suppose you want to buy 500 Microsoft, for instance, and MSFT is 95. Instead of buying the 500 shares at 95, you buy only 250 shares at 95; MSFT goes down to 90 and you buy 250 more shares, averaging down. Instead of paying 95 for the 500 shares, your average cost is $92\frac{1}{2}$.

This strategy works well in theory, but not always very well in practice. Buying as a stock goes down is risky business, because before you are in a profit position the stock has to trade up above your average cost.

In this momentum market over the last 20 years, averaging up has been a rewarding strategy. In averaging up, using the MSFT example, you buy

250 shares at 95; if MSFT goes down, hold your 250 shares; the stock is down but you only have 250 shares with a loss versus the 500 you plan to buy. If MSFT trades up to, say, 100, purchase another 250 shares. Your average cost on the 500 shares would be 97½, which is less than the present market price of 100. You don't have to wait for the stock to rebound (if it ever does) to be in a profit position.

## Sector Investing

There have been studies that conclude that sector selection can account for as much as 80 to 90 percent of a portfolio's performance. You could divide your portfolio into different sectors that look promising. For risky, aggressive growth, you could buy stocks in the technology, Internet, and biotechnology sectors.

Peppered throughout this book are the names of stocks in the Internet sector. Often the same stocks reappear in the various indexes and exchange shares and institutional portfolios in this book. Look over the portfolios and see if any of these companies make sense to you. You can buy those stocks that are in the portfolios you wish in order to have representation in a certain sector. For real representation you would have to buy 10 to 20 names. You don't have to have all the names, however. You could invest in some of the funds mentioned here or check with your investment adviser for the names of other funds. Then buy the funds of your choice, and also buy some of the stocks you like in addition to the fund investments. This is called overweighting in a sector.

Using exchange shares, you could buy into a sector, consider holding a percentage of exchange shares long term, and perhaps trade some exchange shares on a more active basis. What percentage you trade and hold long term depends on the amount of funds you can comfortably risk, and how much risk you can emotionally accept.

Conventional portfolio management suggests putting about 70 to 90 percent in stocks and keeping the remainder in cash. Consider keeping a larger percentage of cash, perhaps 50 to 60 percent. With the smaller amount of cash, you could get more aggressive in the sectors you select. Having 30 percent of your portfolio in Internet stocks and 70 percent in cash, for instance, may make more sense for your risk profile than having 70 percent in "conservative" stocks, 10 percent in Internet stocks, and 20 percent cash. The larger Internet exposure will have risk, but also a sizeable profit potential. With less of your overall fund invested in stocks, the risk exposure may be about the same, holding a large Internet sector and a large amount of cash.

## Considering Internet and Other Growth Nasdaq Stocks

The perceived wisdom that "conservative" stocks have less risk can be questioned. Some of my larger losses for clients and myself have occurred in so-called lower-risk, lower-P/E stocks.

For many years, people scoffed at Internet, biotechnology, and other growth stocks as being overvalued, pie-in-the-sky stocks and a bubble about to burst. When the decline in these groups happened, skeptics were glad they had avoided the group. But some companies made good gains even considering the market decline, and others may gain in the future.

This book has shown that there are some fundamental reasons for the advances in the growth groups. Whether these sectors will continue to grow, only time will tell. But having representation in the growth sector, according to one's risk profile and desire for risk profit, is worth considering.

## Zero-Coupon Bonds Hedged with Growth Stocks

To offset the risks incurred with buying growth stocks, consider buying zero-coupon bonds as a hedge. A zero-coupon bond is issued at a deep discount to its face value; the face value is the amount received at maturity. No interest is paid quarterly, hence the term "zero" coupon. Bonds usually sell in $1000 face value increments, with minimum purchases of $5000.

The difference between the issue price and maturity value is deemed to be income to the bondholder by the IRS. For example, if you buy a 20-year zero-coupon bond at 60, the amount of accretion, or march to maturity of the bond, is 2 points per year for 20 years, or 40 points at maturity. This is "phantom" income; you receive no interest but still have to pay taxes each year on the 2-point accretion.

You can avoid paying interest by buying tax-free municipal zeros. Or consider buying U.S. Treasury zero "stripped" bonds, commonly called "CATS" for Certificate of Accrual on Treasury Securities. State taxes are exempt on U.S. debt instruments, although you must still pay federal income taxes. In Table 7-1, taxes, commissions, and markups have been disregarded.

The zero-bond strategy can take the edge off of investing in growth and emerging growth stocks. Considering your investment to be on a 20-year basis, you can buy Internet, biotechnology, or other higher-risk, higher-reward stocks. You know that in 20 years the least you will have is your original investment, in this example $100,000. Even if your stock portfolio shrinks to zero, which is hard to imagine, you will still have the same

CHAPTER 7   DISCIPLINE: THE KEY TO SUCCESS

**Table 7-1** Zero-Coupon Tax-Free Municipal Bond (Original Investment, $100,000)

| *Stocks, year 2000* | *Bonds, year 2000* |
|---|---|
| $50,000 growth, emerging growth, speculative and seasoned | $50,000 zero-coupon municipal, 20-year maturity, $100,000 face value (cost, 50) |

| *Stocks, year 2020* | *Bonds, year 2020* |
|---|---|
| Value unknown | Value $100,000 |

amount you started with. Of course, shorter- or longer-term bonds can be bought, and the calculations on the strategy will change.

This hedge can be used with interest-sensitive growth stocks as well. If interest rates go up, interest rate sensitive stocks such as retailing and financials will decline, and the bonds will also decline. But held to maturity, the bonds will go to par (face value), and your bond investment will be returned, no matter what interest rates do in the interim. If interest rates go down, the price of the zeros will appreciate, returning a short-term profit. Also the interest sensitive stocks in the portfolio will advance. In this strategy, the zeros are held as a hedge to return the original investment, no matter what the markets do before the bonds mature.

## The Risk in Low-P/E Stocks

This book has covered various ways to consider P/Es when relating them to technology and other high-growth stocks. P/Es are *a* way of measuring companies, not *the* way of measuring companies.

Investors can and do have losing trades by buying low-P/E stocks, thinking that there is downside support with the P/E. This support has often proved to be illusory at best. A low-P/E company can have a drop in earnings, or even have a loss, and downside support is gone. A 10-multiple stock can have its earnings drop and can become a 30-multiple stock, for instance. Anyone who has been in the market any length of time has had a stock that went down; and probably everybody has experienced a stock decline in what was thought to be the least likely stock to drop.

Money put into the stock market should be looked upon as risk capital; a conservative, safe stock market investment, I think, is close to being an oxymoron.

## THE NATURE OF THE STOCK MARKET

The stock market reflects the capitalist system. The nature of this system dictates that stronger companies will swallow or destroy weaker companies. And one of the main arbiters of which companies will survive is a company's profit margin. Companies have to carve out a niche to have wide profit margins. Once they do, other companies will come into that industry and compete with the original companies, and this competition usually drives down profit margins. Or a big company will buy up a small company with a good margin, therefore lessening competition. Once the smaller company is merged, its profit margin will be absorbed into the bigger company's margin, again driving down the smaller company's margins. These takeovers are ongoing. Consider that there have been 740 changes in the S&P 500 Index in the last 36 years, a remarkably large number of changes.

The stock market reflects corporate competition. The recent bull leg may seem to be investor friendly, but these higher prices are a by-product of competitiveness and an almost ideal economic environment. The market is a competitive arena that reflects what goes on in the business world on a minute-by-minute basis. Knowing this helps investors on a longer-term basis. Capitalism will struggle on, the weaker companies will be vanquished by the stronger, and efficiencies will prevail. That is why the indexes are making new highs: the market keeps growing to reflect increasing efficiencies and profitability.

The rise of technology, and the growth of the Internet, is not a new phenomenon, but a continuum of a long-term growth cycle. It is hard to imagine the genie going back into the bottle. The market is reflecting the quickening pace of innovation and growth in the economy on a worldwide basis.

## RISK AND MOMENTUM

Capital risk is prevalent in up markets and down markets, but do not be afraid of declines. The same hedge fund managers, the day traders, the speculators, will follow the momentum of the markets on the way down and take the short side. You may want to put in some shorts along with them.

But before going on the short side, understand why sorting is risky. Shorting is dangerous because your loss is unlimited. If you buy a $10 stock, the most you can lose is 10 points. You can short a $10 stock and may have to cover at 50 or higher. You do not have a limit to your loss.

Because risk is greater on the short side than the long side, you may not want to short; your risk profile may suggest that you don't have the temperament or knowledge or capital to short. Then by all means don't. But if you can short, there are many good strategies to use on the downside.

A strategy may be to short the weakest stock in a group, against your long position. Say that you are long Microsoft, Inc. (MSFT), and you like the company for the long term, but fear that tech stocks will get hit. You could short a tech stock, one that is competing with MSFT, has less earnings than MSFT, and has a weak financial position. If the tech stocks keep going up, MSFT will probably go with them; your short position will go up also, probably giving you a loss position. If tech stocks go down, however, MSFT probably will not go down as much as a more speculative stock: MSFT is in many of the indexes, so there is probably some downside support; the company is a giant in its field, and stronger companies such as MSFT should be among the better performers.

This technique is not foolproof and by no means eliminates risk; but doing your homework, you may be able to reduce your risk profile somewhat.

## Hedging with Different Styles

This ongoing bull market has spawned a dichotomy between value stocks and growth stocks. This difference, with the growth stocks mostly advancing while value stays flat or goes down, has been very pronounced, but is changing.

Along with growth Nasdaq stocks, you may want to consider buying some old-fashioned blue-chip NYSE stocks, figuring that growth may continue to decline, and buyers may continue to scurry to value stocks for appreciation. This scurrying may last awhile, continuing a trend back to value stocks. But there is no hard and fast rule; market exuberance can flow over from one sector to another. Value investing could spill over into investors buying more growth, and vice versa.

You may not trust growth stocks and want to position yourself for the market continuing to come around to your viewpoint—that growth stocks will continue down, and value, up. This is a dicey proposal, trying to figure out what the market sentiment will be. But to accomplish this investment posture, you could buy value stocks and, in addition to buying value, consider shorting some of the high-flying Nasdaq stocks. Then if people sell growth and buy value stocks, which is your view, you will win on both sides. Your value stocks will advance, and your short stocks decline. Also, you might think that growth couldn't advance again without value stocks also advancing. Growth will go up, and sentiment will continue spilling over into value. So your short position of growth stocks may not appreciate more than your long position of value stocks. This would be a risky posture to take, but there is certain logic to it, and it may prove profitable.

## Traders Disguised as Investors

In the tech sector investors many times buy on momentum trends rather than on an objective evaluation of an expected reasonable rate of return. The problem with momentum investing is that this technique gauges past performance rather than the fundamental outlook for a company and an appraisal which sets a realistic stock price. It should be pointed out that "realistic stock price" is a didactic term and may not work as a practical matter.

Momentum investing supposes that if a stock has been going up, it will continue up. On the downside, momentum strategies suggest stocks that are going down will continue down. This is not investing; it is trading.

Trading is fine, at least for a portion of your funds, if this is what you want to do, and if you have the temperament and knowledge and capital to trade. But investors can get trapped into being traders and think that they are investing.

## Avoiding the Herd Mentality

To stay away from buying with the crowd, especially in these days of high valuations, an investor might ask himself how much success the company will have to have to justify its current prices.

If a company is priced at 40 to 50 times gross revenues (P/GR), for example, how much growth would the company have to achieve over the next 3 to 5 years in order to have a P/GR ratio that is in line with its peers, given some reasonable assumptions about how successful its sales might be?

Going through this thought process you might think that a stock's price makes sense; prices of other stocks may strike you as being so out of line so as to appear rather silly. It is helpful to go through this thought process to arrive at a level of conviction before you buy, sell, or short. Right or wrong, you will have something other than momentum to base your investment decision on after going over the fundamentals. After all, momentum is just a reflection of the herd mentality at a certain time.

The most profitable time to buy is when others are selling or avoiding certain stocks or sectors. Also the best time to sell is when others are clamoring to buy and bidding up stocks. This is not a comfortable way to invest, but is often a profitable way. Markets do not reward comfort; markets do not generally reward those who buy and sell with the herd.

You can step apart from the herd in two ways. First, if you want to buy technology stocks and they are making new highs, try to wait for a pullback; on a pullback, buy when others are selling. For example, on April 4, 2000, the Nasdaq market broke, dropping over 500 points. At the lowest point after the sell-off, you could have bought stocks down 20 percent or more from their prior day's highs. Nasdaq rebounded to close down just a little over 70 points that day; many Nasdaq stocks closed up strongly from their day's close. There were 30 percent or more swings on some stocks on that Tuesday. The phones were ringing off of the hooks, both to buy and sell. Fear and greed were on open display. Now that was a good time to buy.

Another way to avoid the herd is to do some research and buy stocks that have been overlooked, no matter what sector. Everyone keeps up with the news on the favorite sectors, but lesser known stocks and sectors are often left languishing. There are stocks selling at reasonable valuations, with lower levels of risk on the downside; a news item or two can send an overlooked stock soaring. Even if you do not take short-term profits and prefer to hold for the long term, short-term upward moves are good for the psyche.

## Measuring Valuations

The new economy is at the present time very big and, yet, is only in its nascent stage. This technology-spawned information revolution could prove to be as big and important as the industrial revolution. The new economy has already swept away old ways of doing business in some sectors.

An investor has to ask herself, How much should be paid for stocks that are part of this revolution? What is a reasonable valuation for companies of a new frontier?

The risk is that you pay too much for a growth stock, and that the price of this stock will not appreciate enough to be profitable for many years. The valuations of many companies are questionable at the time of their IPOs; many stocks with IPOs would not have come public in the markets of years ago. Instead of having an IPO, in the past, small companies would have gotten "bridge" loans; these loans would have been made to give the companies operating capital. Later, when they were more seasoned, these small companies would have had their IPOs.

But time is more compressed now, and there existed recently an active investor appetite for new and fledgling companies in the new economy. This is in spite of the fact that many of these companies have little earnings; many companies may also have little in the way of sales.

Public appetite for these issues has waned. When the herd abandons a group that was hot, you don't want to have paid too much and be left holding stocks at losses. Although the group's fall from favor may be temporary, temporary could stretch out for years. Also, when holding stocks, there is an opportunity cost—your money is tied up in stocks that may pay off down the road, but you may not have more funds with which to take advantage of new opportunities. So valuations must be considered even though you are a longer-term investor.

## The Value of Research

The Nasdaq Composite Index had a stunning run for about 24 months before correcting. Many technicians are predicting a trading range, perhaps about 2300 on the low side to 4000 on the high side. A trading range this wide could set up opportunities for long-term investors to profit from buying and selling at opportune points.

Profits can be made by being in technology stocks, and if you do your homework by, among other things, studying research about the companies you are interested in, you may increase your profits and lower your risk. There are expectations that tech companies will do better than anticipated. If a company beats expectations, it is usually rewarded; if earnings or sales or other performances come short, the stocks of these companies can fall sharply.

Taking the time to do this research should help your performance. Or concentrate on sectors and buy the exchange shares. Then, because you own a basket of stocks, a disappointment in one or two of the companies in the sector will not matter so much; if you are right on the sector, your purchase or sale or short sale will probably be profitable.

# CHAPTER 8

# STRATEGIES FOR THE LONG-TERM INVESTOR

## A LONG-TERM OVERVIEW

In the present environment, one in which so many investors and traders have access to computers, and at the click of a mouse can fire off trades all day long, there is much market volatility. The volatility measurements in the Nasdaq Composite Index have been rising exponentially, along with greater volume. This is somewhat caused by the ease at which people can now trade in and out of positions. Also the speed and easy availability of information makes for greater market volatility; when people have information, they think they are smart, and can make money with that information. Many times in the market that is not true; markets don't move in the ways that logic would dictate. Having information is often not a reason to trade. Besides, with today's communications, it is almost impossible to have information before others.

It is doubtful that many people are now making, or ever have made, money day trading. Studies have shown that most day traders lose money. Without getting into the psychology of why people trade while they continue to lose money, which is outside the scope of this book and much literature is available on this subject, the long-term investor should understand that day trading is helping to drive the volatility in this market. The long-term investor must not get swept up into day trading, but must look beyond the short-term swings and try to capitalize on them while aiming for a longer-term profit.

Although the best of the long-term investors know they should not get swept up into trading, even for them it is hard not to get swept up. As investors, we all break down every now and then and get caught up in short-term thrills. Perhaps speculating with a small portion of your portfolio will help with that itch. But for serious money, the long-term investor stays with the long-term picture. The better long-term investors do.

Day traders buy when stocks seem to be headed up, and sell when stocks look like they are going down. The long-term investor should capitalize on the volatility by buying quality longer-term holdings when the stocks are down and headed lower. And when the day traders are causing good quality stocks to get ahead of themselves, long-term investors should look to hedge themselves against the stock's decline, either by selling part or all of their holdings and/or by shorting.

## Market Sentiment and the Long-Term Investor

It is difficult to do, but long-term Nasdaq investors can increase their performance by gauging market sentiment and using their judgment of market sentiment in timing their commitments. It is important for Nasdaq stock investors, especially those who buy into the Internet, biotechnology, and other growth areas, to try to buy in panic-type situations. After a downturn of 15 percent or so in the Nasdaq Composite, and when the day traders and market savants bemoan the Nasdaq markets and stress how poor the outlook is, the long-term investor can consider stepping in to buy some Nasdaq stocks at a discount. After that, when the markets have advanced over a period of time and are frothy, the long-term investor might consider paring back her portfolio. Not being in a hurry to take action on either side can help during those panic times when you just don't know which side to take, if any.

So long-term investors measure sentiment, which is a judgment of how optimistic people are about Nasdaq or how fearful they are. There are many ways to measure sentiment, and it is up to each investor to develop his own ways. After gauging market sentiment, a long-term investor can consider taking action, which consists of doing the opposite of what she thinks the rest of the market is thinking and doing. Going with the herd will only yield mediocre results. Buying when the market has been strong and indicators are pointing even higher, and selling when everybody is panicking and the market has been collapsing for a while, will render at best an average performance.

Although the long-term investor will get good results over a period of time if he stays in good stocks, her performance could be enhanced by buying and selling at opportune times, if only with a portion of her funds.

Trading at opportune times is also a way to manage risk. Probably you will not be in or out of the market 100 percent at any one time; but being in the market heavier at higher levels and being out of the market at least partially during market shakeouts can increase results. Investors can be successful by investing in the right sector at the right time. Investors can also make money sticking to one sector, and buying when nobody wants to buy into that sector, and selling when the sector becomes strongly into favor.

## Which Market Sector in Which to Invest

From time to time there is a shift from the old-economy stocks and into the new-economy stocks, most of which are listed on the Nasdaq. Another way to decide which sectors you want to be in is to divide the market into the old-economy, more value-oriented stocks, or the new-economy, growth-oriented stocks.

Looking out over the next 10 years or so, many investors think that growth is the place to be, at least for the major portion of your investment funds. Also in a bull leg, usually growth leads the advance; in bear markets, value seems to be more favored. If you see a bear market looming, perhaps you want to get more conservative. But what has worked over the past 10 years has been the growth-oriented view. It is difficult to see at this juncture events that will change this outlook.

As a harbinger of the continuing momentum of capital committed to market areas of growth, it was reported on March 30, 2000, that stock mutual funds drew $39.1 billion in net new money in February 2000. This was a record for net new money taken in for a month. Also, just over $10 billion of this capital went to the Janus funds. These funds were known for their aggressive momentum investing. One of the Janus aggressive growth funds is explored in Chap. 7 of this book.

Signs such as these dispute any slowdown for growth in this sector. But these signs have to be watched and considered ways of measuring market sentiment.

## Investment Timing and Market Events

When an event such as a record of capital inflow into mutual funds is announced, there could be a short-term rise in the growth stocks. In the above example, Janus probably took at least a portion, and invested in the stocks that it already owned, which were aggressive growth issues.

An event such as this can also lead to a sharp advance in growth stocks, which ultimately can lead to a blow-off phase, at least in the short run, and can cause quite a bit of pain for those investors who chased these issues. In other sectors and for investment trends in general, this can happen: People will chase stocks for a couple of months before the trend plays out and there is a pullback or even a panic.

As a long-term investor, you may want to back off of a sector after a sharp rise; it could take a year or longer for a sector to recover after a sharp rise and subsequent blow off. The strategy of a long-term investor is to be in a sector as it flattens and not just before a blow off.

> *Try as one might to "hang in there" with a losing stock or stocks, perhaps down 50 percent or so, one may not be able to. Fear and disappointment may be too overwhelming, or one may not have the financial staying power. Avoiding getting caught in this situation, although it may be difficult to avoid, should be foremost in an investor's mind.*

As an example, Mexican stocks, such as Telefonos De Mexico (TMX) were in great demand early in 1994. Throughout 1994 Mexican stocks stayed hot, with the sector written up as a buy in virtually every periodical. This hot streak ended in late 1994 with the Mexican peso devaluation, and subsequent dumping by investors of Mexican stocks.

Although a person may have been a long-term investor, she would have encountered a large measure of pain and financial loss if she had bought at the top; the top was when the stocks were selling at their highest and the buy recommendations were at their most vociferous.

It took years for the Mexican stock sector to return, and when the sector did return many of the stocks that had been favored in the prior advance were not the stocks that came to favor in the later advance.

## Short-Term Pain

It is hard for a long-term investor to have an attitude of "I don't care what the market does short term; I am in for the long term," without experiencing moments of self-doubt, regrets, and sometimes having to later acknowledge using bad judgment about "not caring." Many of those long-term investors who bought Mexican stocks near the top probably discovered that they cared very much about the Mexican market's decline. It's a lousy feeling a year later to see a portion of your portfolio down 30 to 40 percent. At that point, you *do* care, and there is no telling when buying in that sector will come back, if ever.

Even long-term investors reach a pain threshold that just becomes too great, after his stocks are down for a while. At this point many give up and get out. Sometimes giving up is the right thing to do.

The thing to do, which is not easy, is to avoid situations where market sectors can go against you, and you are trapped. To foresee a potential problem and to avoid that problem takes one more step in the investing process. This step is to understand your risk tolerance and to weigh your financial resources. To not get into trouble, it helps to lighten up or hedge when market sectors get overblown and buy or add to positions when other investors are fleeing.

For an example of market timing with sector allocation consider the price performance of QQQ in 1999. An investor, rather than purchasing QQQ and just holding it through up and down markets, might have employed a timing method. QQQ had three downturns of between 8 percent and 10 percent in 1999. Each time the dip was only for a brief period, and an investor could have taken advantage of these dips if she had had cash in hand at those times. Also, one could have sold off all or a portion of QQQ every time QQQ sold at 10 percent above its old high, for instance. And the funds could be held to purchase QQQ each time it breaks 10 percent or lower than the seller's selling price.

For instance, QQQ breaks down 10 percent, to 102. A long-term investor could buy QQQ at that price and hold for the long term. If QQQ continues down another 10 percent, the investor can continue holding for the long term. Suppose QQQ goes from 102 to 112, and then makes a new high, at 115; then QQQ goes to 120. A long-term investor could sell some off at 120, keeping the funds available for a pullback in QQQ. In the year 2000, with its sharp sell-off in QQQ, the investor would probably have a loss, if the market stayed near a bottom. Even so, buying after a pullback would have saved the investor money.

Although this borders on trading, which is not what a long-term investor wants to get caught up in, there are differences from trading. The long-term investor will take profits and buy on dips with just a portion of his assets. And, unlike a trader, who is looking only at shorter-term moves, the long-term investor plans to hold long term. He thinks that QQQ long term will do fine because growth stocks will continue going up. There will be dips, and these dips could last for years, but his time horizon is 5 years or longer for a portion of his funds.

A short-term trader's time horizon is 5 minutes or weeks or months, but certainly not years. And as for the fundamental long-term future of growth stocks, a trader could not care less. Price is her only consideration.

Long-term investors should not turn into stealth traders. But markets have changed, and strategies have to be changed to adapt to these changes, or at least to not suffer from the changes. Today's markets are extremely volatile, and price patterns have been compressed, accompanied by extremely high volume. Living through periods of pain, with portfolios down 50 percent, is not pleasant or prudent for the long-term investor. Avoiding these situations can best be done by anticipating them.

## Growth Areas to Watch and Buy on Dips

As a long-term investor, you can also look for value as well as growth, no matter what market sector or country or stock in which it appears. You are not chasing the latest fads that traders are piling into; you are searching for the areas that are the most likely to blossom because of good fundamental reasons.

Consider that technology is not the only area to explore. About 70 percent of the Nasdaq-100 stocks are technology; but there are also retailing, consumer goods, and other sectors in the index; the companies in these other sectors can be bought for long-term growth. There is also a time to buy energy stocks, utility stocks, gold stocks, and stocks in other sectors. The best time to buy is when these sectors are cold and no one wants them.

For example, the medical and health-care sectors are promising on a long-term basis, and representation there seems prudent. Health care should be a growth area over the next 10 years. All demographics studies show that the aging of the baby boomers is spurring demand for new and better products and facilities for health care of this huge number of people. One company, Allscripts (MDRX), is an example of the new technology that is changing the way companies in this sector are operating. The company provides prescription management and uses the Internet to facilitate its operations.

Health care and biotechnology are closely allied. When biotech stocks correct, as they did in late March 2000, opportunities to purchase these stocks at bargain prices appear. Human Genome Sciences (HGSI), for instance, is mapping out the human genome, and within that framework, the company is discovering why diseases act a certain way on humans. HGSI is getting the big drug companies to commit to purchasing the findings of HGSI. Stocks such as this can be bought on dips. HGSI ran from 50 to 225 over about a 5-month period, ending in mid-March 2000. The stock pulled back to about 82 in late March.

Viropharma, Inc. (VPHM), is another stock of the type that could be a success over a longer period of time. The company started out looking for ways to cure the common cold. The company has branched out into getting patents on products to treat diseases such as hepatitis C; this disease has not received much attention in the past, but will become more prominent as our citizenry ages. The company has some products in phase III trials with the FDA. VPHM has declined sharply, going from about 111 to 22 in late October 2000.

There are options to look beyond just technology and biotechnology, the strongest growth sectors of the past. But if you just want to buy in Internet stocks, there are many subsectors in this sector to choose from, and many companies within each subsector; for example, in the Internet sector there are Internet Business to Consumer (B2C), Business to Business (B2B), Internet architecture stocks, and other areas. Also there is the related wireless and telecommunications area. Each of these subsectors experience times when they get hot and times when they get cold. And investors in the Internet area must try to not get trapped in a sector just before it gets cold, and to buy when the sector is cold to participate in a move upward.

## Sectors to Consider for Long Term

To purchase for growth over the next decade, long-term investors should look for value, both in the old-economy stocks and in the stocks and sectors of the new economy.

If you want to buy new-economy stocks, one sector to consider is Internet B2C stocks. The potential for B2B companies appears bright. International Data Corporation (IDC) estimates that $15 billion in goods and services was exchanged between business and consumers in 1998. IDC estimates that B2B e-commerce has much more potential than B2C; this market is predicted to grow from $35 billion to over $1.1 trillion by 2003 in goods and services transactions. The companies to consider to participate in this growth are the facilitators of B2B commerce.

Ariba, Inc. (ARBA) is a company that should benefit from B2B growth.

Another company to consider is Commerce One, Inc. (CMRC). Both stocks had good gains in 1999, but pulled back with the sector in 2000.

CMRC deals with the major aerospace companies and is setting up an online exchange for transactions in aerospace and airplane parts. By moving their transactions online, Aerospace companies calculate that they can lower costs, gain other efficiencies, and speed up their delivery cycles. The aerospace industry is one of the "bigger-scale industries" going into B2B. These are industries that deal in bigger size. A similar industry is the auto industry, which is also developing its B2B capacity for online transactions.

B2B commerce seems destined to develop in the bigger-scale industries first, and then filter down into smaller-scale industries, eventually radically changing the ways that business gets done.

The financial industries sector is also turning more to the Internet for its growth and efficiencies.

One company that illustrates the changes in this sector is S-1 Corporation (SONE). The Royal Bank of Canada initially funded SONE. SONE originally was to become an Internet banking portal. SONE has evolved to where it is now, which is building the infrastructure that will allow a standard for the Internet banking sector. It competes with the in-house Internet divisions of major banks. SONE is receiving contracts from major banks because it has been successful in convincing major banks to operate through SONE's standard, rather than going to the expense of creating their own platforms. SONE is also buying up other financial-related industries on the Web. One of the companies that it recently absorbed will allow SONE to be a major player on the Web in offering insurance products. This type of growth could lead SONE to become a financial services conglomerate.

## Swings from Optimism to Pessimism and Back

Among the widest swings in sentiment, from optimism to pessimism to optimism again, will be in Nasdaq stocks in the technology and biotechnology group. This is due to the fact that the earnings stream of companies is what investors ultimately follow. Many companies in these groups have forecasted earnings but at the present have very little or no earnings. This situation heightens the anxiety of holding the stocks and increases the greed to move one to buy the stocks.

As a long-term investor, a way to leverage the sentiment between optimism and pessimism that regularly occurs in the market, particularly in this type of stock, is to take advantage of people fleeing these stocks, and to buy these stocks on dips. The important ingredient here is the investor's own temperament: How hard is it to live with the greed and fear that inevitably results from investing in the market? Also, how much money can one realistically afford to lose while waiting for a rebound?

Most people, maybe almost all, get scared when markets are crashing. No bottom seems in sight, and the fear of losing more takes over. Concurrently, most people, when the markets are soaring, feel as if they are missing out, and jump in, wanting to participate in the good times. Usually, this is at or near the top.

Easier to say than to do, but the long-term investor must turn these events and responses around: When the markets or chosen sectors are crashing, the investor jumps in with some or most or all of her risk capital; and when the markets or sectors are going through the roof, the investor takes a profit with all or a portion of her capital.

The drops in big companies, particularly in the growth sectors, throughout 2000, are not just anomalies; drops of 50 percent or more in growth stocks have become commonplace.

The long-term investor has to develop a strategy that will enable him to benefit from this pattern or at least not be a casualty. It is painful and costly to buy these volatile stocks at the top and sell them near the bottom. Doing this, the long-term investor will not survive long enough to enjoy the good market times.

Do not underestimate how hard it is to be a long-term investor: Holding stocks through 50 percent declines can test anybody, and few can stay in there. And even if one can stay in there, it may prove not to be the right thing to do; the stock may go down more.

Being able to lighten up and waiting for opportunity is one of the soundest ways to stay in for the long term. Diversifying helps also. An investor should buy several stocks for sector representation or purchase exchange shares. There are many sectors in which baskets of stocks are put together, giving the investor sector representation.

## How Many Stocks in a Portfolio?

Probably the best answer to how many stocks one should have in a portfolio is as many as the investor can comfortably keep up with. I say *comfortably* because it is difficult and time-consuming to keep current with the daily events of companies. With communication being as swift and available as it is today, it is imperative that you be among the first to know of a company's good or bad fortunes; but this is difficult because a world of investors are out there who will know as soon as you do.

About five issues in a portfolio is as small a universe that seems prudent, allowing you representation in sectors without being too concentrated in one or two issues. About 10 issues are as many companies as one can handle, and this is *not* to say comfortably: 10 issues is a great number of companies to keep up with.

Definitely consider using exchange shares for representation in sectors and industries. Exchange shares have been modeled by savvy investment houses such as Barclays Global Investors and Merrill Lynch. These firms have taken the important companies, those that form the guts of the industries or sectors, and put them in packages so that a buyer will have representation in that industry or sector. Buying an exchange share literally takes the guesswork out of choosing which companies will give the most representation; the exchange share sponsors have already done that work for you.

In 1999, there were about 35 exchange share products; in 2000, they now number about 100, offering a wide choice of sector representation to investors. Some of the new products, such as Merrill Lynch's Internet B2B HOLDRs and Internet Architect HOLDRs, contain companies many investors are not familiar with; these companies have just recently come to the fore as their industries have grown.

Exchange shares do not replace individual stocks; exchange shares are used as an adjunct to individual stock selection. Suppose Internet stocks have had an 80 percent correction, and let's say that you want representation in the group, but don't know which stock to pick. You also realize that if you start researching companies, it could take a lot of your time. So you could purchase YHOO and AMZN, names that are familiar, and the Internet HOLDRs Trust (HHH). You would be overweighting in YHOO and AMZN in this case and would have a broad-based representation in the Internet group.

# CHAPTER 9

# STRATEGIES FOR THE SHORT-TERM INVESTOR

## LEVEL II TRADING

There has always been Level I. In the "old days," that is, before the rise of online trading, and with its higher level of sophistication among traders, all market participants would go to Level I. Level I shows the highest bid and lowest asked among all of the traders in a stock. Level II, which was only in the past used by institutions, professional traders, and market makers, is now widely watched by a larger universe of players: People sitting at home day trading, hedge funds, scalpers, and others watching the moment to moment market gyrations tune in to Level II.

All the bids and all the offerings for stocks are shown on the Level II screen. The inside market is the quote between the dealers, or market makers, that is the highest bid and the lowest offer. On any stock there might be as many as 20 market makers on each side of the bid and offer. For instance, on Microsoft (MSFT) there might be the best market of 100 bid,

100½ offered; the 100 bid is Merrill Lynch, the 100½ is Herzog. Then in columns throughout the screen are the other bid/offers; a trader can glance at the screen and see at what price each market maker is willing to buy or sell. Also, size is shown along with the bid/offers. Size is the amount of shares a market maker will trade—such as on a 100 to 100½, 10 by 30, the market maker will buy 10,000 shares at 100, and will sell 30,000 shares at 100½.

When a market maker changes his bid or offer, it is shown on Level II instantaneously. Also when the top bid or offer changes, the firm making the top bid and lowest offer moves up to the top of the screen.

## Level II and Level III

Level II is offered as part of a package of additional services by many on-line brokerage firms. This package is offered to clients who trade more often, or have a certain amount of assets in their account, or for other reasons. Also, there are services that traders can pay a fee to and receive Level II.

Market makers use Level III for trading. Market makers employ different services to input their quotes, such as Nasdaq Work Station. Level III allows the market maker to input his bid/offer "market," and the market maker adjusts his market throughout the trading day. For example, the best market on MSFT is 100 bid, offered at 100½; a market maker may be in "the box" (shown on the computer screen) at 99½ bid, offered at 100¾; the market maker would be shown on the screen, but he would be "out of the way," and not shown as the best market.

If the market maker decides to become the best market, he would go on to Level III and adjust his quote to 100⅛ bid, 100⅜ offered. This best quote would also be reflected on Level I, where people can see the market maker's quote.

A retail (individual) Nasdaq customer has the ability to improve the quote by putting in an order to buy or sell stock through an NASD member firm or through an ECN. Under the rules, the Nasdaq market maker or ECN has to show the customer's limit order, including size. This results in making the customer directly involved in the markets reflecting all bids and offers. The customer may end up being the best bid and offer.

### The Importance of Indications in Trading

One of the importances of Level II is for an individual trader to see the indications, which are the bids and offers of the market makers, and to observe the directions and patterns of these indications.

For example, if MSFT is quoted at 100 by 100¼, and there are five market makers on the bid side, and there is more size shown on the bid side than the offer side, obviously the stock is stronger on the bid side. Conversely, if the offering side shows a number of offerings, all with large size, the offering side is weak because there is a lot of stock for sale. The buyer may then opt to wait for lower prices before buying. Indications are good signals to watch for in determining stock price direction.

## *Trading Using Level II*

A trader, either institutional representing billions of dollars or a part-time trader trading $10,000 of her own money, can sit in front of her computer, scan the price activity of different stocks, and look for trends, something to catch her eye. Maybe MSFT is taking off on the upside or CSCO is getting bombed. Whatever.

She sees something: WCOM is taking off and there is no news to explain the activity. She goes into the stock's "chat room." Yahoo, AOL, and almost all the other portals have chat rooms in which market players discuss what they are hearing. These chat rooms are not to be underestimated—there is a plethora of discussion, much of it off the mark. But it is nothing short of amazing how accurate some of the information is. Then she checks the charts of WCOM—again, it is remarkable how available all this information is on today's computers. Much of this information would have been costly just a couple of years ago—to see if the stock should be sold, shorted, or if there is nothing to be done.

Then the trader will go back to Level II; she will watch the stock to see if there is volume coming in on the upside. She will see who the players are, if Merrill or Goldman or the other giants are buying, or just some smaller firms. If the majors are buying, that is promising, because these firms can move markets with their big size. She sees that Merrill, who opened at high bid, stays at high bid all morning, not dropping its bid; this could mean that Merrill is representing a buyer of serious size. Then the stock starts trading off of its offering price; then Merrill goes up an ⅛ on its bid; then Merrill goes up another 1/16 on its bid, perhaps indicating that Merrill has more to buy.

Slowly the trader forms her opinion: Merrill has more stock to buy; something's going on; WCOM is noted for its deal making, maybe it is about to buy another company or announce a contract. She notes that the other telecommunication companies are starting to move; maybe it's a sector move, but who cares; she doesn't care why WCOM's moving, she just wants to participate. She buys.

Also it is important for a trader to watch every "print" or trade. Perhaps Merrill is buying stock all day in small pieces, then Merrill buys a block on Merrill's offer side; and Merrill stays on the offer or increases its offer. This could indicate that Merrill's buyer is not finished and has more to buy, or the buyer has a higher buy price in mind. Or perhaps another giant, such as Morgan Stanley or Goldman Sachs goes up on its offering, matching Merrill's offer or higher than Merrill's offer. This could indicate that something is afoot, and the giants are onto it.

None of this trading review is foolproof, and is not meant to make trading look easy. Trading is not easy, and most traders spend years or decades

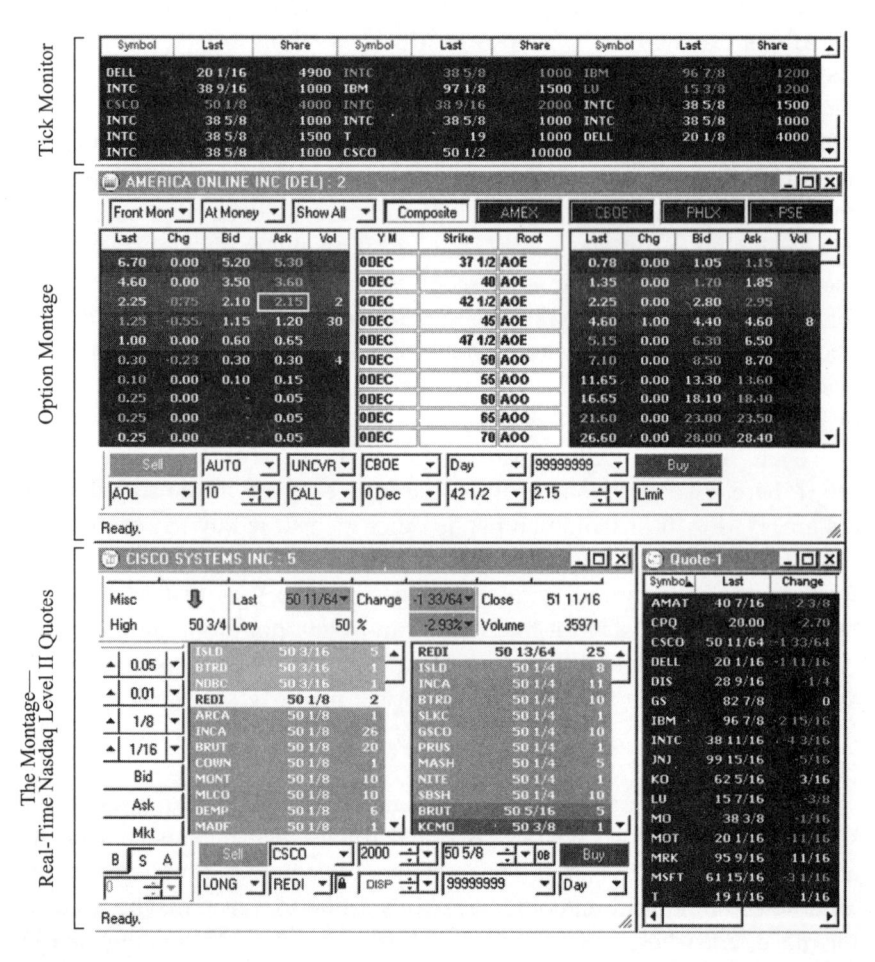

**Figure 9-1** Level II Quote Source

getting good at this task. But the tape doesn't lie: buying with the trend has worked for years in this bull market; buying with the tape on the upside, or shorting on the downside, is one of a trader's main strategies.

There are many products offered to retail and institutional market participants for their use in accessing Level II. Figure 9-1 shows some of the features offered on a product from the REDI Products Division of Spear, Leeds & Kellogg.

## USING CHARTS

Trading or investing only on fundamentals or sector preference without glancing at a chart is passing up an opportunity to get a snapshot that may change your mind about buying or selling. The chart may not change your decision, but it is a tool that should be understood and used.

There are no hard and fast rules regarding the use of a chart, although there are plenty of schools of thought on the subject. But the conclusions of some chartists may surprise you. For instance, one of the oldest market axioms is to buy low and sell high. Many chartists would tell you this is exactly the wrong action to take, especially in a bull market. Much money made over the last several years has been made buying stocks on breakouts, and selling the stocks at even higher levels. And, as this book has covered, some new-economy stocks, such as the Internet and biotechnology, have reported improvements in growth and earnings or exciting new or potential products. These events have spurred high-priced stocks even higher. Waiting for stocks, especially those that are growing their earnings, to come down to a desired buying price is often difficult. And waiting for the environment to change is often a difficult strategy in which to prosper also.

Many traders examine the charts of a market leader. These traders are not afraid to buy after breakouts, when stocks reach new highs. They follow the strategy of buying stocks at high levels and are ready to sell out if the stocks start to look toppy. It could take awhile for new traders to feel comfortable to trade in this way.

### Trading Relative Strength with Charts

Charts can be used as a simple way to reinforce or question your decision regarding investing in a stock or sector or style of investing. Suppose you believe in the Internet sector and decide to buy Yahoo for representation. A quick glance at the chart of YHOO will tell you if the stock is keeping up with the sector, outperforming the sector, or underperforming. If an Internet sector chart shows the group strengthening and YHOO slumping, you might rethink the decision to have this stock as your choice for the group. Perhaps YHOO is a laggard and will catch up; but if you are "bottom fishing" for laggards in the group, that is a whole other market strategy. You should know that you are bottom fishing, not momentum trading. If the other Internet stocks are slumping or an Internet group chart shows a downward spiral, and YHOO is going up, you may want to reconsider buying the group now: It is hard for a single stock to buck its group trend for long. Or perhaps YHOO is even a better buy because it is bucking its sector trend. Another chart you might look at is the chart of the exchange shares, such as the Internet HOLDRs (HHH), to measure the group's performance.

A quick glance at a chart can tell you much; you might want to buy YHOO, thinking it will continue bucking the trend, but at least, after looking at a chart, you have another piece of information to help in your investment decision.

If you have the right stock and the right industry, most of the time you will make money. Studies have shown that perhaps 90 percent of investment success comes from being in the right sector. It is difficult to make money buying Internet stocks when the group is getting pounded: It is far easier to short the group in that atmosphere.

Comparisons using charts can be used in many ways. Suppose you don't like Internet stocks, but think the rest of the market will soar. And charts bear out that this is presently true: Internet charts show those stocks headed for the floor; charts on financial services and consumer stocks are headed up. Then buy the financial services stocks of your choice and avoid or short Internet stocks.

Or use exchange shares. Merrill Lynch has produced Internet HOLDRs such as HHH, which contains many of the retail Internet names the public is familiar with, such as YHOO and Amazon.com (AMZN), the Internet Architecture HOLDRs (IAH), the Internet Infrastructure HOLDRs (IIH), and the B2B Internet HOLDRs (BBH). Purchasing an exchange share relieves you of the research to find the right issues in these groups to buy or short. Also you are not at risk by owning only one name; if one company goes counter to the group, it won't fully distort the performance of the group.

Exchange shares could be used with group trading or investing also. Sometimes, for instance, the MidCap SPDR (MDY) will move in the opposite direction of the Dow Jones (DIA) or the SPDR (SPY). Both the SPY and MDY contain many Nasdaq stocks, so participation in Nasdaq is not missed by buying into the exchange shares. If the charts show MDY taking off and SPY and/or DIA staying flat or declining, this is an excellent show of relative strength. You could buy MDY; to get more aggressive, short SPY and/or DIA.

## HEDGING STRATEGIES USING OPTIONS

Nasdaq stocks, because of the sorts of companies listed there, are very volatile. As a result of this volatility, engaging in hedging techniques with Nasdaq stocks, especially stocks in the new-economy growth area, are among the most expensive to do because of the high cost of premiums. So a key to hedging in the growth Nasdaq stock sector is to find ways to reduce the cost of hedging.

If the cost of premiums were not so high, you could purchase a put. Let's say that you bought Qualcomm, Inc. (QCOM), at 150, and that is where the stock is selling right now; you like the stock long term, but are afraid that over the next 6 months or so QCOM could get hit. You don't care if it goes down a few points, but don't want to sustain a major loss. The purchase of a put allows you to put, or sell, the stock to the put seller for a price, called the strike price. In this example, let's say that the strike price is 130; also there is an expiration date on the put; in this example the expiration date is 9 months away. For this right to put the stock to the seller, you must pay a premium; in this example, you pay 10 points. Also, because you can put QCOM to the seller at 130, and the stock is now 150, you are *out* of the money; you are out of the money by 20 points. If you could put QCOM to the seller at 160, for example, the put would be *in* the money by 10 points. Because out-of-the-money puts have no intrinsic value, the premium sometimes trades at a more reasonable premium; in-the-money puts, because they have intrinsic value as well as speculative value, often have very high premiums.

Buying an out-of-the-money put when you hold the stock, if the put sells at a reasonable premium, is a way to protect you against a major decline. But in Nasdaq stocks, which have gone up, the premiums have also increased. Buying puts have been a lousy proposition for buyers for a while because stocks have gone up, rendering puts worthless. When Nasdaq growth stocks have gone up, not making it profitable for put buyers to exercise puts, the put buyers have had losing trades. For this reason, out-of-the-money puts are harder to find and have high premiums.

### Using a Bear Spread

A way of reducing the cost of buying a put against a long position, a trader or investor could consider entering into a transaction known as a put bear spread. In this transaction, not only will you buy an option on a stock, but also at the same time, you will sell an option. The option you sell will be at a lower strike price than the option you purchase. So instead of buying a put outright, which would entail a high premium cost, you will sell a put also; the premium that you receive from the sale of your put will reduce the cost of the put you purchase. The amount of funds you will actually render is the difference between the amount you pay for the put you buy and the amount for the put that you sell (at the lower strike price).

For instance, if you are holding QCOM, say that you buy a put on QCOM and pay a premium of 30; also you sell a put on QCOM at a premium of 20 (remember, because it is a lower strike price, the option costs less); the amount that you pay is 10 points. If the strike price differential is 50 points, then you will have a 50-point profit potential with a 10-point cost, for a 40-point net difference. This is a 4 to 1 potential in the trade.

## USING EXCHANGE SHARES FOR NASDAQ REPRESENTATION

Hedging techniques can be used on individual stocks or surrogates for the technology and Nasdaq growth groups. Somewhat of a surrogate security for the Nasdaq stocks is the S&P 500 Index. The S&P 500 has about 30 percent of its index in technology stocks; technology stocks sometimes trade closely to Nasdaq stocks. The exchange share representing the S&P 500 is SPY. Check App. D to see a listing of Nasdaq stocks in the S&P index.

A closer surrogate to the Nasdaq growth stocks is the Nasdaq-100 exchange shares, which trade on the Amex under QQQ. Purchasing this exchange share gives investors and traders representation in a basket of Nasdaq growth issues, without the one risk of holding only one stock.

For example, let's say that you own 100 shares of QQQ, and that QQQ is selling at 117; you buy a 100 put and sell a 50 put simultaneously for a debit of 10 points, meaning you are out of pocket 10 points. You can make money the following way. If the QQQ goes down to 50, that means that the long 100 put is worth 50 points. It has to be worth 50 points; you could put QQQ to the seller at 100, keeping the 50-point difference between the 100 price at which you can put QQQ to the seller and the present price of 50. At the same time, the 50 put that you sold is worthless; the buyer of the put can sell it in the open market at 50, so he would not put it to you at 50. So the difference between the two positions is 50 points, less the 10-point spread between the 2 positions, which nets 40 points. Forty points is

CHAPTER 9  STRATEGIES FOR THE SHORT-TERM INVESTOR    133

the maximum you can make in this position, because, remember, you sold a put as well. If QQQ goes to 40, you will make 60 points by putting QQQ to the seller at 100; but the buyer of your put will put QQQ to you at 50, costing you 10 points, and then you must deduct your 10-point cost. Because you paid 10 to create the position, your breakeven point is 100 minus 10, which is 90. So you start making money on this position when QQQ is 90 or lower.

This strategy is a worst-case bear market spread. It is insurance at the lowest cost. If the market continues up, the insurance is not needed. If QQQ goes to 200, you still have the stock. The put you bought will expire, and the put that you are short and would have to honor would also expire, because the put buyer can sell QQQ in the open market at 200 instead of putting it to you at 50. The cost to you for this insurance was 10 points, a cheaper cost than just buying a put.

## HEDGING STOCKS THAT GAP UP AND DOWN

Another technique can be used for stocks that move up and down in gaps, such as biotech stocks. Consider the chart in Fig. 9-2 on Protein Design Labs (PDLI), a Nasdaq biotech stock.

The question is: What can one do to protect oneself against the sharp market down swings such as this stock experienced? A person could put in

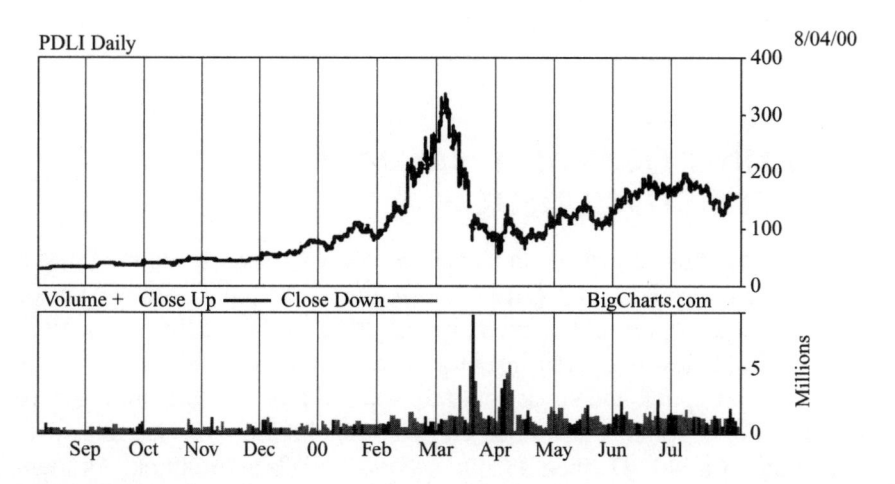

**Figure 9-2** Protein Design Labs stock savings. (*Courtesy of Zacks Investment Research.*)

stop-loss orders. This order is used to prevent further losses in a stock. A stop-loss order is an order that becomes a market order once the stop price is reached; the stop price is set under the current market price. For instance, if MSFT is selling at 110, and a stockholder wants to risk only five points, the stockholder will tell her broker to sell MSFT at 105 stop. If MSFT touches 105, it becomes a market order to sell.

The problem with using a stop order with PDLI, or a stock as volatile, is that the holder may get stopped out only to see the stock rebound sharply.

> *Protecting yourself against a catastrophe, using options, makes sense, especially when dealing with highly volatile stocks. But if you don't thoroughly understand the use of options, consult with a specialist in the field.*

Another way to protect against a plunge in a stock is to buy some deep out-of-the-money puts, perhaps 50 or so points out of the money. These puts would act as disaster insurance, helping only if there is a catastrophe in the stock—which can happen with a volatile stock. As an example, a 50-point out-of-the-money put, maturing in a few months, could cost about 15 points or so; a 9-month or so put could cost about 30 to 40 points. The problem is that because of the short maturity, a put buyer would have to turn around and buy another put at the put expiration date. This would get expensive over a period of time.

But a glance at the chart shows that this expensive insurance may be worth it: PDLI tumbled a couple of hundred points, which would have paid for many short-term, deep out-of-the-money puts.

## SHORTING QQQ AS A NASDAQ GROWTH STOCK HEDGE

QQQ can be shorted just like a stock. In fact, QQQ can be shorted better than a stock because QQQ can be shorted on a downtick. Stocks can be shorted only on upticks. An uptick, or plus-tick, is a trade that takes place higher than the last trade. For instance, a stock sells at 40, 40, then 41. The 41 trade is an uptick and stock could be shorted there. Also there is a zero uptick trade, at which trade stock can also be shorted. For example, with stock trading at 40, 41, then 41, the second 41 is a zero uptick. As mentioned, SEC rules require that stock can be sold short only on an uptick. QQQ, along with other exchange shares, is exempt from this rule.

When selling short, you must get stock protection so that stock will be available for you to purchase when you want to cover the position. Your broker can arrange for this. In the case of QQQ, because the exchange shares trade so actively, there is virtually no problem in reserving shares for buying back.

An investor or trader can hedge a portfolio of Nasdaq stocks by shorting QQQ. If the Nasdaq stocks stay strong, then QQQ will go up, cutting down some on the profits of the stocks that the trader holds in his portfolio. But if the Nasdaq market gets hit, as it sometimes does, QQQ will go down, hedging against the losses in the trader's portfolio.

How much a market participant wishes to hedge is up to his risk profile. He may feel the market is low and will trade higher; in that case perhaps a 25 percent short position is comfortable. If the market climbs and his portfolio goes up 25 percent, perhaps he will want to increase his short position to 50 percent. If the market continues up and he believes it is due for a correction, then he may want to increase his short position to 75 percent or 80 percent of his long portfolio.

Shorting is risky, and you should check with your investment professional when undertaking this strategy, especially if you are relatively new to the market. Shorting QQQ is preferable to shorting individual issues because the risk of shorting individual stocks is higher than shorting a portfolio of stocks, which offers diversification.

If, instead of shorting QQQ you shorted a handful of Nasdaq Internet stocks, you may not have mitigated your portfolio risk. Suppose one of the Internet stocks you shorted gets "taken out," which means taken over by another company. You are short the stock at 30 and a bid comes from another company at 60. Trading is fierce and by the time your order to cover gets executed, you have lost 20 points. In this scenario, you lose money on your short side, not the result that you entered into the position to achieve.

## USING OPTIONS FOR INCOME

Another strategy you may employ using Nasdaq stocks is to write calls against long positions. When you write, or sell, calls and you are long the stock, you are in a covered position. This position is no higher in risk than owning the stock. If you are long a Nasdaq stock and feel comfortable with the position, you can sell options and receive income.

Your risks in this position are: the price of the stock declines more than the premium you receive for writing the call; the stock is called from you, and after that proceeds to appreciate manyfold. Remember, your appreciation is limited to the strike price at which you write the call. Look at the example in Fig. 9-3.

| |
|---|
| Buy 100 shares MICROSOFT (MSFT) @ 103. |
| Sell one MSFT call July 110 @ 7½. |

**Figure 9-3** Covered Call

In the example in Fig. 9-3 you received a premium of $750 for writing a call on MSFT. For income tax purposes, usually premium income is regarded as normal income. Check with your tax consultant for your own tax consequences of using these strategies. If MSFT goes down, you will have a loss on MSFT; you would have had a loss anyway if you had been long the stock. But now you have an extra $750 you would not have had if you had not written the option. If MSFT goes up, the stock will be called from you at 110, limiting your gain to 7 points, or $700. But you also have the $750 premium.

Because many Nasdaq stocks are volatile, there are sometimes large premiums offered to those who are willing to sell calls. But the risks are high in holding these stocks. Before engaging in any transaction such as call writing, check with your investment adviser. You should understand what exactly you are getting into and the risks involved.

## SELLING CALLS NAKED

As scary as selling calls naked sounds, that is how scary the transaction can be, unless you know what you are doing and understand the risks involved. With that knowledge, the transaction can make some sense.

Suppose you are convinced that the Nasdaq Internet or technology stocks will go lower, there is no question in your mind, and you are willing to take the risk that you may be wrong. A strategy that fits this profile is to sell calls naked, or uncovered. Instead of buying MSFT and selling a call against it, for example, you would merely sell the call. Brokers require that you put up margin funds. Commonly, you are required to put up enough funds to cover the purchase of MSFT if, in fact, MSFT is called from you.

If MSFT is not called from you, the premium received is usually regarded as income. If you sell an MSFT 110 call, and MSFT is selling at 105 at the call expiration date, you merely keep the premium income. If MSFT is selling at 115, you will have to buy the stock at 115 and it will be called from you at 110, netting you a 5-point loss. But you have the premium you received for selling the call. This position is risky and is essen-

CHAPTER 9  STRATEGIES FOR THE SHORT-TERM INVESTOR                    137

tially the same position as being short the stock. Your potential loss in this position is unlimited.

## SELLING COVERED CALLS AND USING MARGIN

Say MSFT is selling at 110. When you buy 100 shares of MSFT and sell one call against the position, at most brokerage houses you could put up margin funds instead of the entire purchase price. At the present time the initial margin is 50 percent.

So in your calculations, you can cut the funds employed in half. In the above example, the funds put up would be $5500, half the $11,000 cost of buying MSFT. Commissions and taxes are disregarded in these examples. The risk is increased because you borrowed the funds to initiate the position, but the potential income is enhanced. Because you put up half the funds, your income is generally doubled. If the return on invested cash would be 12 percent with a fully funded purchase of the stock to cover a written call, this 12 percent would become roughly 24 percent.

Buying stock on margin and selling calls against the margined stock is risky; the stock could go down, necessitating your putting up additional maintenance funds. Brokerage firms, complying with federal regulations, require one to maintain certain equity in an account. So if your stock goes down, you will get a maintenance, or house, call requesting you to put up more funds. If you do not meet the call, the brokerage firm, per the margin agreement you signed when you opened a margin account, will sell enough stock to satisfy the call.

But understanding this risk, and having the financial profile to accept the risk, might lead you to use this strategy, which can offer a very decent return.

---

Sold short 100 QCOM @ 150
Buy 9-month call, QCOM, 170 strike, 10-point cost

QCOM @ 190 with option
Call stock at 170, $2000 loss, premium paid, $1000 = $3000 loss

QCOM @ 190 (no option)
Sold short @ 150, over 190 = $4000 loss

---

**Figure 9-4**  Selling Short with a Call

## Reducing the Risk of a Short Stock Position

To reduce the risk of selling a stock short, you could buy a call. The strike price would vary, depending on how much risk you want to take, the price of the call, and the volatility of the stock. Look at the example in Fig. 9-4.

The example shows that you sold short 100 shares of QCOM at 150. At the same time you purchased a 9-month call of QCOM at a price of 10, 170 strike price. If QCOM goes down, that is fine, you are in a profit position; you will lose only the premium that you paid for the call, which will expire worthless. If QCOM goes up to 190, you will lose the amount you paid for the premium, and the difference between the short and the strike price is $3000. With the called stock you can cover the short.

This loss of $3000 is less than the $4000 you would have suffered without purchasing a call. And also QCOM can go much higher, giving you an unlimited loss if you did not hold the call. No matter how high QCOM goes, for the life of the call option you purchased, you can purchase the stock at 170 and cover the stock you sold short.

CHAPTER 10

# PUTTING IT ALL TOGETHER: NASDAQ AND THE OVERALL PORTFOLIO

## HOW MUCH TO PUT INTO NASDAQ STOCKS

To calculate how much of your portfolio to put into Nasdaq stocks you have to look at your risk profile and investment objectives: How much are you willing to risk to receive what you want out of your investments?

Nasdaq stocks run the gamut of degrees of risk and reward, because Nasdaq stocks cover virtually all industrial sectors. Also, there are smaller, growth companies on Nasdaq. For these companies you should commit only your more aggressive capital. The Nasdaq market appears to house many of the stocks of the big hit potential, stocks that can turn into 3 to 5 baggers. Working with an investment professional you should assign your goals, knowing, of course, that the loftier the goals, the greater the risk.

Normally, small companies grow faster than big companies in terms of earnings and sales. This usually causes a premium in the price of smaller companies. Investors will generally pay more, in terms of P/E, or price to sales, or multiple of sales, or other measurements, for a company that has much of its growth ahead of it.

However, some of today's valuations are so high that in many cases it is hard to compare them to any valuations in the past, especially in the hotter sectors such as biotechnology, technology, telecommunications, and pharmaceuticals. Internet stocks are a subsector of technology, and, although the group has sharply corrected, valuationwise it could still be placed with biotechnology.

The different sectors should be in your portfolio with weightings that relate to your ability to take risk, and according to your investment objectives. There is no "cookie-cutter" formula; every person has a different shading of risk profile and objectives. Whether 10 percent or 90 percent of a portfolio should be exposed to the higher risk sectors is a serious question that might take some time to answer. Working with an investment adviser is always advisable in ascertaining one's financial universe.

## Lower-Valued Nasdaq Sectors

With attention focused on the stronger sectors of the Nasdaq market, some of the other sectors are going unnoticed. There are companies selling with P/E multiples of 5 to 8 times, with good fundamentals, yet those stocks have very little volume or trader interest.

So in this split-valuation Nasdaq market, where some new-economy stocks still boast high valuations and the rest of the market receives comparatively little attention, the quieter sectors, such as utilities, banks, and energy could be combed looking for value. Also, from time to time the small-cap companies go relatively unnoticed. At those times some small-cap companies offer real value; usually the tip-off that small-cap stocks are undergoing a loss of investor sentiment and should be looked at is when volume in the sector has slowed substantially.

## Remember Taxes

In considering whether to buy, sell, short, or hold, fundamentals of a company and the stock's future price direction should be the overlying investment consideration. But tax consequences should also be weighed.

If you hold a stock longer than a year (it could be a year and a day), the profit becomes long term. Held less than this period, a gain in a stock is short term. There is roughly a 100 percent difference in the taxation treatment, which is a large difference. Including federal and state taxes, long-term profits are generally taxed at 20 percent; short-term profits, in the higher earnings brackets, go up to about 39.6 percent.

Every tax situation is different. Check with your tax professional about your specific circumstances.

## Mutual Funds and Taxes

A mutual fund, in reporting its performance, usually does not include the tax consequences to its holders. This could be of major importance to you.

If a fund you purchased returned a sparkling 50 percent return, and 85 percent of that profit is short term, and you are in a higher tax bracket, you would realize about 60 percent of that gain, or about 30 percent after you pay your taxes. A 30 percent return is nothing to denigrate, but it is not the 50 percent you thought you were getting. Also, to achieve that high a return, the fund took some risks. And on a risk-adjusted basis, perhaps a 30 percent return after taxes for a fund that traded volatile stocks is not as good as it first appeared.

The funds that have made the big gains over this bull market have been mostly the new-economy stock funds. A glance over the statistics of these types of funds shows high turnover ratios, indicating that the funds do not hold the stocks very long. This suggests a large amount of short-term profits that will have to be paid by investors in growth funds.

## Stealth Short-Term Gains Taxes

Because many growth funds have a higher turnover rate, the fund's gains are usually more short term than long term. This situation could set up tax consequences for the new buyers of the fund. The buyers would be buying into a tax liability when they purchase the fund and may not even know it.

To illustrate, suppose that a growth fund has had many investors buying into the fund; and let's also suppose that the stock which the fund holds has appreciated. This will probably make the cost basis of the shares in the fund selling below the net asset value (NAV) of the fund. For example, the NAV, which is usually the market price of the fund, plus any markups, is $10; in this example this is also the market price of the fund. The cost basis of the stocks held by the fund, let's say, averages $5. This means that there are short- and/or long-term gains, and concomitant tax liability, to any new buyers.

Let's say people want out of the fund and start to sell. The fund will probably have to sell off some of its low-priced stock to meet redemptions. And because the fund is selling off low-priced shares, the holders of the fund are incurring a short-term tax liability. The fund does not pay this liability; it passes it on to holders of the fund. At the end of its fiscal year, the fund will send a check to its holders and will inform them of their tax liability. Holders of the fund would be charged with the short- and/or long-term capital gains distribution.

To clarify, let's suppose that a new fund is created and priced at $50 a share. Your husband purchases the fund at $50. The fund goes up and your husband suggests that you buy the fund, and you do, paying $75.

The market then goes down, and many holders unload the fund. The fund sells off some low-priced stock it is holding, to cover redemptions. When the fund sells these shares, it incurs a short-term gain of, say, $15 a share. Your husband sells the fund, taking a profit. You hold the fund, and the fund sinks to $30 a share.

The fiscal year appears, and the fund manager distributes the gain of $15 a share. You receive a check for $15, and a notice that the gain is short term and that you must report it to the IRS. So you now have a $45 unrealized loss and a $15 short-term gain. The gain comes with a tax liability; the unrealized loss has no tax benefit.

This example is not a happy after-tax result. And this event is not that rare. The popularity of mutual funds, like stocks, goes in cycles. When the sector that a fund is invested in, such as biotechnology or technology, goes out of favor, redemptions occur. Often this is usually at the worst possible time because the fund, which is now out of favor, has to sell its stock, which is also out of favor.

Be cautious before chasing an in-favor fund. Not only can it fall out of favor, but also the tax consequences can be onerous and also a surprise.

### Exchange Traded Funds (ETFs)

Many ETFs do not have this tax liability problem because the shares, due to their creation and redemption process, redeem in kind. Essentially this means that the securities of the trust take their cost basis with them when they are redeemed out of the fund. So volatile ETFs such as Internet HOLDRs, which contain Nasdaq stocks such as YHOO and AMZN, will not surprise the buyer with a capital-gain obligation.

## Trading Nasdaq Stocks with Other Markets

Generally, Nasdaq stocks are for that portion of your portfolio that seeks newer, more growth-oriented issues. How much of your portfolio you dedicate to this type of growth is dependent upon how much risk you can stand. Whether zero or 50 percent or 80 percent or 100 percent of your funds belong in Nasdaq stocks is up to your risk profile and investment objectives.

Nasdaq contains stocks of companies that are small, some in the $50 million or less range in terms of revenues; some of these companies can grow tenfold over the next 5 or 10 years to become $500 million revenue companies.

If you want growth but also want to put 10 to 20 percent of your funds into slower, larger capitalized companies, certainly your search should include stocks on Nasdaq as well as the NYSE and Amex. But, however you apportion your funds, doing your research in order to be comfortable that you are choosing companies which match your investment objectives makes sense.

No matter which markets you are trading, certain things should be looked for in the companies in which you are considering investing.

1. *Sales.* In Nasdaq stocks the sales of some companies are more dramatically increasing. Many Nasdaq stocks are young and small, and in that case it is not unusual to see faster-growing sales.

2. *Balance Sheet and Profit and Loss (P&L) Statement Items.* Following are some items that one should look at before investing.

    *Profit Margins.* This is the difference between the amount a company receives for its goods and services and the amount it costs to produce them. There is a pretax profit and an after-tax profit usually reported by companies. This refers to corporate federal taxes. Profit margins are important items, especially in the new-economy companies; these companies are expected to maintain high margins.

    *Return on Equity.* This item is calculated by dividing common stock equity into net income, after the payment of preferred stock dividends but before common stock dividends. This figure tells stockholders how effectively their money is being used. The amount is expressed as a percentage. Stockholders can compare the percentages against different periods and also consider the trend of the return.

    *Debt.* The amount that a company owes its creditors. Debt can be in the form of bonds, notes, mortgages, and other instruments. The debt may be secured by corporate property or unsecured; if unsecured, it is backed by the promise of the company to pay. Too much debt can strangle a company; too little debt can hinder its opportunity to grow. Debt should be considered in proportion to the other balance sheet items.

*Cashflow.* This item includes a company's net income with non-cash charges, such as depreciation, added back. Another way to look at this item is to consider it as cash earnings. Annual reports usually include a statement of cashflow, which analyzes all items that affect the cash of a company. Negative cashflow occurs when more cash goes out than comes in; positive cashflow is the opposite. Companies with weak financial conditions have to watch their cashflow to make sure they can meet current obligations.

*Company Commitment to Its Pension Plans.* When stock markets go down, a company's pension funds, if the funds are invested in the markets, can experience a value decline. Pension funds traditionally have been invested in stocks of more mature companies. These stocks have not performed well over the last 12 months or so. Companies have to fund their pension funds every year according to actuarial tables; the tables ensure that the companies can meet their obligations to retiring employees. The companies have to earn pretax profit so that they can keep their pension funds fully funded. If a company loses 10 percent in a year in its pension fund investments, for example, it has to make these funds up by funding from pretax profits.

Pension funds funding details can be found in the company's balance sheet. The details are usually in the footnotes, so it often takes some work to dig them out. The balance sheet as well as the income statement and other financial information can be found in the 10-K and 10-Q.

3. *Earnings.* Earnings of some of the companies listed on the Nasdaq are dramatically increasing because these companies are young and small. Earnings usually slow as companies increase in size.

## 10-Ks and 10-Qs

The result of operations and a general picture of a company's activities are filed with the SEC 4 times a year.

The yearly report is called a 10-K. This report is part of the public record and is available to all investors. The quarterly reports are referred to as 10-Qs. Investors can download most 10-Ks and 10-Qs online.

> Much can be garnered by perusing a 10-K or 10-Q. As much as anything, an investor or trader can get a feel for a company; perhaps a piece of information will click and spur a market participant to buy or sell or short.

Additionally, virtually all companies report quarterly and annually to their shareholders. Copies can be received by request from the reporting companies. Included in the report are the balance sheet and income statement details, as well as the company developments and outlook.

## Debt and Burn Rate

An item to pursue when looking at a company's balance sheet, particularly smaller companies, is its debt.

In the old-economy stocks, a company's debt may not be that big an issue. As long as a company is making enough money to repay its debt in a timely manner, debt should not be a threat.

In new-economy companies, debt takes on heightened importance. Many of the newer companies, especially in the faster-growing fields such as biotechnology and Internet, have no sales and, consequently, no earnings.

This could become a problem. The rate at which a company "burns up" cash versus the rate at which a company receives cash is referred to its burn rate. If a company, because of debt repayment and other operating expenses, has a burn rate of $300,000 a month, for example, and the company has $3.6 million cash on hand, the company will run out of money in 12 months. If the company cannot raise more cash, it will go under.

Exacerbating the problem is that, when a company gets low in its cash position, the company's options for raising new cash are often limited. The stock of a company low on cash would probably be down, so issuing new shares is not an option because selling low-priced stock is too dilutive for the company. Debt financing, because of the company's questionable future, carries a high rate of interest, if debt financing, in fact, can be found.

The investor and trader must be careful when considering investing in this type of company. It is for high-risk capital only.

CHAPTER 11

# BEHAVIORAL FINANCE AND SENTIMENT SHIFTS

## A NATION OF STOCK TRADERS

Trading days start early on the West Coast, at 6:30 a.m. Usually I'm up and on the way to my office by 6:00 a.m. or so, with the sun just starting to show. One morning, as I wiped sleep from my eyes, barely awake, I listened to the blare from the television. On the screen a smiling, pleasant-looking woman was extolling her opinion that last week's market strength would probably not follow through, and that stocks could be weak early in the week, but strengthen toward the middle of the week. Like delivering a weather report, the woman patiently explained how pending midweek economic reports would probably drive the market higher.

I wondered if there is that large an audience out there that cares about what the market will do this week! There must be, I concluded, otherwise this woman would not be on the screen, what with the cost of television time being so high. Do people really think that the market, like the weather, can be predicted with any kind of certainty? I guess so, I decided.

Getting dressed, I remembered when I first attended meetings at which market prognostications were readily received and disseminated. Back in the mid-1960s, early in the morning, I was sitting in a conference room at a Merrill Lynch office in Houston, Texas. A newly licensed broker, I heard from over the speakerphone as a trader extolled us to sell stocks to customers because the market, after swooning for several days, was about to rebound sharply. Later in the week, he assured us, the market should have a good run.

The thing that occurs to me now, is that in that conference room, about 35 years ago, we were a small group. There were only about 25 of us, interested in the near-term market prospects. And, also, we were all professionals. We would take this information and make telephone calls, or go see investors in person, trying to get buy orders. The market for this information was not very big back then. Few people were interested in what the market would do—this week. Stock trading, for all but a very few, was a peripheral thing.

But back to the present: Do many people really think that this week's market performance can be known? And also, is the audience that huge that market prognostications are beamed out so early in the morning, when people have barely had a cup of coffee? Have we become a nation of stock jockeys? I suppose in many ways we have. Certainly the rise of online trading has exploded the market for stock information and opinions, much of which finally turns out to be little more than "noise."

As far as the size of online trading, Forrester Research, Inc., [Punishill (1999)] projected that there will be over $3 trillion managed online by 2003, in over 20 million online accounts. This will represent almost 19 percent of total retail investment assets. So there really is a huge and growing market for doing the trading and investing themselves.

Does this constant dispersal of investment information help investors, or does it distract investors by taking up their time? Do people make more money by taking more time with their investments? This is part of a bigger question of whether people are trying to make money in the market, or are just developing a habit of trading.

## The Market Compulsion

Like many people, I find the market very compelling. When I buy a stock and it goes up, sometimes I get carried away. I start thinking that there is, after all, justice in the world, and I am being rewarded for my intelligence and market wisdom. Then I come back to earth by quickly reminding myself of the past losers I've had. Other people feel good after picking winners as well. I'm sure that they experience that sort of high after buying a stock that goes up; the quicker and higher the stock goes, the greater the thrill.

This excitement in trading the market is unique. But this excitement can be dangerous, if not recognized and understood.

## The Dentist

In a recent television commercial, a dentist informs his patient, a young, arrogant-seeming professional on Wall Street, that he, the dentist, retrieves market quotes as quickly as does the professional. And this is just before the dentist instructs the professional to open his mouth—the power that the dentist, an individual investor, has over the professional Wall Street "type" is obvious.

The dentist, glowering, says that he gets his quotes at the same time as the Wall Street patient gets his and, also, as the market is moving—as if that, in itself, is an advantage. The implication is that the dentist, because he can trade as quickly as the professional, with the same information as the professional, can compete or even vanquish the Street professional.

It is somewhat interesting that the dentists can trade in this manner, but is this manner really important? The question to be answered is whether having the means to trade more quickly leads to making more money in the market. There is evidence to conclude that the answer to this question is no.

Even more sobering is the evidence that the wealth of information found online and the means to act on this information via online trading can result in a worse performance than one would experience if one did not have this plethora of information and the click-quick means to complete transactions.

## BEHAVIORAL FINANCE

Behavioral finance is involved in empirical fact-gathering—studying the facts regarding the activity of people as related to their trading and investing. The premise of behavioral finance is simple: People, when they invest, act as people, not as the rational prototypes that financial theorems postulate. People who invest and trade take their nonrational, human qualities with them, for better or worse, when involved in these endeavors. And behavioral finance studies what people *do*, not what they say or *think* they do.

Behavioral finance is a fast-growing specialty, gaining adherents rapidly. Part of the reason for this growth is probably a reaction to the "efficient market" theory. This theory concludes that markets are rather perfect. All the news and information that there could be about a company has already been reflected in its market price, the theory postulates. Investors and traders, the theory continues, have ready access to information and will absorb this information and act rationally with it, which is to say, buy or sell or short or hold stocks on the basis of a rational interpretation of this news.

That is a nice-sounding theory, but it has trouble explaining big market advances or declines, say in the 500- to 600-point range. The theory cannot explain a company's decline on good news or a company's advance on bad news, actions which happen all the time.

As behavioral finance grappled with events such as these, certain trading patterns emerged. Behavioral finance considered these events more from the standpoint of people's trading patterns. And these patterns exposed large gaps in what could be called rational behavior. Rational behavior dictates that people, when confronted with data, should act one way; but people often act in nonrational ways. People act like people.

## ONLINE TRADING

Terrance Odean and Brad M. Barber at the University of California at Davis studied some of the facets of my example of the hubris of the "powerful" dentist. Their study is entitled "Online Investors: Do the Slow Die First?" This study investigates online traders and delves into the results of people using the powerful online investing and trading tools. Put into the hands of individual investors, do these tools make people more money? And, as measured against other groups, what sorts of traders and investors go online?

In their study Odean and Barber found that it is mostly younger people who go online, and that they are predominantly male. A majority of these young men are active traders; they have a relatively high amount of nonmarket income; they are more likely to favor trading smaller-cap growth stocks, the sorts of stocks that have a higher degree of market risk; they have stock portfolios that are a small portion of their total net worth.

### Before and After Going Online

Before switching to online trading, the study shows, the average online investor that it used in its sampling beat the market by 4.2 percent annually, not counting trading costs. Beating the market by this amount, the study concludes, gave these investors confidence in their investing abilities.

After switching online, these traders did not perform as well. Their gross returns underperformed the market by about 1.2 percent a year. Before switching online, these investors did not trade that much. In the 2 years prior to going online, these investors had an average annualized portfolio turnover of about 70 percent. One month after switching online, these investors increased their portfolio turnover to 120 percent annualized.

One has to wonder. Online trading has definite advantages; one can sit down and with a click receive reams of research information; another click buys and sells stock quickly, efficiently, and cheaply. So why, at least in this study, does performance lag when investors go online?

Prior studies by Odean and Barber, as well as research done by other behavioral finance practitioners, point to investment success leading investors to overconfidence, which further leads to overtrading, resulting in poorer investment returns. Overtrading is made even easier by the lack of trading "friction." Trading friction refers to the steps involved in trading; these steps are present in offline trading but not in online trading.

For example, when trading offline you have to call your broker, and your broker may or may not be available. Then, usually, you will discuss a trade with your broker, and this discussion may weaken your resolve to make a trade. If you make a trade with your broker, usually you will wait for a trade report before doing another trade. Your broker will have to call you back with the report, taking more time. Also, the commission costs with a telephone broker are usually higher, another hindrance to making a trade.

All these factors create friction in completing a transaction and may change your mind about whether or not to trade. And if you want research to help in your investment decision, and don't utilize online sources, the trading decision again is delayed, if not abandoned. By the time a broker mails out your requested research, your will to trade may have evaporated.

None of this friction exists in online trading. You can download research, a mountain of it if desired, point and click and . . . done; virtually instantaneously the trade is completed and report furnished.

## OVERCONFIDENCE AND LOWER RETURNS

Odean and Barber found that strong performances such as those reported by investors before going online are consistent with a self-attribution bias. That is, investors and traders take the credit for their success, thinking that their stock-picking ability is the major reason for their market success. The notion that the market just happened to go their way never occurs to them.

The more market success, the more likely the investor can become overconfident. Being overconfident in bullfighting, stock trading, as well as many other things, can lead to a gouging, or financial loss.

Also, when an overconfident market participant, convinced that because she is smart and can beat the market consistently, downloads the research that is relevant to her trading interest, she can easily end up anticipating that she should be even more successful; she figures that now she has more knowledge backing up her overconfident "trading abilities."

This downloaded data can lead an overconfident investor or trader to the illusion that possessing all this research will lead to even more profitable trades: The illusion that possession of this research can produce even more winning trades can lead to even more overconfidence. This vicious cycle can lead to more and more trading which, studies have borne out, leads to a lessening of market performance.

All of which takes us back to the dentist. The dentist has Wall Street in his chair in the form of a young, arrogant male. The dentist points out to the professional that the dentist's stock quotes are gotten as quickly as the Wall Street professional gets his stock quotes.

The issue that it is questionable—whether getting stock quotes quicker is, in fact, an advantage—is never raised; studies that show that this "advantage" leads to lower performances never enters the discussion. But this commercial is to sell a service, not to explore evidence regarding the pitfalls of being too confident and trading too much.

## SPECULATING TO FIND SAFETY

Another television commercial that can lead a trader or investor astray is one in which an older couple with white hair are embracing; the couple say to each other how fulfilled they are to be able to enjoy their retirement with financial security. In the advertisement the couple states how Social Security did not pay enough for their retirement plans but, rather, their own successful stock investing over the years is financing their retirement dream.

The implication is that Social Security will not be there at retirement time. And if Social Security is still alive, the benefits it offers will not be sufficient to offer people the amount that is necessary to retire in a comfortable way. This constant doubting of Social Security's solvency that we hear from politicians, television commercials, and other sources can lead people to believe that they may lose the benefits that Social Security has offered over the years. This loss can affect people to the extent that they will be willing to take extra risks to replace the Social Security benefit that they fear they are losing.

Feeling the pressure that they must retire with a large amount of money, and that this retirement will give them loads of free time to be happy (a questionable premise in itself), people might understandably get nervous. And this nervousness may move people to think that they must make more money with their investments.

Commercials put out by the investment community constantly suggest that more financial gain is possible if one buys a certain fund, or trades online with a certain firm, or subscribes to a certain letter. This barrage of aggressive marketing is everywhere: on television, in magazines, on the Internet.

So the dynamics are there to move people to take bigger risks to receive bigger rewards: the fear that Social Security will not be adequate, even if extant; the lure of how wonderful retirement can be with more money; the suggestion that if greater risks are taken, if certain products are purchased, greater rewards might be forthcoming.

Well, sadly, as Odean and Barber's report finds, online trading tools do not necessarily lead to more investing success. They often lead to overtrading which can lead to less success.

> *Odean's study finds that there seems to be a cycle that trading success leads an investor or trader to overconfidence which leads to going online, trading every more actively, and achieving less success than before going online.*

There is also empirical evidence for the premise that aversion to loss, such as the fear of losing Social Security benefits, can lead to taking greater risks. Daniel Kahneman and Amos Tversky ["Prospect Theory: An Analysis of Decision under Risk," *Econometrical* (46): 171–185, 1979] came to the conclusion that people will take greater risks to recover to a status quo position. This suggests that people will buy riskier stocks to make more return to make up for their loss of Social Security.

## ONLINE TRADING AS ENTERTAINMENT

Sitting down in front of a computer and clicking a mouse and seeing a trade instantly completed can be fun.

There is an element of entertainment to online trading. When stocks go up, this fun can be confused with having an easy way to make money.

When stocks go down, online trading can be seen for something else: a risky venture that can lead to financial disaster if taken too far.

Although there are a number of people at any give time who are trading for entertainment, Odean's study finds that those who are trading the most are overconfident investors who expect to be successful. A rational, not-overconfident trader would see that the price of this entertainment is a below-average market performance and would quit trading. A rational person would conclude that there are cheaper ways to be entertained. A rational person would take up golf or bowling or do something other than trading.

Or a rational person would continue trading for entertainment, which has its own fun value. Just be aware that if you trade for fun, know that you are taking risks and that you can lose all or part of your funds, and be sure you can financially and emotionally take a loss. Also keep your entertainment funds a small portion of your portfolio, perhaps 5 percent or so.

Or maybe put about 50 percent of your investment funds into lower-multiple stocks, those stocks that you think have long-term staying power. And take 10 percent of your money and play with it, knowing that this is your play money. If it is play money, that is, if you can afford to lose it, go ahead and indulge yourself by buying highly volatile, high-risk stocks. If you are looking for trading thrills, the highly volatile stocks are where you will get it. And your 50 percent is also at risk, but not to the same extent as the 10 percent risk money.

> One should differentiate more serious, longer-term money from trading less serious money. Unless you are a professional, keep the trading money portion a small part of your overall portfolio.

As for online trading, if you are a serious, not-overconfident investor, there are many advantages to trading online versus trading over the phone. Almost all the reasons overconfident traders go online and trade too much, such as quick and low-priced stock transactions, speedy execution reports, and an endless supply of top research material, are valuable tools and can help rational investors that have reasonable expectations succeed.

Online trading should be used by all investors who wish to trade with a minimum of friction between themselves and the trade. Investors should stay conscious that this lack of friction can cause them to overtrade, get more speculative, which can then lead to a drop in their investment performance.

## THE CARD DEALERS

Dealers in casinos know that the odds are with the house, and the more one gambles against the odds, the less chance one has of winning. That is good knowledge to have but, unfortunately, knowledge counts for little in games of chance. The stock market is not a game of chance, but there are similarities between an investor and a card dealer regarding the limits of knowledge. Having knowledge has some influence on winning and losing, but not the ultimate influence.

After a period of time, a card dealer knows the feel of the green felt upon which she places the cards; she knows the odds of hitting or staying; she knows the chances of busting or not busting; glancing around the table, she can pretty well tell which are winning hands and which hands will lose. But the overriding question, and the question of paramount importance, is what the next card she turns over will be.

She may know the type of paper used to make the cards, the style and color of ink used to print the cards, and how many queens and other suits are in each deck. But she doesn't know if she'll bust on the next turned-over card.

A market trader, especially if he is trading short term, is in a similar situation. He may know everything about the company down to the name of the CEO's dog or cat; he may know the size of the company's backlog, and its average backlog for the last 20 years; the company's debt repayment schedule; the chances of the company's group advancing in the present market cycle; and so on. But he doesn't know what the market or that company's stock will do tomorrow or in the short term. And only an overconfident investor would be sure that he did know.

## HIGH-MULTIPLE AND LOW-MULTIPLE STOCKS

You can buy high-multiple and lower-multiple stocks; they both have a place in your portfolio. Both types of stocks have risks and potential rewards. But before buying either you should consider how well equipped you are to deal with these two very different types of stocks.

Buying Internet stocks is not like buying auto stocks, for example. A buyer of high-multiple Internet stocks is buying into a particular scenario or set of scenarios regarding what the future might be like. This is unlike buying an auto stock. If you buy General Motors (GM), the question is what will GM be making 5 years from now? You can be pretty sure that

GM will be making cars and trucks. You know that GM has the capacity to make cars, and that people will be buying cars 5 years from now; people may be buying bigger cars or smaller cars or more cars or fewer cars, but they will be buying cars.

The range of uncertainty is much more constrained with a known quantity such as GM than with a newly publicly issued technology company that, for example, has never earned any money, doesn't own a factory but leases its space, is just starting a Web site, and has no one at the company over 30 years old. You are hoping that this company will be the next Microsoft; there is also a good chance that in 5 years the company will be gone and forgotten.

There is a huge amount of uncertainty with buying a technology start-up company. Is the company pursuing the technology that everyone will buy 5 years from now? And, if so, is the company going to be the dominant player in the field? These questions have to be answered before an investor can feel confident about buying the stock. But the question is virtually unanswerable.

Lower-multiple stocks also can have a degree of uncertainty about their future. But, at least if it appears as if its earnings will continue, the earnings can act as a buffer against future problems.

## The Problem with Valuing No- or Little-Earnings Stocks

Let's look at where the P/E multiple comes from. If the denominator (earnings) in the P/E ratio is small enough, the multiple will always calculate into a high P/E ratio. If there are no significant earnings, the P/E ratio will always be huge; with negative earnings there is no reason to even speak to a P/E ratio. A reason for the large numbers of high P/E stocks trading recently is that many technology companies are going public with little or no earnings. The companies have useful products and high expectations of producing earnings, but have not yet settled into a steady state of generating earnings.

Also there is uncertainty about the future of these companies; the companies operating in the rapidly changing Internet and technology industries mostly cause this uncertainty. This high degree of uncertainty makes for many differences of opinion regarding valuations.

A sure sign of widely divergent views of a company's future stock performance is when there is a large amount of short interest in a company. Short interest is the number of shares of stock that have been sold short. The higher the short interest in a stock, the higher the expectation that the stock will decline. But because stock has to eventually be bought back to cover a short, a high short interest is also a potential source of buying pressure.

A high short interest, therefore, shows that many people think a stock is overvalued. This contrasts with the people who are holding the stock, who think that the stock is not overvalued. This high level of differing opinion is routinely found in low-earnings stocks. Conversely, the short interest in a more predictable stock, such as GM, is usually much lower.

## The Numerator and the Denominator in the P/E Ratio

To a much greater extent, usually with lower-multiple stocks you know what you are buying, earningswise, than with higher multiple stocks. And for this lack of earnings uncertainty you pay a price. The price is that usually low-multiple stocks do not increase their earnings sharply; sharp earnings advances are usually what propel stock prices higher. So it is thought that big winners are rare in low-multiple stocks.

In a P/E ratio there is a numerator and a denominator. The change in the denominator that would reduce the P/E is higher earnings. The factor most likely to bring down the numerator is lower earnings expectations; if the price of the stock (numerator) declines, the P/E ratio concurrently declines.

Put another way, the denominator discloses the present reality regarding earnings; the numerator indicates what the market thinks will happen to those earnings in the future.

## The Appeal of Lower-Multiple Stocks

Often lower-multiple stocks, those between 5 and 10 times earnings or so, are stocks of companies that have fallen out of favor. People often buy them because they think that the stocks are a bargain. Often these companies are not exciting; but they have good earnings relative to their market price.

This type of stock buying is considered a "value" approach to investing. Value investing, unlike growth investing, does not consider earning as the important factor. Rather, value investing looks to items concerning the valuation of assets; it looks for "hidden" items such as overfunded retirement plans, and other not easily found gems. And a company is considered a good buy when its stock price is less than its value.

The growth approach to investing has been all the rage for the last few years, although this has changed recently with a return of interest toward value investing. The new economy has spurred investors to focus in on earnings; investors want a piece of the action in the fast-growing new economy. This has left many value stocks to go begging, which has created opportunities for investors in the low-multiple group.

## Lottery Tickets and Low-Multiple Stock Returns

Behavioral finance studies the investment practices of people. This range of practice can be as wide as people putting money in a bank or buying a lottery ticket.

Highly priced, negative earnings technology stocks are not lottery tickets, but in some ways resemble the gambling associated with lottery tickets. Conversely, investing in, for example, a natural gas company that sells at 4 times earnings is not depositing money in a bank, but in some ways is closer to making a bank deposit than is buying a technology stock with negative earnings. There is certainly a difference in the element of risk between the two investments.

With the low-multiple stock you can, however, receive a lottery ticket type payoff. The natural gas company in the prior example could have its earnings double over time, and the multiple could go to a more reasonable 10 times earnings. This would make the stock a five bagger, a return usually associated more with high-risk technology stocks.

The stock market advance over the last several years has left many people wondering why they were left out. The Nasdaq Composite Index has made a huge gain, even after its retracement. Mostly high-valued technology and biotechnology stocks led the composite's advance, with the advances in stocks in the other sectors very spotty, indeed.

## The Lower Risk of Lower-Multiple Stocks

Those traders who are technologically savvy are doing much of the investing activity that has gone on online. This is changing as online trading, as well as computer usage generally, spreads to those not as literate computerwise.

The technological sophistication of the earlier online investors gave these investors a natural bias toward technology, and their investments have reflected wherein lies their interest: technology and technology-related stocks.

> Just because a stock has a low multiple does not mean that it cannot perform and produce a handsome return over time. Sentiment can change, making out-of-style sectors and groups and stocks popular once again.

But more basic companies, those that are not technology-related, should not be overlooked as investment opportunities. Although old-economy companies may not look as exciting as technology-type companies, do not underestimate the profits that can be made in old-economy stocks.

Through market cycles it becomes obvious that overlooked, obviously undervalued companies in a sector can become profitable once market sentiment settles on this sector. Even in a sector such as insurance or transportation, once discovered, the group can make impressive and even spectacular gains.

And the advantage in the old-economy stocks, especially those with low multiples, is that often their downside is not that great. If the timing is not there, instead of advancing, these stocks may sit still; but that is better than a one-third or two-thirds or more decline that some of the hotter groups have experienced in the recent past.

If you can uncover a stock that is undervalued, the stock can advance even without its sector advancing. There are always stocks to be found that are undervalued and overlooked. And finding a stock 5 or 6 times earnings that is later discovered by the investing public can be as exciting as seeing an Internet stock climb.

## Some Low-Multiple Trades

Recently I made a couple of lower-multiple trades for myself and customers that worked out really well, and I want to show them as an example of how low-multiple stock picking can be profitable. I may or may not still be holding these stocks at publication date, and I'm not suggesting that any reader should buy these stocks for himself or herself.

In the spring of 2000, investors abandoned the biotech group with a vengeance. It was as if the group, which heretofore was an investor's dream, turned into a nightmare. Some stocks in this group plunged 90 percent!

I looked through the group, searching for bargains. Knowing names of stocks that I had watched climbing, I now looked up the current price of these stocks. I went to Zack's Investment Services, Hoover's, and other sites, looking for:

1. *Fundamentals.* Specifically, what did the company do. I wanted companies involved in the area of the human genome because (a) that area seems to hold great promise in a very fundamental way; (b) genetics can be a window into treating disease in a very new way, much as the Internet has revolutionized the processing of information; (c) genetics is a blind item. Markets get excited about blind items. Stock salespeople can get on the phone and, themselves excited about a new area, can excite and move their customers into buying stock in which there is the expectation that something really new is going on. Some of this forward-looking expectation may not have substance. But in genomics, I think, there

can turn out to be quite a bit of substance. I also went over the capitalization of the companies, but not in an accountant in-depth way. I looked to see if anything jumped out which could hurt the companies, such as, a preponderance of too much short-term debt. Which leads me to:

2. *Earnings.* I like earnings; I feel more comfortable buying stocks in which there are presently earnings. If a company sells at 50 times earnings or even higher, at least some earnings are there to sustain the company. Earnings often make stock analysis easier in that if there are earnings, other factors such as the amount of a company's debt recede somewhat in importance; earnings show that the company is profitable, which is a company's first hurdle to staying alive and growing. I realize that the earnings forecasts of companies are often best guesses by analysts and company officers. But if a company has present earnings, that factor speaks louder than all the rosy promises that investor relations firms can trumpet. I know that earnings can evaporate or at least be off the mark. I expect it. You can get the latest 12-month earnings, and future earnings estimates by going to one of the many financial sites. If a company has good earnings now, but will not next year, better use next year's earnings in your analysis. Which brings me to the last factor that I explored while scrolling through Web sites, ruminating and wondering which companies are truly among the bargains.

3. *Recent Events.* Very important to check, and very simple to do. On probably every Web site that gives financial information there are the latest corporate developments. Click on and read the information; go back a couple of quarters. Is there anything new that sends up red flags to you, either positive or negative? Also be a bit wary of companies that continually announce new contracts, especially small contracts. The company may just have an investor relations firm working the media to get the company publicity. Or the company may have internal problems. I have seen companies send out a spate of good news, only to see the stock crash later, when the companies ran out of good news to report. Also, check with sources such as suppliers and competitors in the industry in which you are investing. It is surprising how much information is available. After this: sleep on it.

4. *Timing.* I know it is very much *de rigueur* to do research, then, using online trading capabilities, to put those capabilities to work by firing off an order. The television ads tell us to beat the crowd;

well, what if the stock goes down right after you buy it? You would have been better off being slower on the execution; the slower buyers are getting a better price. Unless you are day trading, the speed of your execution will make little difference, if any. So after you do your research, and you are not sure about what to do, think about it. Go to the movies, do the dishes, ruminate about the company, your portfolio, see if there is something there eating at you which will come to consciousness after a while. If you don't buy and the stock jumps up, well, such is life; you will have to pay more if you buy later. If the stock goes down, great; being quick on the trigger is important in a gunfight but not, necessarily, in stock investing or trading.

After looking around for a while, I came across a biotech company that I had watched climb from about 4 to over 36 in the prior few months' period. The whole time it had climbed, in the past, I regretted not having bought it. The stock was a participant in the frenzied buying of the biotech companies in early 2000. After, investors abandoned the group, and the stock plunged to about 5½. In the investment business, with gallows humor, we call this price action a round-trip. The stock was BioSource, Inc. (BIOI).

I liked some things about BIOI. The company worked in the human genome field; it was a small-cap company, and it wouldn't take major buying to move the stock; it had earnings and was estimated to have better future earnings; the stock sold about 17 times earnings. I wondered: What has changed in the stock to make it 5½ instead of 36? Only market sentiment, I concluded.

I called the company. The investor relations person was a pleasant-sounding woman who did not seem to be hyping the stock at all. Nothing major was pending, she said, and she confirmed the future earnings estimates. That was okay, I reasoned. A company with 17 times earnings shouldn't have much downside risk; not in the biotech group. I also checked with sources in the industry. No negative comments were expressed about the company.

I bought the stock. An institutional brokerage firm later came out with a buy recommendation, boosting the stock to about 12; the stock then ran to over 20. I had bought for a long-term hold and had never seen a short-term trade developing. After the stock started running, the decision about holding the stock or selling developed. The decision of when to sell is often a tougher decision than at which point to buy. Holding a winner is a lot easier than sitting with a loser; and selling a little early is acceptable.

Better to leave something on the table for the next buyer than to try to pick the top, risking a loss.

Another successful trade developed when an officer of a company that I was interested in showed up in my office for a second time. To retrace, about a year earlier I had covered an investment banking conference for *The San Francisco Examiner.* At that conference I had come across a company that was selling for about $1.50; the stock was up from selling at under $1 a share. I couldn't get the fact that the stock was selling so low out of my mind, even though I kept reminding myself that I didn't deal in penny stocks.

I remembered being attracted to the company years before when it had gone from about $3 a share to over $30 in a fairly short period of time. In the past I had regretted not buying the stock, and now it was back down.

The company was Chesapeake, Inc. (CHK), a natural gas company. The company had taken on a lot of debt; it used the money from the debt to purchase more gas properties. The price of natural gas had collapsed, along with the price of oil. Natural gas generally follows the price of crude oil. Crude had sold at about $25 a barrel; now crude was about $10 a barrel. So CHK had much gas and much debt and little earnings; questions abounded as to whether the company could make it.

I had, back then, called a company officer and asked him about the CHK's prospects. He was very candid, and said that the company could make it, that is, if oil prices would firm up. Tell me where oil prices will go, he reflected to me, and I'll tell you where the price of the stock will go. He thought that the price of oil would go up, and the natural gas price also.

A few months later, the officer came to my office. He was more bullish about the outlook for gas prices, and he told me why. He outlined that he thought CHK, which was now about 2½ would continue to go up with oil prices. The company did have the fundamentals to survive, I decided, if oil prices stayed firm. But it was still too speculative for me.

As I said at the beginning, the officer then came to see me about a year later. Oil was now about $25 a barrel, and with that, natural gas prices had moved higher. CHK was selling at 3½, and the officer showed me opinions from major brokerage firms to buy the stock. Also, there were estimates out that CHK could earn $1 a share or more in the next fiscal year. Now, to my way of thinking, 3½ times earnings is a reasonable risk for a speculative stock. I ruminated about it, still not liking the risk. I also checked with people in the industry, looking for something negative to offset my positive instincts.

Over the next several weeks, oil stocks and natural gas stocks firmed. CHK jumped in price one day. No news was out on the stock, but there was a jump in volume. The stock moved up to about 4¼. That is still a reasonable multiple, I figured. Also the stock was getting up to the $5 area. The NYSE and the NASD set minimum equity that must be carried in brokerage accounts. Brokerage firms set additional minimums. Often firms will not allow stocks under $5 to be calculated for minimum requirement purposes.

The change in a stock being carried for maintenance can do two things. One, brokers could buy the stock on margin. The margin aspect makes the stock more attractive for brokers to suggest to aggressive traders and investors; they can buy roughly twice the amount of shares utilizing margin. Second, people who already hold the stock can double up: they can buy more shares without putting up any cash; they simply use the shares they presently hold for collateral. This could be a source of large potential demand.

Considering the maintenance margin factor, and with the stock selling at only about 4 times earnings, I figured buying the stock was worth the risk. Besides, I liked that the company had an officer out exposing the stock to potential buyers. If the company did well, the story would get out. I bought the stock.

Over the next several weeks, the price of oil stayed strong, natural gas continued up in price, and the stock moved about 1½ points higher. Buying a stock this cheap could lead to having a real winner. It is not out of the question that CHK could go to 10 times earnings and over time increase its earnings. Also, market sentiment could come into the group. If all of this happened, not an impossibility, certainly no more of an impossibility than some of the scenarios sketched for some of the Internet companies, the stock could rise substantially. In a few years out, CHK might earn $1.50 a share; market sentiment could drive its multiple to 20 times. If all this happened, the stock could sell in the $30 area.

I don't know if CHK will get to $30, or fall back below $5, or even if I'll hold it beyond next week. Things change, information is a constant, insight shifts. I could get an inkling that it is time to get out of CHK for whatever reason, and I'll sell. The stock market is not a place for rigid postures.

These are a couple of my winners. I've had my losers, too. We all have.

## THE UNKNOWN OF FUTURE MARKET OPPORTUNITIES

Try as we might, as market traders and investors, we cannot guess the future with any real degree of accuracy. In managing our investments, we want to stay as current as possible to present trends and try to calculate the future. But the future in economic matters, as in most things, does not evolve in a straight line but, rather, in fits and spurts. And knowing where to look for future investment opportunities is a constant work in progress, with not a whole lot of assurance of being accurate.

As an example, let me relate some of my experience as a stockbroker and vice president of Lehman Brothers back in the late 1970s. Back then anything having to do with oil was all the rage. Oil drillers, service, producers, explorers, were all in demand. Because of an OPEC-induced worldwide oil shortage, the price of crude had climbed from about $12 a barrel to above $30 a barrel. There were long lines at gas stations, and people angrily waited their turns to fill up; gas was being rationed, and at some gas stations you could receive only about half a tank; everybody *knew* that gas was going to $50 a barrel, on its way to, perhaps, $100 a barrel. There was no stopping the fact that inflation was here to stay. Oil was king, and nothing was of value except hard assets such as gold or land; stocks were dead because they were not a hedge against inflation.

At Lehman Brothers, as in every other brokerage firm, we were trading small- and macro-cap stocks of oil exploration companies. These stocks had no earnings and probably would not for years. But if you extrapolated the future of these companies out several years, using the commonly held belief that oil would be $50, the stocks one day would have big earnings. And at $75 or $100 a barrel, the stocks were selling at low levels, indeed.

Now, doesn't all of this sound familiar? We hear the same claims for many technology and biotechnology stocks. Granted, the Internet revolution is not commodity based, as was the oil craze. Also the Internet era has fostered a fundamental information change, whereas the oil craze was merely a supply/demand ratio that got out of kilter for a while.

Still, the tendency to extrapolate present factors and trends into the future is a strategy that is usually fundamentally flawed. To invest and trade the market believing that trends will continue in a straight line can be dangerous to your financial well-being.

Ultimately the oil craze played out. Oil did not go up to $50 a barrel; it went down to about $9 a barrel; homes and raw land and office buildings in the "Oil Belt" that were financed by oil interests plunged in price as people moved out; real estate projects were abandoned; many people involved in the oil business sought protection of the bankruptcy courts. Many small-cap oil stocks went down to pennies a share, then disappeared. There is a similarity to the oil companies of the past and many of today's dot-com companies.

Much of the crash of the oil stocks in the 1980s has been forgotten by now, just as people will forget today's dot-com craze and crash in the future. And lurking out there somewhere is a new craze, just waiting to get started. That's the way it's always been and will always be.

## LOOKING FOR GOOD TRADES

Just as potential busts are shaping up, potential booms are developing. There is no telling from where the opportunity is coming but, invariably, it will come.

Looking back at good and bad trades I've made over the years, it strikes me that each year I would come across one, maybe two, really good trades. These stocks would maybe double over the year, and some did even better than that. But good trades come sparingly. And when you do make a good buy, try to the hold the stock for a while and receive all the benefits you can from making that good buy.

My biggest regrets come from doing the research, buying, and taking what I thought was a good profit, only to see the stock go up several more times; sometimes the process of a stock working out can take several years.

After all the effort of making a good purchase and seeing the stock work, don't be in a big hurry to sell. Not unless you are actively trading. Do more research, call the company, keep current with company developments, think it over.

## SEARCHING FOR LOW-MULTIPLE BARGAINS

Although the Nasdaq market is known for its high-multiple growth stocks, there are low-multiple stocks also trading in this market. Appendix A is a sampling of low-multiple stocks, arranged by industry. This sampling could be a starting point for you to investigate another area of the Nasdaq stock market: lower-multiple issues.

# PART IV

# NASDAQ RESOURCES

APPENDIX A

# NASDAQ STOCKS WITH LOW P/E MULTIPLES

There are many stocks today with high P/E valuations. This makes it easy to think that high P/E stocks are all there are, especially on the Nasdaq market, which has many growth, new-economy stocks. This is just not true. This appendix lists stocks that are selling at modest multiples, some as low as five times earnings. The companies are in diverse industries, such as computers, insurance, and industrials. If earnings estimates are provided for a company, they are courtesy of Zacks Investment Management (*www.zacks.com*). Price/earnings multiples are based on the last 12 months' actual earnings.

This Appendix A is just a sampling of companies; there are many more low-multiple companies listed on the Nasdaq market. A buy or sell opinion is not given here, but researching these stocks as well as perusing the Nasdaq market for other low-multiple issues would yield some investment possibilities.

Lower-multiple stocks often have less downside risk than higher-multiple stocks. The upside potential with lower-multiple stocks is that there will be a multiple expansion, particularly if earnings grow.

Good companies could have been overlooked with the stampede of investors pouring money into the high-tech areas. Also, small-cap companies have been generally disregarded with the rush toward bigger, stronger technology stocks.

It takes some time and effort to go through ferreting out good values in the low-multiple stocks listed on the Nasdaq, but one or two winners could make it time well spent.

## COMPUTER INDUSTRY

**TSR, Inc. (TSRI)** *Price/earnings multiple: 6.36 times.* The company is a provider of computer programming consulting services. Its specialty is in finding technology professionals for assignments of a temporary basis; it works mostly with Fortune 500 companies. There is a great shortage of computer programmers nationwide, which the company feels is a great opportunity for them with its ability to place personnel. The company believes there is much growth in consulting services.

**Cadmus Communication Corp. (CDMS)** *Low earnings estimate: $1.56; high earnings estimate: $1.65; mean earnings estimate: $1.68; price/earnings multiple on mean estimate: 5.07 times.* Cadmus is the largest producer of medical, scientific, and technical journals. The company helps publishers around the world produce both electronic and printed periodicals. Its magazine group offers production solutions for publishers of special interest, such as business-to-business, alumni, and other specialty magazines. It also offers print outsourcing, Web architecture, and other services.

**Amlicon, Inc. (AMPI)** *Price/earnings multiple: 7.34 times.* The company has been in the leasing business since 1977. It has helped people lease over $1.7 billion in capital assets. The companies it has helped have operated in the fields of law, health care, post-secondary education, and other fields. Amlicon works with both large and small companies in order to help the companies obtain the capital assets they need. The company also helps in the financing of installation and training costs.

**Cellular Technical Services Company, Inc. (CTSC)** *Price/earnings multiple: 4.42 times.* CTSC is a leading developer, marketer, distributor, and supporter of a wide range of services and products for the telecommunications industry. Among its services it provides real-time management solutions and information processing; it also offers integrated solutions for fraud management. In June 2000 the company received $1.2 million in a legal action settlement.

**ePresence, Inc. (EPRE)** *Price/earnings multiple: 6.84 times.* The company is a leader in Internet and directory technology; it offers services that include Web site and Web portal designs and implements these services. The company also offers directory and security planning and network optimizing. It also owns a 40 percent interest in Switchboard, Inc., which is an Internet-based network interconnecting customers and merchants.

**Casino Data Systems (CSDS)** *Price/earnings multiple: 7.14 times.* The company is a leading designer, manufacturer, and distributor of proprietary technology products for the casino gaming industry. Among its products are online slot accounting and player tracking games; also it offers multisite linked progressive jackpot systems and meters. A wholly owned subsidiary, TurboPower Software, acquired OfficePartner from DeVries Data Systems.

**Formula Systems (1985), Ltd. (FORTY)** *Price/earnings multiple: 6.16 times.* This company is listed both on the Tel-Aviv Stock Exchange and on Nasdaq. Its business units are divided into two divisions: Information Technology Services and Proprietary Software Solutions. Additionally, the company has a division that is involved in venture investments which is named Formula Ventures. It also offers hardware-related services through its Sintec subsidiary.

## TELECOMMUNICATIONS INDUSTRY

**Talk.com, Inc. (TALK)** *Price/earnings multiple: 6.34 times.* This company is a leader in providing e-commerce telecommunications; it is the founder of AOL Long Distance, which is AOL's most successful partner. TALK has reduced the cost components for long-distance service by using online elements. TALK also has its own national telecommunications network, One Better Network. The company signed an agreement to have Quintel Communications, Inc., market its services.

**Modern Times Group MTGNY (ADR)** *Price/earnings multiple: 4.65 times.* This company is traded on the Stockholm Stock Exchange and Nasdaq. It started the first commercial channel on television in Sweden. It operates in several media arenas, including radio, newspaper publishing, television, the Internet, and other media services. It brings together companies for production in media ventures. The company has experienced good growth.

## TRANSPORTATION INDUSTRY

**Marten Transport, Ltd. (MRTN)** *Price/earnings multiple: 6.37 times.* This company is a dry-freight carrier. It also specializes in the transportation of foods, chemicals, and other products requiring temperature-controlled or insulated carriage. It strives to be the premium supplier of transportation services in the field. The company is one of the top four temperature-protected freight haulers in America.

**P.A.M. Transportation Services, Inc. (PTSI)** *Price/earnings multiple: 7.56 times.* This company is a holding company that owns subsidiaries that operate irregular route contract and common motor carriers. These subsidiaries are authorized to transport, throughout Ontario, Quebec, and the United States, general commodities. The company is based in Tontitown, Arizona. It has been profitable for the last 4 years, and has a market cap of about $71 million.

**Emons Transportation Group, Inc. (EMON)** *Price/earnings multiple: 7.67 times.* This company is involved in freight transportation and distribution services. It operates in the mid-Atlantic and Northeast regions; through a subsidiary it serves Quebec, Canada. It owns five short-line railroads, operates rail/truck facilities and a rail intermodal terminal. Among its services is providing customers with warehousing and logistics services for storage of freight.

**Old Dominion Freight Line, Inc. (ODFL)** *Price/earnings multiple: 5.65 times.* The company is an interregional and multiregional motor carrier. It transports shipments that comprise less than a truckload of commodities such as textiles, capital goods, and consumer goods. It serves the southeast, south central, northeast, midwest, and western regions of the United States. The company recently has had to contend with higher prices for fuel and other petroleum products.

**USA Truck, Inc. (USAK)** *Low earnings estimate: $0.80; high earnings estimate: $1.15; mean earnings estimate: $0.98; price/earnings multiple on mean estimate: 5.50 times.* The company is a medium haul, contract and common carrier; it specializes in truckload quantities of general commodities. It operates in all of the 48 contiguous states of the United States, and the provinces of Ontario and Quebec in Canada. It also operates in Mexico through the gateway city of Laredo, Texas. The company can work on single or multiple destinations on an as-needed basis.

**Arkansas Best Corporation (ABFS)** *Low earnings estimate: $3.05; high earnings estimate: $3.15; mean earnings estimate: $3.10; price/earnings multiple on mean estimate: 4.96 times.* Among this company's subsidiaries is one of the biggest and most experienced of the motor carriers. It services all 50 states in the United States, nine provinces in Canada, Guam, and Puerto Rico. It also offers broad service in Mexico. The company provides time-definite shipments and guaranteed expedited service. Also the company offers international service to over 130 other countries, through 230 ports.

**Amtran, Inc. (AMTR)**   *Low earnings estimate: $1.39; high earnings estimate: $2.85; mean earnings estimate: $2.16; price/earnings multiple on mean estimate: 5.06 times.* This company has as its subsidiary ATA. ATA is the eleventh-largest airline in passenger travel; it is also the largest operator of commercial and military passenger charters. ATA goes to popular resorts and major business centers from its gateways in Chicago–Midway and Indianapolis. Its quoted fares are for one-way, off-peak travel days; generally fares are not available during high-volume travel periods.

**Great Lakes Aviation, Ltd. (GLUX)**   *Price/earnings multiple: 6.58 times.* The company operates both Beechcraft 1900D and 1900C, and 30-passenger EMB-120 Brasilia model of planes. Its charter services division offers charters for passenger and corporate use. Also the company fills shipping and small package needs. It increased its weekday flights at O'Hare Chicago airport in June 2000, and has added additional flights to Michigan, Illinois, and Indiana.

**Boyd Bros. Transportation, Inc. (BOYD)**   *Price/earnings multiple: 7.64 times.* This is one of the largest flatbed trucking companies in the United States, and operates countrywide. It provides transportation services to time-sensitive, high-volume customers. Its customers are mostly in the building materials and steel industry. Some of the factors that can affect the company negatively are a shortage of qualified drivers, higher fuel prices, and adverse safety experience.

**Transport Corporation of America, Inc. (TCAM)**   *Price/earnings multiple: 10.70 times.* The company provides a variety of logistics and truckload freight carriage service to customers who are located in the United States and Canada. It provides responsive and time-definite services, using its technology. In 2000 the company opened a commercial driver's license school; it plans to use the school to facilitate a number of new drivers into its system.

**Railworks Corporation (RWKS)**   *Price/earnings multiple: 1.70 times.* The company is comprised of rail industry service and product providers throughout the United States. It has taken over other companies, including Breaking Technology Corporation, Hovey Industries, Ltd., and assets of Western Tar Products Corporation. Its subsidiaries provide the New York

City rail and civil construction markets and also manufacture railway switch heaters.

**Genesee & Wyoming, Inc. (GNWR)**  *Price/earnings multiple: 6.00 times.* GNWR is a leader in operating short-line and regional freight railroads in the United States, Canada, Mexico, and Australia. The company also is a provider of freight car switching and related services. It increased its Australia traffic as a result of its contract with Broken Hill Proprietary Company Limited. The company operates in four countries on over 3750 miles of owned and leased track.

**Pioneer Railcorp. (PRRR)**  *Price/earnings multiple: 3.55 times.* This is a short-line railroad holding company, operating 15 railroads totaling over 440 miles in nine states. It serves some of the largest corporations in the United States. Through a subsidiary the company owns more than 1400 items of railroad equipment. Through other subsidiaries it provides agency and accounting services and real estate management to present and future railroad subsidiaries.

## INSURANCE INDUSTRY

**Intercontinental Life Corporation (ILCO)**  *Price/earnings multiple: 6.17 times.* The company is mostly engaged, through subsidiaries, in marketing and underwriting personal life insurance and annuity products. It also administers portfolios of individual and group life insurance, annuity products, and credit life and disability insurance policies. ILCO has purchased a number of companies, including Grinnell Life, State Auto Life, and Meridian Life.

**Financial Industries Corporation (FNIN)**  *Price/earnings multiple: 4.96 times.* The principal subsidiary of FNIN is Family Life Insurance Company. Family Life is a Seattle-based mortgage protection life insurance provider. Included in the company's net income calculation includes FNIN's equity in the net income of its InterContinental Life Corporation affiliate. The company is also involved with ILCO, owning about 47.5 percent of its outstanding stock.

**Atlantic American Corporation (AAME)**  *Price/earnings multiple: 5.31 times.* This company is an insurance holding company. Its subsidiary companies are involved in the markets of life, health, property, and casualty insurance industries. America Southern Insurance Company, American Safety Insurance Company, Associated Casualty Insurance Company, Association Risk Management General Agency, and Self-Insurance Administration, Inc., are some of its subsidiaries.

**American National Insurance Company (ANAT)** *Price/earnings multiple: 7.79 times.* Galveston, Texas, is the headquarters for this major insurance company. Its assets exceed $9 billion. The company is rated A+ (superior) by A.M. Best. Its major insurance subsidiaries include American National Life Insurance Company of Texas, Standard Life and Accident Insurance Company, Garden State Life Insurance Company, and Standard Life and Accident Insurance.

**National Security Group, Inc. (NSEC)** *Price/earnings multiple: 9.97 times.* This company sells property/casualty and life insurance in Arkansas and other southern states. Almost all of its revenues derive from its property/casualty unit. The unit sells fire and windstorm insurance to homeowners. It also sells nonstandard automobile insurance and small-business commercial insurance. The life insurance unit sells term, health, and accident insurance.

**National Western Life Insurance Company (NWLIA)** *Price/earnings multiple: 4.83 times.* NWLIA sells individual, whole, universal, and term life insurance. The company also sells endowments and flexible-premium and single-premium annuities. Its market includes customers in 43 states and the District of Columbia, Central and South America, the Caribbean, and the Pacific Rim. Many operations are through 7900 independent broker agents.

**Investors Title Company (ITIC)** *Price/earnings multiple: 9.60 times.* This is the holding company for Investors Title Insurance and Northeast Investor Title Insurance; both companies underwrite land title insurance for owners of land and mortgages, and also sell reinsurance to other title companies. It serves customers from offices in 28 cities in North Carolina, and 1 office each in Michigan, South Carolina, and Virginia. Its agents are in 14 additional states.

**Insurance Management Solutions Group, Inc. (INMG)** *Price/earnings multiple: 5.26 times.* Through its subsidiaries, Insurance Management Solutions and Geotrac, this company provides policy and claim outsourcing services to property and casualty insurance companies; its focus is on the flood insurance market. The company's customers include its Bankers Insurance Group affiliate as well as unaffiliated insurers. It also provides flood zone information.

**Delphi International, Ltd. (DLTDF)** *Price/earnings multiple: 2.99 times.* This Bermuda-based insurance company provides excess loss and quote share reinsurance. The company provides mostly reinsurance for group employee benefit insurance items; this includes long-term group disability and excess workers' compensation insurance. The company provides reinsurance to its subsidiaries, but is also developing a third-party book of customers.

**ACMAT Corporation (ACMTA)**   *Price/earnings multiple: 8.80 times.* ACMTA provides insurance and surety-bond coverage for professional workers in the environmental and construction fields. Its insurance products are sold in the 50 states of the United States. The products are sold through insurance brokers, some of which are Marsh & McLennan, Aon, and Willis Corroon. More than two-thirds of its revenues come from two subsidiaries.

**Citizens Financial Corporation (CNFL)**   *Price/earnings multiple: 3.03 times.* This insurance holding company sells individual and group life insurance and annuities, and accident and health insurance, in 19 states and the District of Columbia. The life insurance products include universal life, whole life, and term life. The company also provides insurance for hospitalization, surgical expenses, death, and dismemberment. Its group plans cover short- and long-term disability.

**Bancinsurance Corporation (BCIS)**   *Price/earnings multiple: 6.65 times.* Through its primary subsidiary, Ohio Indemnity, this insurance holding company underwrites insurance products. The company sells ultimate loss insurance, which provides financial protection to lenders and auto dealers by insuring collateralized property against theft and damage. Another subsidiary administers self-insurance programs for businesses' workers' compensation plans.

**Professionals Group, Inc. (PICM)**   *Price/earnings multiple: 8.99 times.* This holding company provides professional liability coverage for lawyers and health-care providers. It is the second-largest medical malpractice insurance carrier in Michigan, and also serves Florida, Illinois, Indiana, Ohio, and Pennsylvania. Most of the company's insured physicians practice primary-care specialties. These physicians are often required to be "gatekeepers" in managed medical care.

## FINANCE INDUSTRY

**Royce Focus Trust, Inc. (FUND)**   *Price/earnings multiple: 4.47 times.* An adviser that has more than 25 years of investing in small-cap and microcap stocks manages the fund. The average weekly trading volume of this fund is low, averaging just about 130,000 shares. The daily net asset values for the fund are available on its Web site and online through most ticker symbol lookup services. Also the net asset values can be found under the symbol XFUNX.

**Consolidated Mercantile Corp. (CSLMF)** *Price/earnings multiple: 3.00 times.* This merchant banking and venture capital firm invests in durable good companies, owning stakes in companies that produce specialty covers, furniture, packing, and pool products. The company works with the management of its holdings to increase their performance and profitability. It also has holdings in Polyair InterPack and Distinctive Designs Furniture. The president owns 25 percent of the company.

**Bando McGlocklin Capital Corporation (BMCC)** *Price/earnings multiple: 6.34 times.* This company is a real estate investment trust (REIT). It operates in a number of industries and does a number of functions: vinyl doll manufacturing, clock making, and loan portfolio and real estate management. Its portfolio is secured by first and second mortgages; the portfolio consists of loans to small businesses primarily in Wisconsin. The company also has two land parcels under development.

**JB Oxford Holdings, Inc. (JBOH)** *Price/earnings multiple: 10.79 times.* This company provides brokerage and financial services to institutions and individuals through three offices in the United States. Its primary subsidiary is JB Oxford and Company. This company offers discount and online brokerage services, including securities, mutual funds, annuities, and other products. It acts as a clearing agent for over 30 broker dealers and also makes markets in about 500 companies.

**BF Enterprises, Inc. (BFEN)** *Price/earnings multiple: 11.72 times.* This company is still developing. Its basic business is developing the Meadow Point tract of land in suburban Tampa. It owns about 30 percent of this 1700-acre development, and is selling its other holdings in commercial and residential lots. Also this company owns 21 acres of undeveloped land in Nashville and owns a 220,000-square-foot commercial building in Tempe, Arizona, as well.

**Doral Financial Corporation (DORL)** *Low earnings estimate: $2.00; high earnings estimate: $2.05; mean earnings estimate: $2.02; price/earnings multiple on mean estimate: 8.23 times.* The company recently changed its name from First Financial Caribbean. It is a leader in mortgage banking in Puerto Rico. DORL purchases and sells mortgages on single-family homes and issues mortgage-backed securities for sale and investment. Its principal revenues are from loan servicing and origination fees and interest. Among its holdings is Doral Bank.

**Santa Fe Financial Corporation (SFEF)** *Price/earnings multiple: 8.12 times.* This company owns an almost 50 percent interest in the Justice Investor Limited Partnership. The partnership owns the land improvement and leaseholds at 760 Kearny Street in San Francisco. This site holds the Holiday Inn of Chinatown and the financial district. It also owns a 55 percent interest in a 100-unit apartment complex in Cincinnati. InterGroup Corp. owns almost half of SFEF.

**Source Capital Corporation (SOCC)** *Price/earnings multiple: 6.70 times.* Through subsidiaries, this company makes direct commercial loans. The loans are mostly secured by real estate or personal property. Its commercial lending activities include secured lines of credit, construction and development loans, and real estate loans. The company has a financial subsidiary that provides accounts receivable financing to manufacturers, wholesalers, and others in Spokane, Washington.

**ADVANTA Corporation (ADVNA)** *Low earnings estimate: $2.20; high earnings estimate: $3.50; mean earnings estimate: $2.85; price/earnings multiple on mean estimate: 3.99 times.* This company provides consumers and small businesses with products and services via direct and indirect, cost-effective delivery systems. The company originates and services business credit cards, small-ticket equipment leases, credit insurance deposit products, and other goods and services. It utilizes customer information, usage patterns, and other characteristics to enhance proprietary information to match customer profiles with appropriate products.

## BANKING INDUSTRY

**Republic First Bancorp, Inc. (FRBK)** *Price/earnings multiple: 7.22 times.* This is the holding company for First Republic Bank and Republic First Bank of Delaware. These bankers serve businesses and individuals from nine branches. Eight of the branches are in Philadelphia and southern New Jersey, and one branch is in northern Delaware. The banks offer standard deposit products such as checking, NOW, savings accounts, money market accounts, and other accounts.

**Fidelity Bancorp, Inc. (FSBI)** *Price/earnings multiple: 6.49 times.* This is the holding company for Fidelity Bank. The bank serves small to midsized businesses and individuals in the Pittsburgh, Pennsylvania, area. Its products include savings, checking, money market, and NOW accounts. More than half its loan portfolio is made up of one- to four-family residential mortgage loans. The bank invests a portion of its deposits in mortgage-backed securities.

**National Mercantile Bancorp (MBLA)** *Price/earnings multiple: 7.58 times.* This bank caters to wealthy individuals who are associated with the television, music, and film industries; also the bank serves its customers' production companies and talent agencies. Deposit services include savings and money market accounts and certificates of deposit. It also offers health care and access to community-based not-for-profit organizations to its target market.

**Century Bancorp, Inc. (CNBKA)**  *Low earnings estimate: $1.90; high earnings estimate: $1.95; mean earnings estimate: $1.93; price/earnings multiple on mean estimate: 7.43 times.* This is the bank holding company for Century Bank and Trust. The bank is Massachusetts based and serves small and medium-sized businesses; also it provides deposit services to about 100 municipalities in Massachusetts. The bank makes residential real estate, construction, commercial, consumer, and home equity loans. It operates 15 banks in the state and offers investment and other services.

**PVF Capital Corp. (PVFC)**  *Price/earnings multiple: 7.58 times.* This is the holding company for Park View Federal Savings Bank; it operates 10 offices in greater Cleveland. Its services include checking and savings, NOW accounts, IRA accounts, and money markets. Its loan portfolio is about 95 percent in the Cleveland area. The bank also offers consumer loans to its customers. It has a subsidiary that acquires and develops real estate.

**Sterling Financial Corporation (STSA)**  *Low earnings estimate: $1.74; high earnings estimate: $1.82; mean earnings estimate: $1.79; price/earnings multiple on mean estimate: 6.44 times.* This is the holding company for Sterling Savings Bank. It operates in Washington, Idaho, Oregon, and Montana through 75 branches. The bank works with individuals and businesses. About a quarter of its portfolio is in one- to four-family residential mortgages. It has a mortgage subsidiary and an investment subsidiary, and Harbor Financial Services, which works in investment products.

**People's Bancshares, Inc. (PBKB)**  *Low earnings estimate: $3.33; high earnings estimate: $3.50; mean earnings estimate: $3.42; price/earnings multiple on mean estimate: 4.92 times.* The company is a holding entity for People's Savings Bank of Boston. It serves the Brockton and New Bedford area in southeastern Massachusetts through 14 branches. These branches offer checking and savings accounts, money markets, CDs, and IRAs. The bank sells some of its loans and retains the servicing. It has subsidiaries that deal in securities and foreclosed real estate.

**First Citizens BancShares, Inc. (FCNCA)**  *Price/earnings multiple: 9.06 times.* This holding company operates 354 branches for First Citizens Bank & Trust. It operates in the Virginias. It also includes Atlantic State Bank, which operates 31 branches in Georgia and Florida. It offers banking services such as deposit and checking accounts, as well as trust services. The bank's portfolio includes commercial, consumer, and lease financing loans.

**Ipswich Bancshares, Inc. (IPSW)** *Price/earnings multiple: 6.58 times.* This is the holding company for Ipswich Savings Bank, which operates seven branches in Beverly, Essex, Ipswich, Marblehead, North Andover, Rowley, and Salem, Massachusetts. More than 80 percent of the bank's loans are from residential mortgage loans. Also the bank makes commercial real estate, construction, and home equity loans. It offers checking accounts and other services.

**First Defiance Financial Corp. (FDEF)** *Price/earnings multiple: 6.25 times.* This bank operates First Federal Bank of the Midwest; it has 14 branches serving northwestern Ohio. Its primary business is offering residential mortgages funded with deposits gathered from checking and savings accounts and CDs. About two-thirds of the bank's loan portfolio is for single-family homes. The bank also offers consumer, home equity, multi-family real estate, and other loans.

## THE INDUSTRIAL SECTOR

**Baltek Corporation (BTEK)** *Price/earnings multiple: 5.64 times.* This company supplies materials including balsa wood, PVC foam products, and nonwoven polyester mats, to manufacturers for lamination between fiberglass or metal skins. This material is used in a number of products, from model airplanes to boating, to aircraft flooring. Its core materials are sold through the Americas, Europe, and the Pacific Rim. Its materials are also used for sandwich structures.

**American Locker Group, Inc. (ALGI)** *Price/earnings multiple: 3.94 times.* This company sells plastic clusters of mailboxes to the United States Postal Service. The Postal Service uses them in housing developments and apartment complexes. About 70 percent of its sales are to the Postal Service. It has also developed a coin-operated baggage cart system for use in airports. The company has assembly and maintenance operations in the United States and Canada.

**Chattem, Inc. (CHTT)** *Low earnings estimate: $1.05; high earnings estimate: $1.65; mean earnings estimate: $1.35; price/earnings multiple on mean estimate: 7.01 times.* The company makes a number of over-the-counter (OTC) pharmaceutical and personal-care products and dietary supplements. Over half its sales comes from items such as toiletries, cosmetics, and supplements. Products include Flexall joint and muscle pain reliever,

Pamprin menstrual symptom reliever, Melatonix sleep aid, and Mudd clay-based facial mask. It is also making acquisitions.

**Kimball International, Inc. (KBALB)** *Price/earnings multiple on mean estimated earnings: 10.61 times.* This company makes furniture and cabinets. It also produces wood and metal home, office, lodging, and healthcare furniture, TV cabinets, and panel systems. Its electronics division produces contract assembly services for customers in the computer, automotive, defense, medical, and telecommunications industries; also it sells furniture components to other manufacturers.

**Helen of Troy Limited (HELE)** *Price/earnings multiple on mean estimated earnings: 10.34 times.* HELE sells licensed personal-care products and accessories; its brand names are Vidal Sassoon, Revlon, WIGO, Karina, and Helen of Troy brands. Its hair-care items include hair dryers, curling irons, brushes, and mirrors. Manufacturers in Asia make the company's products under contract; the products are marketed primarily to retailers such as warehouse clubs and grocery stores.

**Federal Screw Works (FSCR)** *Price/earnings multiple: 4.62 times.* This company manufacturers fasteners and related items primarily for the auto industry. About 45 percent of its sales are to Ford Motor Corporation and 20 percent to General Motors. Items such as locknuts, bolts, and piston pins are sold. Its seven manufacturing plants are located in southern Michigan. Also the company has nonautomotive sales; these sales are mostly to manufacturers of durable goods.

**Scott Technologies, Inc. (SCTT)** *Price/earnings multiple on mean estimated earnings: 11.13 times.* This company makes Scott Air-Pak self-contained breathing devices, air-purifiers, gas detection instruments, and oxygen masks. Its primary customers include firefighters and aviation personnel and passengers. Its major customers include distributor Aviall and the U.S. government. The company also provides respiratory products maintenance and overhaul services.

**American Pacific Corporation (APFC)** *Price/earnings multiple: 4.05 times.* APFC makes launch rockets, propel missiles, deploy airbags, and fire suppressors. Customers include commercial satellite launchers, Cordant Technologies, which is about 40 percent of sales, NASA, and the U.S. military. About 90 percent of its sales are in the specialty chemical field. The company is the only U.S. manufacturer of ammonium perchlorate, which is a rocket fuel oxidizer.

**Escalade, Incorporated (ESCA)** *Price/earnings multiple: 7.50 times.* This company derives about two-thirds of its sales from sporting goods and the rest from office equipment. It makes basketball backboards, ping-pong tables, archery equipment, and dart cabinets. Sears, Roebuck accounts for about 25 percent of its sales. It also makes paper trimmers, folding machines, and check signers. Some of its brand names are Indian, Harvard, and Stiga.

**Knape & Vogt Manufacturing Company (KNAP)** *Price/earnings multiple: 7.92 times.* This company is a manufacturer of drawer slides, shelving systems, closet rods, and other hardware items related to storage; the company also makes ergonomic office products. It sells its products primarily to other manufacturers and to specialty distributors in the United States and Canada. Drawer slides account for almost half its sales. It also sells directly to consumers.

**K-Tron International, Inc. (KTII)** *Price/earnings multiple: 7.30 times.* KTII makes and sells gravimetric and volumetric feeders; these allow manufacturers worldwide to control the flow of solid bulk and liquid materials in the manufacturing process. Its pneumatic conveying equipment, sold under the Hurricane brand, includes filterless and powder hopper loaders. Its line also includes products that deliver precise control of the flow of ingredients.

**Lindberg Corporation (LIND)** *Price/earnings multiple: 6.66 times.* Lindberg heat-treats metal components to improve their mechanical properties, durability, and wear resistance. Its customers are in the automotive, defense, and consumer products industries. Twenty-four percent of its sales are in the commercial aerospace field. Its heat-treating processes include hardening, tempering, and annealing. Most of its operations are in the United States.

**STV Group, Incorporated (STVI)** *Price/earnings multiple: 4.65 times.* This company designs airport facilities, light-rail systems, and highways. It also provides architectural and engineering consulting and design services for governmental and industrial clients. Accounting for about 35 percent of sales is civil, highway, bridge, airport, and port engineering accounts. The company also works directly with construction firms on design–build projects.

**Sonesta International Hotels Corporation (SNSTA)** *Price/earnings multiple: 7.09 times.* Sonesta owns or operates 22 hotels in Bermuda, the Caribbean, Egypt, Italy, Peru, and the United States. The luxury properties it is associated with cater to upscale business and leisure travelers and are designed to show the culture and history of the exotic locations in which they are set. The company plans expansion, moving into places such as Atlanta, Houston, and New York City.

**Roanoke Electric Steel Corporation (RESC)**  *Price/earnings multiple: 5.45 times.* The company has a Shredded Products subsidiary that processes junked autos to supply the company's steel minimills with raw materials. Other subsidiaries use the merchant steel to produce joists used in construction. Steel of West Virginia, another subsidiary, makes customer steel for heavy machinery, guardrails, joists, and billets. The company serves customers in 21 states.

**PACCAR, Inc. (PCAR)**  *Price/earnings multiple: 4.99 times.* This company is the number three maker of trucks in the world, based on worldwide production. It trails DaimlerChrysler and Navistar. It makes light-, medium-, and heavy-duty trucks; these include the Kenworth, Petervilt, Dam Keykand DAF, and Foden lines. The company also produces aftermarket truck parts. It operates an online marketplace for the trucking industry.

**Park-Ohio Holdings Corporation (PKOH)**  *Price/earnings multiple on mean estimated earnings: 4.71 times.* PKOH provides logistics services and makes engineered products for the railroad, aerospace, auto, and other industries. Its aluminum products unit makes castings for the auto industry. The Ford Motor Corporation accounts for about 13 percent of sales. Its also makes forged and machined products, induction heating systems, and industrial rubber products.

**Napco Security Systems, Inc. (NSSC)**  *Price/earnings multiple: 7.35 times.* This company makes fire alarm controls, door alarms, digital-access control locks, alarm control panels, and infrared-heat detectors. It also manufactures panic buttons, which are personal emergency-response items; these can help an individual summon police or medical help. A majority of its products are sold to independent distributors and wholesalers.

**Village Super Market, Inc. (VLGEA)**  *Price/earnings multiple: 4.62 times.* This supermarket chain operates 21 ShopRite stores in New Jersey and one in northeastern Pennsylvania. It also operates, under the Village Market name, a former ShopRite. Village Super Market is a member of Wakefern Food, the largest retailer-owned food cooperative in the United States. Most of its operations are superstores; they average about 55,000 square feet.

**Waters Instruments, Inc. (WTRS)**  *Price/earnings multiple: 11.62 times.* WTRS makes electrical fence controllers for animal containment through its American FarmWorks Division; this division contributes 60 percent of its sales. It also makes electromechanical assemblies, printed circuit boards, and wiring harnesses. Its Waters Network Systems is soon to be merged with Garrett Communications. The company has contracted to make wiring harnesses for Winnebago.

**BCT International, Inc. (BCTI)** *Price/earnings multiple: 9.38 times.* This holding company has a subsidiary, Business Cards Tomorrow, which is a franchise printing chain; the subsidiary has about 90 locations in the United States, Canada, and Argentina. The franchise makes business cards, letterheads, and labels, and sells them to retail printers. The company also offers its customers, which include Kinko's and Office Max, delivery in 48 hours.

**Marsh Supermarkets, Inc. (MARSA)** *Price/earnings multiple on mean/estimated earnings: 9.46 times.* This is the leader of supermarket operators in Indianapolis; it operates about 90 March supermarkets and small, limited-service LoBill Foods stores in central Indiana and western Ohio. The company also operates about 1890 Village Pantry stores in that area, a distribution business that supplies those convenience stores, and about 1300 unaffiliated stores in nine states.

**McClain Industries, Inc. (MCCL)** *Price/earnings multiple: 6.66 times.* This company, through subsidiaries that include Galion and E-Z Pack, manufactures baling equipment, transfer trailers, sludge and detachable roll-off containers, compactors, and bodies for garbage and recycling trucks. It sells to distributors and others. It also operates a steel-tube mill and processes and warehouses steel products. The company sells its truck chassis to customers as well.

**RCM Technologies, Inc. (RCMT)** *Price/earnings multiple: 5.33 times.* The company offers information technology services; these services include design and implementation of technology and software systems, project management, and outsourced solutions. It also offers engineering consulting and services, as well as temporary staffing for office, clerical, and light industrial positions. RCMT operates in 26 states and Canada in over 70 offices.

**TBC Corporation (TBCC)** *Price/earnings multiple: 4.78 times.* This is the largest independent tire distributor in the nation, and it also sells and services tires through about 440 Big O Tires stores; most of these stores are franchised. The company distributes tires through more than 200 centers located across the United States and in Canada and Mexico. Its stores are located in about 20 states, mostly in the western United States and Canada. One customer accounts for about 10 percent of sales.

**Nash-Finch Company (NAFC)** *Price/earnings multiple: 5.41 times.* This company is a wholesale distributor; this activity accounts for about 80 percent of sales. The company also supplies fresh produce, frozen foods, meat and dairy products, and nonfood goods such as health and beauty aids, tobacco, and other products to about 2000 independent supermarkets and military bases. Its customers are in about 30 states, mostly in the Midwest, Southeast, and mid-Atlantic.

**Deb Shops, Inc. (DEBS)** *Price/earnings multiple: 7.20 times.* This company sells moderately priced sportswear, dresses, coats, lingerie, accessories, and shoes. Most of its customers are 13- to 18-year-old junior and plus-size females. It operates about 300 stores, located in over 35 states and primarily in malls. It also operates about 200 bookstores under the Atlantic Book Warehouse and Atlantic Book Shops names; books account for only about 7 percent of sales.

**Minntech Corporation (MNTX)** *Price/earnings multiple on mean estimated earnings: 8.60 times.* This company makes medical devices, sterilants, and water purification products; its products are sold under the names of Minntech, Minntech Renal Systems, and Minnetech Fibercor. Accounting for almost 70 percent of its sales are its kidney dialysis products; open-heart surgery products account for about 20 percent of sales. It produces other products that are used by the medical and other industries.

**S&K Famous Brands, Inc. (SKFB)** *Price/earnings multiple: 6.99 times.* This company sells men's suits, sportswear, and accessories at discount prices. It operates about 240 S&K Famous Brand Menswear stores in malls, shopping centers, and outlet centers in 27 states. Most of its stores are in the Midwest and South. It sells clothing bearing its own private labels, such as Roberto Villini and Tailors Row; along with the private label, it sells names such as Ralph Lauren and Bill Blass.

**American Physicians Service Group, Inc. (AMPH)** *Price/earnings multiple: 5.28 times.* The company manages malpractice insurance companies, medical practices, and investments. Its subsidiaries manage American Physicians Insurance Exchange, an exchange that writes insurance for subscribers in Texas and Arkansas; subscribers contribute to the exchange's surplus. It also offers brokerage and investment services.

**Isramco, Inc. (ISRL)** *Price/earnings multiple: 3.47 times.* The company operates the Shederot Venture, which has one onshore drilling license. It also operates the Negev Med Venture, which has five offshore drilling licenses, and the Yam Ashdod Carveout Venture, which has one offshore license. The company owns Jay Petroleum; this operation has proved reserves of 103,000 barrels of oil and 2.6 million cubic feet of gas in Louisiana, New Mexico, and other states.

**P&F Industries, Inc. (PFIN)** *Price/earnings multiple: 5.50 times.* This company sells air-powered tools, including sanders, grinders, drills, and saws; these products account for about two-thirds of sales. Sears and W.W. Grainger are important customers, accounting for about 45 percent sales of its Florida Pneumatic Manufacturing subsidiary, which sells the above products. Also the company makes baseboard heating products and other items.

**Integral Vision, Inc. (INVI)** *Price/earnings multiple on mean estimated earnings: 6.25 times.* INVI makes optical inspection equipment and software to improve the quality of manufactured equipment and the efficiency of the production process. The company recently sold its resistance-welding controls and systems division to Weltronic-Technitorn Corporation. About 73 percent of sales were from welding controls.

**NPC International, Inc. (NPCI)** *Price/earnings multiple on mean estimated earnings: 8.88 times.* The company is the largest franchisee of Pizza Hut restaurants in the world: it has almost 850 restaurants and delivery kitchens in 27 states. NPCI accounts for about 20 percent of the Pizza Hut franchises, and over 10 percent of the Pizza Hut system. Most of the restaurants are located in the southern United States. Also the company owns a 20 percent interest in Roma Restaurant Holdings.

**Intermet Corporation (INMT)** *Price/earnings multiple: 6.25 times.* This company makes castings for automakers; it is one of the largest independent manufacturers of this item. Among its castings are ductile iron, gray iron, and aluminum castings. These items are used for brake parts, steering components, differential cases, camshafts, and crankshafts; these items are used in passenger cars and lights trucks, heavy trucks, railroad, and other equipment.

**Ramsay Youth Services, Inc. (RYOU)** *Price/earnings multiple: 8.93 times.* This company was a mental-health-care provider that now offers youth services; its services are offered mostly through contracts with state and local government agencies trying to cut costs by privatizing juvenile social services programs. The young people it serves have behavioral or psychiatric disorders, substance abuse problems, or other disorders. It operates in eight states.

**Steel Technologies, Inc. (STTX)** *Price/earnings multiple: 4.70 times.* STTX processes flat-rolled steel for customers in the automotive appliance industries; this comprises about 60 percent of the company's sales. It also serves customers in the appliance, lawn and garden, machinery, and office equipment industries. It also makes steel blanks, which are customized steel forms supplied to manufacturers for processing into finished products.

APPENDIX B

# STOCKS OF THE NASDAQ-100 INDEX (QQQ)

| Company name | Symbol | % of index (adjusted) |
| --- | --- | --- |
| 3Com Corporation | COMS | 0.43 |
| Adaptec, Inc. | ADPT | 0.25 |
| ADC Telecommunications, Inc. | ADCT | 0.69 |
| Adelphia Communications Corporation | ADLAC | 0.44 |
| Adobe Systems Incorporated | ADBE | 0.37 |
| Altera Corporation | ALTR | 0.98 |
| Amazon.com, Inc. | AMZN | 0.73 |
| American Power Conversion Corporation | APCC | 0.34 |
| Amgen Inc. | AMGN | 1.7 |
| Apollo Group, Inc. | APOL | 0.08 |
| Apple Computer, Inc. | AAPL | 1.27 |

| Company name | Symbol | % of index (adjusted) |
|---|---|---|
| Applied Materials, Inc. | AMAT | 1.36 |
| Applied Micro Circuits Corporation | AMCC | 0.47 |
| At Home Corporation | ATHM | 0.58 |
| Atmel Corporation | ATML | 0.26 |
| Bed Bath & Beyond Inc. | BBBY | 0.28 |
| Biogen, Inc. | BGEN | 0.85 |
| Biomet, Inc. | BMET | 0.33 |
| BMC Software, Inc. | BMCS | 0.43 |
| BroadVision, Inc. | BVSN | 0.62 |
| Chiron Corporation | CHIR | 0.59 |
| CIENA Corporation | CIEN | 0.59 |
| Cintas Corporation | CTAS | 0.34 |
| Cisco Systems, Inc. | CSCO | 6.61 |
| Citrix Systems, Inc. | CTXS | 0.78 |
| CMGI, Inc. | CMGI | 1.78 |
| CNET, Inc. | CNET | 0.25 |
| Comcast Corporation | CMCSK | 0.93 |
| Compuware Corporation | CPWR | 0.28 |
| Comverse Technology, Inc. | CMVT | 0.6 |
| Concord EFS, Inc. | CEFT | 0.25 |
| Conexant Systems, Inc. | CNXT | 0.83 |
| Costco Systems, Inc. | CNXT | 0.83 |
| Dell Computer Corporation | DELL | 2.05 |
| Dollar Tree Stores, Inc. | DLTR | 0.13 |
| eBay Inc. | EBAY | 0.74 |
| EchoStar Communications Corporation | DISH | 0.53 |
| Electronic Arts Inc. | ERTS | 0.24 |
| Fiserv, Inc. | FISV | 0.28 |
| Gemstar International Group, Limited | GMST | 0.84 |
| Genzyme General | GENZ | 0.27 |
| Global Crossing Ltd | GBLX | 2.22 |
| Herman Miller, Inc. | MLHR | 0.06 |

# Appendix B  Stocks of the Nasdaq-100 Index (QQQ)

| Company name | Symbol | % of index (adjusted) |
|---|---|---|
| i2 Technologies, Inc. | ITWO | 1.06 |
| Immunex Corporation | IMNX | 1.37 |
| Intel Corporation | INTC | 5.58 |
| Intuit Inc. | INTU | 0.95 |
| JDS Uniphase Corporation | JDSU | 3.34 |
| KLA-Tencor Corporation | KLAC | 0.68 |
| Legato Systems, Inc. | LGTO | 0.13 |
| Level 3 Communications, Inc. | LVLT | 1.16 |
| Linear Technology Corporation | LLTC | 0.93 |
| LM Ericsson Telephone Company | ERICY | 0.82 |
| Lycos, Inc. | LCOS | 0.47 |
| Maxim Integrated Products, Inc. | MXIM | 1.07 |
| MCI WorldCom, Inc. | MXIM | 1.07 |
| McLeodUSA Incorporated | MCLD | 0.49 |
| MedImmune, Inc. | MEDI | 0.59 |
| Metromedia Fiber Network, Inc. | MFNX | 0.73 |
| Microchip Technology Incorporated | MCHP | 0.14 |
| Microsoft Corporation | MSFT | 9.4 |
| Molex Incorporated | MOLX | 0.21 |
| Network Appliance, Inc. | NTAP | 0.89 |
| Network Associates, Inc. | NETA | 0.2 |
| Network Solutions, Inc. | NSOL | 0.46 |
| Nextel Communications, Inc. | NXTL | 2.78 |
| NEXTLINK Communications, Inc. | NXLK | 0.37 |
| Northwest Airlines Corporation | NWAC | 0.07 |
| Novell, Inc. | NOVL | 0.72 |
| NTL Incorporated | NTLI | 0.71 |
| Oracle Corporation | ORCL | 3.51 |
| PACCAR Inc. | PCAR | 0.18 |
| PacifiCare Health Systems, Inc. | PHSY | 0.1 |
| PanAmSat Corporation | SPOT | 0.59 |
| Parametric Technology Corporation | PMTC | 0.4 |

| Company name | Symbol | % of index (adjusted) |
|---|---|---|
| Paychex, Inc. | PAYX | 0.54 |
| PeopleSoft, Inc. | PSFT | 0.48 |
| PMC–Sierra, Inc. | PMCS | 0.65 |
| QLogic Corporation | QLGC | 0.33 |
| QUALCOMM Incorporated | QCOM | 6.53 |
| Quintiles Transnational Corp. | QTRN | 0.2 |
| RealNetworks, Inc. | RNWK | 0.53 |
| RF Micro Devices, Inc. | RFMD | 0.37 |
| Sanmina Corporation | SANM | 0.34 |
| SDL, Inc. | SDLI | 0.47 |
| Siebel Systems, Inc. | SEBL | 0.91 |
| Sigma-Aldrich Corporation | SIAL | 0.18 |
| Smurfit-Stone Container Corporation | SSCC | 0.22 |
| Staples, Inc. | SPLS | 0.37 |
| Starbucks Corporation | SBUX | 0.31 |
| Sun Microsystems, Inc. | SUNW | 2.65 |
| Synopsys, Inc. | SNPS | 0.22 |
| Tellabs, Inc. | TLAB | 0.8 |
| USA Networks, Inc. | USAI | 0.41 |
| VERITAS Software Corporation | VRTS | 2.04 |
| VISX, Incorporated | VISX | 0.11 |
| Vitesse Semiconductor Corporation | VTSS | 0.43 |
| VoiceStream Wireless Corporation | VSTR | 0.67 |
| Xilinx, Inc. | XLNX | 0.99 |
| Yahoo! Inc. | YHOO | 2.22 |

# APPENDIX C

# THE TOP 50 CAP-WEIGHTED STOCKS IN THE NASDAQ-100 INDEX

The forward P/E ratio is included in the following list. The P/E is not as relevant an investment measurement to this growth group as a P/E might be to a value listing of stocks. Included also are the phone numbers for the companies, as well as an investor relations person, if one is specified. At virtually all companies investors and traders are encouraged to call and speak with the investor relations representatives as part of a due diligence process, so don't hesitate. Web sites are also included. As part of your due diligence, going to the Web site to get a sense of the company and to learn more about it before investing makes good sense. The earnings estimates are courtesy of Zacks Investment Research.

**ADC Telecommunications, Inc. (ADCT)** *P/E multiple based on estimated earnings for 2001, 32 times. www.adc.com.* Investor relations, 612-939-8080. The company manufactures systems that regulate the transmitting rate of voice, data, and radio signals. The regional Bell operating companies are the main customers. The company's products cover the problems that arise when slower systems connect to high-speed network systems and to end users and also include ADCT design installation systems. The company plans to continue its push into the wireless market.

**Altera Corporation (ALTR)**  *Estimated earnings for 2001, $1.91; P/E multiple based on mean estimated earnings for 2001, 19 times. www.altera.com.* Investor relations, 408-544-8303. The company, for the do-it-yourself customers, makes programmable logic devices that are high density. The company also makes standard integrated circuits that customers can program on their own. The programmable logic devices are made for different markets, one of which is for a system-on-a-chip application. The company sells almost all of its products through distributors; the company's business is international, with almost half its sales outside North America.

**Amazon.com, Inc. (AMZN)**  *Mean estimated earnings for 2001, (loss) $0.68; P/E not applicable. www.amazon.com.* Investor relations, 206-622-2335. The company sells products through its Web site. Thirteen million people in more than 160 countries have shopped at Amazon.com. Amazon is a source of information on over 150,000 movies and entertainment programs, and offers other online shopping services such as drugstore.com, an online retail and information source for personal-care items, pharmacy, and other products; pets.com, the largest pet-supply company on the Internet that also offers information for pet owners.

**Amgen, Inc. (AMGN)**  *P/E based on mean estimated earnings for 2001, 51 times. www.amgen.com.* Investor relations, Carl Rosansky, 1-800-84-AMGEN. The company makes EPOGEN, which is an antianemia drug; the drug Neupogen, which stimulates the immune system; Infergen, a treatment for hepatitis C. Amgen has alliances with companies such as Johnson & Johnson, and Kirin, the Japanese brewer that is also involved in pharmaceuticals. Amgen is a major company in the biotech field. The company makes and markets products for soft-tissue repair, inflammation, and autoimmunity.

**Apple Computer, Inc. (AAPL)**  *P/E multiple based on mean estimated earnings for 2002, 15 times. www.apple.com.* Investor relations, 877-438-2775. Apple makes and markets the Macintosh computer, the multicolored iMac, the Macintosh Operating System, and other computer products. The company is branching out into lower-cost network computers and products for the Web. A subsidiary, File Maker, is involved in database solutions from the desktop to the Web; custom Web publishing that is easy to use is offered. AAPL is coming back from a near-death marketing and sales slump.

**Applied Materials, Inc. (AMAT)** *P/E multiple based on mean estimated earnings for 2001, 13 times. www.appliedmaterials.com.* Investor relations, 408-748-5227. Applied Materials is the leader in manufacturing semiconductor water facilitation equipment. Its customers include Intel, Motorola, and Advanced Micro Devices. Recently the company settled a lawsuit in which it accused a supplier of stealing its blueprint. The company shipped 500 Metal Etech DPS chambers, making it among the leaders in making semiconductor chips. Semiconductor equipment is a dynamically growing industry.

**At Home Corporation (ATHM)** *Mean estimated earnings for 2001, (loss). www.home.net.* Investor relations, 650-556-5000. The company was formed when the broadband access provider AT Home bought Excite, the Web portal. Through a subsidiary, the company offers free Internet access; Excite offers content, e-mail, and search services. At Home announced that Excite search reached a milestone of indexing 250 million Web pages, making it the largest index among the top-ranking portals. ATHM is involved in other aspects of the Internet.

**Biogen, Inc. (BGEN)** *P/E multiple based on mean estimated earnings for 2001, 27 times.* Investor relations, Elizabeth Woo, 617-679-2812. The company researches, manufacturers, and markets biopharmaceuticals to treat many ailments. The company also licenses drugs it has developed to other companies; some of the developed products are alpha interferon and a hepatitis vaccine. The company announced that in a study its Avanen drug slowed down the development of multiple sclerosis so significantly that the study will terminate early. Biogen is one of the major biotech companies.

**BroadVision, Inc. (BVSN)** *P/E multiple based on mean estimated earnings for 2001, 85 times. www.broadvision.com.* Investor relations, 650-261-5100. This company helps companies design their own Web sites for online marketing. Its software, named One-To-One, allows users to complete on-line transactions such as filling orders, billing, and costs services. Included as customers are Cyberian Outpost and Oracle. Forty percent of sales are in Europe and Asia. Broadvision recently announced a number of newer customers and revenue expansion in Europe.

**Chiron Corporation (CHIR)** *P/E multiple based on mean estimated earnings for 2001, 49 times. www.chiron.com.* Investor relations, 510-923-6055. The company develops preventatives and treatments for a number of diseases such as AIDS, cancer, and cardiovascular disease. Chiron carries out its research with educational institutions and large pharmaceutical companies. Recently the company's nucleic acid systems were competitively selected by the Australian Red Cross to screen the country's blood supply.

**CIENA Corporation (CIEN)** *P/E multiple based on mean estimated earnings for 2001, 137 times. www.ciena.com.* Investor relations, 410-865-8500. The company makes MultiWave systems including optical amplifiers, optical transmission terminals, and network management software. Its customers include Sprint, Teleway Japan, and MCI WorldCom. Cienna Corporation created new markets when it developed the first dense wavelength division multiplexing systems (DWDM). Also the company has developed intelligent optical network architecture.

**Cisco Systems, Inc. (CSCO)** *Estimated earnings for 2001, $1.27; P/E multiple based on mean estimated earnings for 2002, 50 times. www.cisco.com.* Investor relations, 408-526-4000. Cisco controls over 75 percent of the global market for products that power the Internet, including routers and switches. The company has made alliances with IBM, Motorola, Sun Microsystems, and others. Routers differ from switches in that they use software for directing data; switches transmit data only. Recently equipment has been developed that blends both functions.

**Citrix Systems, Inc. (CTXS)** *P/E multiple based on mean estimated earnings for 2001, 35 times. www.citrix.com.* Investor relations, 888-595-CTXS. Citrix offers application server software and services that enable users to operate applications or servers that can be accessed from many different devices. CTXS has over 100,000 worldwide customers. The benefits of the company's system are that they extend the reach of any application to any user in any location.

**CMGI, Inc. (CMGI)** *Price earnings based on loss for year 2002, not applicable (loss). www.cmgi.com.* Investor relations, Catherine Taylor, 978-684-3832. The company's business is creating and managing the largest and most diverse network of Internet companies in the world. The CMGI network is comprised of 60 companies; CMGI controls billions of dollars in marketable securities.

**Comcast Corporation (CMCSK)** *P/E multiple based on mean estimated earnings for 2001, not applicable (loss). www.comcast.com.* Investor relations, Marlene S. Dooner at *ir@comcast.com*. The company is the third-largest cable operator in the United States, with about 3.4 million customers; Comcast has a majority interest in QVC, the shopping network.

**Conexant Systems, Inc. (CNXT)** *P/E multiple based on mean estimated earnings for 2002, 25 times. www.conexant.com.* Investor relations, 800-854-8099. Conexant is the world's largest company providing semiconductor products for communications electronics. It uses its mixed-signal processing expertise for a wide number of applications.

**Costco Wholesale Corporation (COST)**  *P/E multiple based on mean estimated earnings for 2002, 20 times. www.costco.com.* For investor relations, go to home page and click on. The company is a major retailer; it operates warehouse-sized shopping stores for retail customers. Among its products are general merchandise, food products, and business and healthcare plans.

**Dell Computer Corporation (DELL)**  *P/E multiple based on mean estimated earnings for 2002, 17 times. www.dell.com.* Investor relations, Ken Kasman, 512-728-7800. The company is one of the world's top PC manufacturers, and the leading direct-sale computer supplier in the world. It also sells computer hardware and markets computer software and peripherals.

**eBay, Inc. (EBAY)**  *P/E multiple based on mean estimated earnings for 2001, 97 times. www.ebay.com.* Investor relations, 409-558-7400. eBay is the biggest person-to-person online trading community in the world. At the company's Web site, a person can bid for merchandise or offer merchandise; there are more than 2 million categories and 2.5 million auctions a day.

**Gemstar International Group, Inc. (GMST)**  *P/E multiple based on mean estimated earnings for 2002, 41 times. www.gemstar.com.* Investor relations, 626-792-5700. Gemstar has licensed its technology to many TV and VCR makers. Its products allow users to review TV listings and use them to program their TV or VCR.

**Global Crossing, Ltd. (GBLX)**  *P/E multiple based on mean estimated earnings for 2001, not applicable (loss). www.globalcrossing.com/index.asp.* Investor relations, Jenson Chow, 800-836-0342. The company is the world's first independent long-distance telecommunications facilitator and service provider. It uses a network of undersea digital fiber-optic cable systems and other sources.

**i2 Technologies, Inc. (ITWO)**  *Estimated earnings for next fiscal year, $1.08; P/E multiple based on mean estimated earnings for 2001, 152 times. www.i2.com.* Investor relations, 214-860-6000. The company produces RHYTHM software that helps manufacturers plan and schedule production operations. Also i2 is becoming a leader in Internet-based production process applications.

**Immunex Corporation (IMNX)**  *P/E multiple based on mean estimated earnings for 2001, 151 times. www.immunex.com.* Investor relations, Mark R. Leahy, 206-389-4363. Immunex is a leading biopharmaceutical company; its products apply immune system science to protect health in humans. The company has many FDA-approved products.

**Intel Corporation (INTC)**   *P/E multiple based on mean estimated earnings for 2001, 21 times. www.intel.com.* Investor relations, 408-765-8080. The company has developed technology to support the computer and Internet revolution worldwide. Intel is a major supplier for networking and communication equipment, computer chips, and other products.

**Intuit, Inc. (INTU)**   *P/E multiple based on mean estimated earnings for 2002, 48 times. www.intuit.com.* Investor relations, 650-944-6000. The company is the pioneer in e-finance by adding online banking and bill payment to its software products. It now offers one-stop shopping for insurance and mortgages; it also offers information to customers on investing and preparing taxes and other financial items.

**JDS Uniphase Corporation (JDSU)**   *P/E multiple based on mean estimated earnings for 2002, 53 times. www.uniphase.com.* Investor relations, 408-434-1800. This high-technology company designs, develops, produces, and markets products for the fiber-optic communications market. The market is comprised of system manufacturers worldwide. End users include those in the telecommunications, computer monitors, and fax machines industries.

**KLA-Tencor Corporation (KLAC)**   *P/E multiple based on mean estimated earnings for 2002, 12 times. www.kla-tencor.com.* Investor relations, 408-875-3000. The company provides the systems, software, and operating knowledge for semiconductor manufacturers. Its yield diagnostics and solution products accelerate solutions by converting inspection and measurement data into critical signatures and sources.

**Level 3 Communications, Inc. (LVLT)**   *Loss estimated for 2001 and 2002. www.l3.com.* Investor relations, Julie Stangl, 877-585-8266. The company offers high-speed connectivity to the global Internet in the United States and Europe; it also integrates its network to provide a solution for routing voice traffic. An international solution provider, the company offers custom tailored IT solutions and also provides infrastructure.

**Linear Technology Corporation (LLTC)**   *P/E multiple based on mean estimated earnings for 2002, 30 times. www.linear-tech.com.* Investor relations, 408-432-1900. LLTC designs, produces, and distributes high-performance linear integrated circuits. Among its applications are telecommunications, notebook and desktop computers, peripherals, cellular telephones, and industrial and automotive controls.

**LM Ericsson Telephone Company (ERICY)** *P/E multiple based on mean estimated earnings for 2001, 42 times. www.ericsson.com.* Investor relations, Stockholm 468-719-000. This company is a leader in telecommunications; it is well known for advanced systems and products for use by the public and private networks in mobile communications. The company also offers Internet-based technology products.

**Maxim Integrated Products, Inc. (MXIM)** *P/E multiple based on mean estimated earnings for 2002, 32 times. www.maxim-ic.com.* Investor relations, 800-998-8800. The company is a leader in designing, developing, and manufacturing linear and mixed-signal integrated circuits. Its products include microprocessor supervisory circuits, data converters, amplifiers, management products, timers, and counters.

**MCI WorldCom, Inc. (WCOM)** *P/E multiple based on mean estimated earnings for 2001, 11 times. www.wcom.com.* Investor relations, 877-624-9266. The company operates in more than 65 countries, providing facilities-based and fully integrated local, long-distance, international, and Internet services. The company is the second-largest long-distance carrier in the United States. Its global network is built for date-intensive communications.

**MedImmune, Inc. (MEDI)** *P/E multiple based on mean estimated earnings for 2001, 62 times. www.medimmune.com.* Investor relations, 301-417-0770. MedImmune is a major biotechnology company. Among its products is Synogis, a drug used to prevent serious lower-respiratory-tract disease. It also has a licensing agreement with Columbia University to develop an antibody against the effects of cocaine overdose.

**Metromedia Fiber Network, Inc. (MFNX)** *Loss expected for 2000 and 2001. www.mmfn.com.* Investor relations, 914-421-6700. The company operates optics networks in Chicago, New York, Philadelphia, and other major cities. It also offers international services. Bell Atlantic uses the company's network; Metromedia Corporation owns a majority stake.

**Microsoft Corporation (MSFT)** *P/E multiple based on mean estimated earnings for 2002, 26 times. www.microsoft.com.* Investor relations, 925-882-8080. Since the company started in 1975, it has created software for the personal computer for school and home. The company is the world's leading software provider; its products include items for use in Internet-related technologies; it is invested in a plethora of other Internet enterprises.

**Network Appliance, Inc. (NTAP)** *P/E multiple based on mean estimated earnings for 2002, 120 times. www.netapp.com.* Investor relations, 408-822-

6000. The company markets and supports high-performance network data storage devices. Its products provide fast, reliable file services for network environments that are data intensive.

**Nextel Communications, Inc. (NXTL)** *Losses expected in 2000 and 2001. www.nextel.com.* Investor relations, 703-433-4300. The company is the world leader in providing fully integrated, guaranteed digital wireless services. It offers all-in-one solutions, integrating voice mail, text, and numeric paging capabilities. Its phone offers a feature that allows a user to contact, at the touch of a button, up to 100 coworkers instantly. The company has about 3.6 million subscribers.

**Novell, Inc. (NOVL)** *P/E multiple based on mean estimated earnings for 2001, 24 times. www.novell.com.* Investor relations, *www.novell.com/corp/ir/index.html.* The company is a leading provider of net services software that delivers services to power and secure networks, both the Internet and intranet. Novell serves wired and wireless users, corporate and private; its products spread across all operating systems.

**NTL Incorporated (NTLI)** *Losses estimated for 2000 and 2001. www.ntl.com.* Investor relations, 800-183-1234. The company has been the backbone in U.K. communications since the 1950s. It provides technology allowing radio and television to enter the house; its systems support emergency services. It supports the biggest Internet services, including Virgin net; over a million homes in the United Kingdom use its cable television.

**Oracle Corporation (ORCL)** *P/E multiple based on mean estimated earnings for 2002, 46 times. www.oracle.com.* Investor relations, 650-506-4073. The company delivers the Internet platform to meet business needs for high availability. The company provides complete high availability e-business from databases to application servers to enterprise applications. Its products make possible buying, selling, and communication over the Internet, allowing access to Web sites.

**PanAmSat Corporation (SPOT)** *P/E multiple based on mean estimated earnings for 2001, 497 times. www.panamsat.com.* Investor relations, 203-622-6664. SPOT operates a global network of 21 state-of-the-art satellites and 7 technical ground facilities. It is the leading commercial provider of communications services that are satellite based in the world. SPOT supplies companies such as the BBC, Discovery Channel, and Disney.

**Paychex, Inc. (PAYX)** *P/E multiple based on mean estimated earnings for 2002, 49 times. www.paychex.com.* Investor relations, Jan Shuler, 716-383-3406. The company provides cost-effective payroll, payroll tax preparation, and human relations solutions for small- and medium-sized businesses. Employees are required to withhold specific employment taxes, and Paychex performs services expediting this task. Almost 4 million Americans depend on its services.

**PMC–Sierra, Inc. (PMCS)** *P/E multiple based on mean estimated earnings for 2001, 60 times. www.pmc-sierra.com.* Investor relations, 604-415-6144. This company develops networking semiconductor parts that improve speed and performance on the Internet and other networks. Cisco Systems, Lucent Technologies, and other companies integrate the company's products into their own networking applications. The company operates globally.

**Qualcomm, Incorporated (QCOM)** *P/E multiple based on mean estimated earnings for 2002, 56 times. www.qualcomm.com.* Investor relations, Julie McClure, 858-658-4813. The company was active in developing code-division multiple access (CDMA) technology. It is a major manufacturer of digital cell phones and is also active in wireless data technology. It is active in a joint venture developing a system of low-orbiting satellites.

**Siebel Systems, Inc. (SEBL)** *P/E multiple based on mean estimated earnings for 2001, 121 times. www.siebel.com.* Investor relations, 650-295-5111. Siebel Systems is a leading supplier of software. Among its customers are Glaxo Wellcome, Lucent Technologies, and Prudential Insurance. The company also offers decision support and client information services across its computer network; it has a global operation.

**Sun Microsystems, Inc. (SUNW)** *P/E multiple based on mean estimated earnings for 2002, 36 times. www.sun.com.* Investor relations, 800-801-7869. This company is a leader in manufacturing UNIX-based storage devices and servers for supplying computer networks and Web sites. The company's computer uses its own manufactured chips. Its JAVA programming language creates software that runs on any kind of computer.

**VERITAS Software Corporation (VRTS)** *P/E multiple based on mean estimated earnings for 2001, 110 times. www.veritas.com.* Investor relations, Dave Galiotto, 650-335-8000. The company is a leading manufacturer of management software. It has gone into partnership with many manufacturers, including Hewlett-Packard and Microsoft. Its software guards against data loss and expedites data recovery. Some of its customers are BMW, Lucent, and Oracle.

**VoiceStream Wireless Corporation (VSTR)** *Losses expected for 2000 and 2001. www.voicestream.com.* Investor relations, 425-653-4600. The company provides PCS service. The company has about 450,000 customers, serving Salt Lake City, Denver, Seattle, Boise, and other areas. It also has a minority interest in a venture with Cook Inlet Regional. VoiceStream has interest in over 100 licenses.

**Xilinx (XLNX)**   *P/E multiple based on mean estimated earnings for 2002, 25 times. www.xilinx.com.* Investor relations, 1-800-836-4002. XLNX makes programmable logic devices. It also distributes the software necessary to customize its chips. The company's chips are used in the telecommunications, data processing, industrial and medical instrumentation, and other markets. Europe accounts for about 25 percent of its sales.

**Yahoo! Inc. (YHOO)**   *P/E multiple based on mean estimated earnings for 2001, 55 times. www.yahoo.com.* Manager, Investor Relations, Andrea Klipfel, 408-731-3300. Yahoo is among the top of the Internet portals; over 36 million people a month visit the company. Recently the company joined with Kmart to initiate an online store. Its site offers e-mail, chat rooms, auctions, and many other features.

# APPENDIX D

# NASDAQ STOCKS THAT ARE IN THE S&P INDEXES

For the following listing, use S&P500 for the S&P 500 Index, MIDCAP for the S&P MidCap 400 Index, and SCI600 for the S&P Small-Cap 600 Index.

| Symbol | Company | Index |
|---|---|---|
| ADCT | ADC Telecommunications | S&P500 |
| AVTC | AVT Corp | SCI600 |
| AXTI | AXT Inc | SCI600 |
| ACDO | Accredo Health | SCI600 |
| ACTL | Actel Corp | SCI600 |
| ACTN | Action Performance Cos | SCI600 |
| ACXM | Acxiom Corp | MIDCAP |
| ADPT | Adaptec Inc | S&P500 |
| ADAP | Adaptive Broadband | SCI600 |

| Symbol | Company | Index |
|---|---|---|
| ADBE | Adobe Systems | S&P500 |
| ADTN | Adtran Inc | MIDCAP |
| ADVP | Advance Paradigm | SCI600 |
| AEIS | Advanced Energy Indus | SCI600 |
| AFCI | Advanced Fibre Communic | MIDCAP |
| ATIS | Advanced Tissue Sciences | SCI600 |
| ARXX | Aeroflex Inc | SCI600 |
| ALEX | Alexander & Baldwin | MIDCAP |
| ALLP | Alliance Pharmaceutical | SCI600 |
| ALSC | Alliance Semiconductor | SCI600 |
| AHAA | Alpha Indus | SCI600 |
| ALTR | Altera Corp | S&P500 |
| AEOS | Amer Eagle Outfitters | MIDCAP |
| AFWY | Amer Freightways | SCI600 |
| AMSY | Amer Mgmt Systems | SCI600 |
| APCC | Amer Power Conversion | S&P500 |
| AMGN | Amgen Inc | S&P500 |
| ALOG | Analogic Corp | SCI600 |
| ANLY | Analysts Intl | SCI600 |
| ABCW | Anchor Bancorp Wisc | SCI600 |
| SLOT | Anchor Gaming | SCI600 |
| ANDW | Andrew Corp | S&P500 |
| ANTC | ANTEC Corp | MIDCAP |
| APOG | Apogee Enterprises | SCI600 |
| APOL | Apollo Group 'A' | MIDCAP |
| AAPL | Apple Computer | S&P500 |
| APPB | Applebee's Intl | SCI600 |
| AMAT | Applied Materials | S&P500 |
| ACAT | Arctic Cat | SCI600 |
| ABFS | Arkansas Best | SCI600 |
| AIND | Arnold Indus | SCI600 |
| ATSN | Artesyn Technologies | SCI600 |
| ASHW | Ashworth Inc | SCI600 |

APPENDIX D  NASDAQ STOCKS THAT ARE IN THE S&P INDEXES

| Symbol | Company | Index |
|---|---|---|
| ASPT | Aspect Communications | SCI600 |
| AZPN | Aspen Technology | SCI600 |
| ASBC | Associated Banc-Corp | MIDCAP |
| ASTE | Astec Industries | SCI600 |
| ASFC | Astoria Financial | MIDCAP |
| ACAI | Atlantic Coast Airlines Hldgs | SCI600 |
| ATML | Atmel Corp | MIDCAP |
| VOXX | Audiovox CI 'A' | SCI600 |
| ASPX | Auspex Systems | SCI600 |
| ADSK | Autodesk, Inc | S&P500 |
| AVNT | Avant Corp | SCI600 |
| AVID | Avid Technology | SCI600 |
| AVCT | Avocent Corp | MIDCAP |
| AWRE | Aware Inc | SCI600 |
| BSYS | BISYS Group | MIDCAP |
| BMCS | BMC Software | S&P500 |
| JBAK | Baker(J.) Inc | SCI600 |
| BKNG | Banknorth Group | MIDCAP |
| BARZ | BARRA Inc | SCI600 |
| BSET | Bassett Furniture | SCI600 |
| BEAV | BE Aerospace | SCI600 |
| BBBY | Bed Bath & Beyond | S&P500 |
| BELFB | Bel Fuse Inc 'B' | SCI600 |
| BELM | Bell Microproducts | SCI600 |
| BILL | Billing Concepts | SCI600 |
| BTGC | Bio-Technology Genl | SCI600 |
| BGEN | Biogen Inc | S&P500 |
| BMET | Biomet, Inc | S&P500 |
| BBOX | Black Box Corp | SCI600 |
| BOBE | Bob Evans Farms | MIDCAP |
| BAMM | Books-A-Million | SCI600 |
| BCGI | Boston Communications Grp | SCI600 |
| CELL | Brightpoint Inc | SCI600 |

| Symbol | Company | Index |
|---|---|---|
| BRCM | Broadcom Corp 'A' | S&P500 |
| BVSN | BroadVision Inc | S&P500 |
| BRKT | Brooktrout Inc | SCI600 |
| TMBR | Tom Brown | SCI600 |
| BMHC | Building Materials Hldg | SCI600 |
| CBRL | CBRL Group | MIDCAP |
| CUBE | C-Cube Microsystems | SCI600 |
| CCBL | C-COR.net Corp | SCI600 |
| CACI | CACI Int'l | SCI600 |
| CDWC | CDW Computer Centers | MIDCAP |
| CHRW | C.H. Robinson Worldwide | MIDCAP |
| CSGS | CSG Systems Intl | MIDCAP |
| CUNO | CUNO Inc | SCI600 |
| CCMP | Cabot Microelectronics | MIDCAP |
| CDIS | Cal Drive Intl | SCI600 |
| CSAR | Caraustar Industries | SCI600 |
| CASY | Casey's Genl Stores | SCI600 |
| CACOA | Cato Corp 'A' | SCI600 |
| CEPH | Cephalon Inc | SCI600 |
| CERN | Cerner Corp | SCI600 |
| CKFR | CheckFree Corp | MIDCAP |
| CAKE | Cheesecake Factory | SCI600 |
| CHCS | Chico's FAS | SCI600 |
| CHIR | Chiron Corp | S&P500 |
| CINF | Cincinnati Financial | S&P500 |
| CTAS | Cintas Corp | MIDCAP |
| CRUS | Cirrus Logic | MIDCAP |
| CSCO | Cisco Systems | S&P500 |
| CTXS | Citrix Systems | S&P500 |
| COKE | Coca-Cola Bott Consol | SCI600 |
| CGNX | Cognex Corp | SCI600 |
| COHR | Coherent, Inc | SCI600 |
| COHU | Cohu Inc | SCI600 |

APPENDIX D   NASDAQ STOCKS THAT ARE IN THE S&P INDEXES

| Symbol | Company | Index |
|---|---|---|
| CMCSK | Comcast CI 'A' Spl(non-vtg) | S&P500 |
| CMIN | Commonwealth Industries | SCI600 |
| CFBX | Community First Bankshares | SCI600 |
| CBSS | Compass Bancshares | MIDCAP |
| CPWR | Compuware Corp | S&P500 |
| CMVT | Comverse Technology | S&P500 |
| CCRD | Concord Communications | SCI600 |
| CEFT | Concord EFS | MIDCAP |
| CNXT | Conexant Systems | S&P500 |
| CNMD | Conmed Corp | SCI600 |
| CPRT | Copart Inc | SCI600 |
| CORR | COR Therapeutics | MIDCAP |
| CPWM | Cost Plus | SCI600 |
| COST | Costco Wholesale | S&P500 |
| CVTY | Coventry Health Care | SCI600 |
| CMOS | Credence Systems | MIDCAP |
| CURE | Curative Health Svcs | SCI600 |
| CYGN | Cygnus Inc | SCI600 |
| CYMI | Cymer Inc | SCI600 |
| CYRK | Cyrk Inc | SCI600 |
| STXN | DMC Stratex Networks | SCI600 |
| DSPG | DSP Group | MIDCAP |
| DMRK | Damark International 'A' | SCI600 |
| DSCP | Datascope Corp | SCI600 |
| DAVX | Davox Corp | SCI600 |
| DELL | Dell Computer Corp | S&P500 |
| DRTE | Dendrite International | SCI600 |
| XRAY | DENTSPLY International | MIDCAP |
| DGII | Digi International | SCI600 |
| DNEX | Dionex Corp | SCI600 |
| DXYN | Dixie Group | SCI600 |
| DLTR | Dollar Tree Stores | MIDCAP |
| DBRN | Dress Barn | SCI600 |

| Symbol | Company | Index |
|---|---|---|
| DRYR | Dreyer's Gr Ice Cr | MIDCAP |
| DPMI | DuPont Photomasks | SCI600 |
| EAGL | EGL Inc | MIDCAP |
| ESST | ESS Technology | SCI600 |
| EGRP | E*Trade Group | MIDCAP |
| EWBC | East West Bancorp | SCI600 |
| EDGW | Edgewater Technology | SCI600 |
| ESIO | Electro Scientific Ind | SCI600 |
| EGLS | Electroglas Inc | SCI600 |
| ERTS | Electronic Arts | MIDCAP |
| ELOY | eLoyalty Corp | SCI600 |
| EMMS | Emmis Communications 'A' | MIDCAP |
| EPRE | ePresence Inc | SCI600 |
| EXBT | Exabyte Corp | SCI600 |
| EXPD | Expeditors Intl, Wash | MIDCAP |
| ESRX | Express Scripts 'A' | MIDCAP |
| FYII | F.Y.I. Inc | SCI600 |
| FTUS | Factory 2-U Stores | SCI600 |
| FAST | Fastenal Co | MIDCAP |
| FITB | Fifth Third Bancorp | S&P500 |
| FILE | FileNet Corp | SCI600 |
| FHCC | First Health Group | MIDCAP |
| FMBI | First Midwest Bancorp | SCI600 |
| FMER | FirstMerit Corp | MIDCAP |
| FISV | Fiserv Inc | MIDCAP |
| FLOW | Flow International | SCI600 |
| FWRD | Forward Air | SCI600 |
| FOSL | Fossil Inc | SCI600 |
| FRTZ | Fritz Companies | SCI600 |
| FULL | Fuller (HB) | MIDCAP |
| GKSRA | G & K Services Cl 'A' | SCI600 |
| GBCB | GBC Bancorp | SCI600 |
| GNCMA | Genl Communication 'A' | SCI600 |

APPENDIX D  NASDAQ STOCKS THAT ARE IN THE S&P INDEXES

| Symbol | Company | Index |
|---|---|---|
| GNTX | Gentex Corp | SCI600 |
| GENZ | Genzyme Corp-Genl Div | MIDCAP |
| GILD | Gilead Sciences | MIDCAP |
| GDYS | Goody's Family Clothing | SCI600 |
| GPSI | Great Plains Software | SCI600 |
| GBBK | Greater Bay Bancorp | MIDCAP |
| GYMB | Gymboree Corp | SCI600 |
| HNCS | HNC Software | SCI600 |
| HGGR | Haggar Corp | SCI600 |
| HAIN | Hain Celestial Group | SCI600 |
| HAKI | Hall, Kinion & Assoc | |
| HLIT | Harmonic Inc | SCI600 |
| HTLD | Heartland Express | SCI600 |
| HSII | Heidrick & Struggles Intl | SCI600 |
| HELX | Helix Technology | SCI600 |
| JKHY | Henry (Jack) & Assoc | MIDCAP |
| HOLX | Hologic Inc | SCI600 |
| JBHT | Hunt(JB) Transport | MIDCAP |
| HBAN | Huntington Bancshares | S&P500 |
| HTCH | Hutchinson Technology | SCI600 |
| HYSL | Hyperion Solutions | SCI600 |
| IDPH | IDEC Pharmaceuticals | MIDCAP |
| IDXX | IDEXX Laboratories | SCI600 |
| IMNR | Immune Response | SCI600 |
| INCY | Incyte Genomics | MIDCAP |
| INFS | InFocus Corp | MIDCAP |
| IRIC | Information Resources | SCI600 |
| IFMX | Informix Corp | MIDCAP |
| INVX | Innovex Inc | SCI600 |
| NSIT | Insight Enterprises | SCI600 |
| INSUA | Insituform Technol 'A' | SCI600 |
| IAAI | Insurance Auto Auctions | SCI600 |
| IDTI | Integrated Device Tech | MIDCAP |

| Symbol | Company | Index |
|---|---|---|
| INTC | Intel Corp | S&P500 |
| INTL | Inter-Tel Inc | SCI600 |
| IFSIA | Interface Inc 'A' | SCI600 |
| INMT | Intermet Corp | SCI600 |
| IFCI | Intl Fibercom Inc | SCI600 |
| ISCA | Intl Speedway 'A' | MIDCAP |
| INTV | InterVoice-Brite Inc | SCI600 |
| INTU | Intuit Inc | S&P500 |
| IFIN | Investors Finl Svcs | MIDCAP |
| ITRI | Itron Inc | SCI600 |
| JJSF | J & J Snack Foods | SCI600 |
| JDSU | JDS Uniphase Corp | S&P500 |
| JAKK | JAKKS Pacific | SCI600 |
| KLAC | KLA-Tencor Corp | S&P500 |
| KSWS | K Swiss Inc 'A' | SCI600 |
| KAMNA | Kaman Corp CI 'A' | SCI600 |
| KELYA | Kelly Services 'A' | MIDCAP |
| KOPN | Kopin Corp | SCI600 |
| KROG | Kroll-O'Gara Co | SCI600 |
| KRON | Kronos Inc | SCI600 |
| KLIC | Kulicke & Soffa Ind | SCI600 |
| LRCX | Lam Research | MIDCAP |
| LANC | Lancaster Colony | MIDCAP |
| LNCE | Lance, Inc | MIDCAP |
| LSTR | Landstar System | SCI600 |
| LVCI | Laser Vision Centers | SCI600 |
| LSCC | Lattice Semiconductor | MIDCAP |
| LAWS | Lawson Products | SCI600 |
| LGTO | Legato Systems | MIDCAP |
| LNCR | Lincare Holdings | MIDCAP |
| LLTC | Linear Technology Corp | S&P500 |
| STAR | Lone Star Steakhouse/Saloon | MIDCAP |
| MAFB | MAF Bancorp | SCI600 |

APPENDIX D   NASDAQ STOCKS THAT ARE IN THE S&P INDEXES

| Symbol | Company | Index |
|---|---|---|
| MSCA | M.S. Carriers | SCI600 |
| MACR | Macromedia Inc | MIDCAP |
| MVSN | Macrovision Corp | MIDCAP |
| MXIM | Maxim Integrated Prod | S&P500 |
| MEAD | Meade Instruments | SCI600 |
| MEDI | MedImmune Inc | S&P500 |
| MBRS | MemberWorks Inc | SCI600 |
| MNTR | Mentor Corp | SCI600 |
| MENT | Mentor Graphics | MIDCAP |
| MRBK | Mercantile Bankshares | MIDCAP |
| MRCY | Mercury Computer Sys | SCI600 |
| MERQ | Mercury Interactive | S&P500 |
| MESA | Mesa Air Group | SCI600 |
| METHA | Methode Electronics 'A' | SCI600 |
| MIKL | Michael Foods | SCI600 |
| MIKE | Michaels Stores | SCI600 |
| MCRL | Micrel Inc | MIDCAP |
| MCHP | Microchip Technology | MIDCAP |
| MCRS | MICROS Systems | SCI600 |
| MSFT | Microsoft Corp | S&P500 |
| MLNM | Millennium Pharmaceuticals | MIDCAP |
| MLHR | Herman Miller | MIDCAP |
| MNMD | MiniMed Inc | MIDCAP |
| MIPSB | MIPS Technologies 'B' | MIDCAP |
| MODI | Modine Mfg | MIDCAP |
| MOLX | Molex Inc | S&P500 |
| NBTY | NBTY Inc | SCI600 |
| NCOG | NCO Group | MIDCAP |
| NAFC | Nash Finch Co | SCI600 |
| NCBC | Natl Commerce Bancorp | MIDCAP |
| NATI | Natl Instruments | SCI600 |
| NATR | Nature's Sunshine Prod | SCI600 |
| NAUT | Nautica Enterprises | SCI600 |

| Symbol | Company | Index |
|---|---|---|
| NTAP | Network Appliance | S&P500 |
| NETA | Networks Associates | MIDCAP |
| NYCB | New York Community Bancorp | SCI600 |
| NXTL | NEXTEL Communications 'A' | S&P500 |
| NDSN | Nordson Corp | MIDCAP |
| NTRS | Northern Trust | S&P500 |
| NOVL | Novell Inc | S&P500 |
| NVLS | Novellus Systems | S&P500 |
| NOVN | Noven Pharmaceuticals | SCI600 |
| NVDA | NVIDIA Corp | MIDCAP |
| NYFX | NYFIX Inc | SCI600 |
| OLOG | Offshore Logistics | SCI600 |
| OCAS | Ohio Casualty | MIDCAP |
| ASGN | On Assignment | SCI600 |
| ORCL | Oracle Corp | S&P500 |
| ORLY | O'Reilly Automotive | SCI600 |
| GOSHA | Oshkosh B'Gosh Cl 'A' | SCI600 |
| OTRKB | Oshkosh Truck | SCI600 |
| OSTE | Osteotech Inc | SCI600 |
| OXHP | Oxford Health Plans | MIDCAP |
| PCTI | PC-Tel Inc | SCI600 |
| PCOM | P-Com Inc | SCI600 |
| PACW | Pac-West Telecommun | SCI600 |
| PCAR | PACCAR Inc | S&P500 |
| PSUN | Pacific Sunwear of Calif | SCI600 |
| PHSY | PacifiCare Health Sys | MIDCAP |
| PALM | Palm Inc | S&P500 |
| PNRA | Panera Bread 'A' | SCI600 |
| PZZA | Papa John's Intl | MIDCAP |
| PMTC | Parametric Technology | S&P500 |
| PRXL | PAREXEL Intl | SCI600 |
| PDCO | Patterson Dental | SCI600 |
| PAYX | Paychex Inc | S&P500 |

## Appendix D  Nasdaq Stocks That Are in the S&P Indexes

| Symbol | Company | Index |
|---|---|---|
| PEGS | Pegasus Solutions | SCI600 |
| PENX | Penford Corp | SCI600 |
| PSFT | PeopleSoft Inc | S&P500 |
| PFGC | Performance Food Group | SCI600 |
| PSEM | Pericom Semiconductor | SCI600 |
| PRGO | Perrigo Co | MIDCAP |
| PPDI | Pharmaceutical Product Devlpmt | SCI600 |
| PTEC | Phoenix Technologies | SCI600 |
| PHTN | Photon Dynamics | SCI600 |
| PLAB | Photronics, Inc | SCI600 |
| PCLE | Pinnacle Systems | SCI600 |
| PIOS | Pioneer Std Electr | SCI600 |
| PLXS | Plexus Corp | MIDCAP |
| PLCM | Polycom Inc | MIDCAP |
| PLMD | PolyMedica Corp | SCI600 |
| PWER | Power-One | S&P500 |
| PWAV | Powerwave Technologies | MIDCAP |
| PHCC | Priority Healthcare 'B' | SCI600 |
| PRGX | Profit Recovery Grp Intl | SCI600 |
| PRGS | Progress Software | SCI600 |
| PSDI | Project Software & Dvlp | SCI600 |
| PDLI | Protein Design Labs | MIDCAP |
| PBKS | Provident Bankshares | SCI600 |
| PFGI | Provident Financial Group | MIDCAP |
| PRHC | Province Healthcare | SCI600 |
| PROX | Proxim Inc | SCI600 |
| QRSI | QRS Corp | SCI600 |
| QLGC | QLogic Corp | S&P500 |
| QCOM | QUALCOMM Inc | S&P500 |
| QTRN | Quintiles Transnational | S&P500 |
| QHGI | Quorum Health Group | MIDCAP |
| RFMD | RF Micro Devices | MIDCAP |
| RSAS | RSA Security | SCI600 |

| Symbol | Company | Index |
|---|---|---|
| RADS | Radiant Systems | SCI600 |
| RSYS | RadiSys Corp | SCI600 |
| RNBO | Rainbow Technologies | SCI600 |
| RATL | Rational Software | MIDCAP |
| RDRT | Read-Rite Corp | SCI600 |
| REGN | Regeneron Pharmaceuticals | SCI600 |
| RGIS | Regis Corp | SCI600 |
| RGBK | Regions Financial | S&P500 |
| RMDY | Remedy Corp | SCI600 |
| ROIL | Remington Oil & Gas | SCI600 |
| RCGI | Renal Care Group | SCI600 |
| RESP | Respironics Inc | SCI600 |
| RETK | Retek Inc | MIDCAP |
| RIGS | Riggs Natl Corp | SCI600 |
| ROAD | Roadway Express | SCI600 |
| ROBV | Robotic Vision Sys | SCI600 |
| RSLN | Roslyn Bancorp | MIDCAP |
| ROST | Ross Stores | MIDCAP |
| RYAN | Ryan's Family Stk Hse | SCI600 |
| SCMM | SCM Microsystems | SCI600 |
| POOL | SCP Pool | SCI600 |
| SEIC | SEI Investments | MIDCAP |
| SPSS | SPSS Inc | SCI600 |
| SAFC | SAFECO Corp | S&P500 |
| MARY | St. Mary Land Exploration | SCI600 |
| SNDK | SanDisk Corp | MIDCAP |
| SANM | Sanmina Corp | S&P500 |
| SAPE | Sapient Corp | S&P500 |
| SAWS | Sawtek Inc | MIDCAP |
| SCHL | Scholastic Corp | MIDCAP |
| SCHS | School Specialty | SCI600 |
| SHLM | Schulman (A.) | MIDCAP |
| SCTT | Scott Technologies | SCI600 |

# Appendix D  Nasdaq Stocks That Are in the S&P Indexes

| Symbol | Company | Index |
| --- | --- | --- |
| SIGI | Selective Insurance Gr | SCI600 |
| SMTC | Semtech Corp | MIDCAP |
| SEPR | Sepracor Inc | MIDCAP |
| SEBL | Siebel Systems | S&P500 |
| SIAL | Sigma-Aldrich | S&P500 |
| SIVB | Silicon Valley Bancshrs | MIDCAP |
| SVGI | Silicon Valley Group | SCI600 |
| SMPS | Simpson Indus | SCI600 |
| SKYW | SkyWest Inc | SCI600 |
| SONC | Sonic Corp | SCI600 |
| SBLU | SONICblue Inc | SCI600 |
| TSFG | South Financial Group | SCI600 |
| SOTR | SouthTrust Corp | S&P500 |
| SWBT | Southwest Bancorp | SCI600 |
| SVRN | Sovereign Bancorp | MIDCAP |
| SLMD | SpaceLabs Medical | SCI600 |
| SPAR | Spartan Motors | SCI600 |
| SFAM | SpeedFam-IPEC Inc | SCI600 |
| SMSC | Standard Microsystems | SCI600 |
| SPLS | Staples Inc | S&P500 |
| SBUX | Starbucks Corp | S&P500 |
| STLD | Steel Dynamics | SCI600 |
| STTX | Steel Technologies | SCI600 |
| SMRT | Stein Mart | SCI600 |
| SSSS | Stewart & Stevenson | MIDCAP |
| SDRC | Structural Dynamics Res | MIDCAP |
| SUNW | Sun Microsystems | S&P500 |
| SUPX | Supertex Inc | SCI600 |
| SUSQ | Susquehanna Bancshares | SCI600 |
| SWFT | Swift Transportation | MIDCAP |
| SYBS | Sybase Inc | MIDCAP |
| SYKE | Sykes Enterprises | MIDCAP |
| SLVN | Sylvan Learning Systems | MIDCAP |

| Symbol | Company | Index |
|---|---|---|
| SYMC | Symantec Corp | MIDCAP |
| SYMM | Symmetricom Inc | SCI600 |
| SCOR | Syncor Int'l | SCI600 |
| SNPS | Synopsys Inc | MIDCAP |
| SCTC | Systems & Computer Tech | SCI600 |
| TROW | T. Rowe Price Assoc | S&P500 |
| TBCC | TBC Corp | SCI600 |
| THQI | THQ Inc | SCI600 |
| TACO | Taco Cabana 'A' | SCI600 |
| TECD | Tech Data Corp | MIDCAP |
| TECH | Techne Corp | SCI600 |
| TECUA | Tecumseh Products CI 'A' | MIDCAP |
| TLCM | TelCom Semiconductor | SCI600 |
| TLAB | Tellabs, Inc | S&P500 |
| WATR | Tetra Tech | SCI600 |
| COMS | 3Com Corp | MIDCAP |
| TSAI | Transaction Sys Architects 'A' | MIDCAP |
| TXCC | TranSwitch Corp | MIDCAP |
| TRMB | Trimble Navigation Ltd | SCI600 |
| TQNT | TriQuint Semiconductor | MIDCAP |
| TRST | Trustco Bk Corp NY | SCI600 |
| USON | US Oncology | SCI600 |
| ULTE | Ultimate Electronics | SCI600 |
| UTEK | Ultratech Stepper | SCI600 |
| UBSI | United Bankshares | SCI600 |
| UNFI | United Natural Foods | SCI600 |
| USTR | United Stationers | SCI600 |
| UNIT | Unitrin Inc | MIDCAP |
| UFPI | Univl Forest Products | SCI600 |
| USFC | USFreightways Corp | SCI600 |
| VLNC | Valence Technology | SCI600 |
| VALM | Valmont Indus | SCI600 |
| VSEA | Varian Semiconductor Equip | SCI600 |

APPENDIX D  NASDAQ STOCKS THAT ARE IN THE S&P INDEXES

| Symbol | Company | Index |
|---|---|---|
| VRTS | VERITAS Software | S&P500 |
| VRTY | Verity Inc | SCI600 |
| VRTX | Vertex Pharmaceuticals | MIDCAP |
| VSAT | ViaSat Inc | SCI600 |
| VICR | Vicor Corp | SCI600 |
| VNWK | Visual Networks | SCI600 |
| VITL | Vital Signs | SCI600 |
| VTSS | Vitesse Semiconductor | S&P500 |
| WDFC | W D-40 Co | SCI600 |
| WFSL | Washington Federal | SCI600 |
| WBST | Webster Financial | MIDCAP |
| WERN | Werner Enterprises | SCI600 |
| WABC | Westamerica Bancorporation | MIDCAP |
| WTSLA | Wet Seal Cl 'A' | SCI600 |
| WTNY | Whitney Holding | SCI600 |
| WFMI | Whole Foods Market | SCI600 |
| WIND | Wind River Systems | MIDCAP |
| WCLX | Wisconsin Central Trans | MIDCAP |
| WCOM | WorldCom Inc | S&P500 |
| XRIT | X-Rite Inc | SCI600 |
| XLNX | Xilinx Inc | S&P500 |
| XIRC | Xircom Inc | SCI600 |
| YHOO | Yahoo Inc | S&P500 |
| YELL | Yellow Corp | SCI600 |
| ZBRA | Zebra Technologies 'A' | SCI600 |
| ZION | Zions Bancorp | MIDCAP |
| ZIXI | Zixit Corp | SCI600 |

APPENDIX E

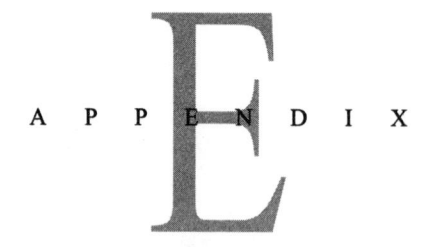

# HELPFUL INVESTOR WEB SITES

See *www.yahoo.com* for news on companies, charts, quotes, chat rooms, message boards, and more.

*www.amex.com*—offers information dealing with interest on Nasdaq and American Stock Exchange matters. Exchange shares are found here also.

*www.barchart.com*—gives technical analysis and charting of stocks and commodities; a good site for traders.

*www.bigcharts.com*—covers stocks, funds, and indexes; offers indicators, quotes, and more.

*www.bloomberg.com*—has research, quotes, company flashes, and other helpful information.

*www.dorseywright.com*—offers everything regarding technical analysis, including stock patterns and buy and sell indicators.

*www.edgar-online.com*—brings down information on government filings on virtually every firm. Quick and easy.

# Appendix E  Helpful Investor Web Sites

*www.exchangesec.com*—the author's Web page; included is information on exchange shares and published articles on the market.

*www.hoovers.com*—provides good thumbnail sketches of companies, including Web pages and financials.

*www.marketguide.com*—gives company sketches, charts, news, projections, and stock screening.

*www.mta-usa.org*—items dealing with technical analysis are covered; the page is sponsored by the Market Technician Association.

*www.ragingbull.com*—deals with many facets of the market, including research and market analysis.

*www.redherring.com*—this is the site linked to the magazine *Red Herring,* and it offers venture capital information.

*www.techstocks.com*—deals with tech stocks; anything that has to do with tech stocks can be found here.

*www.techtool.com*—provides data on indexes, futures, foreign exchanges, and many more markets and funds.

*www.thestreet.com*—features market news, analysis, company forecasting, and market discussions. A good site to browse.

*www.wired.com*—find anything that has to do with the digital age and technology is here; a cutting-edge site.

*www.zacks.com*—offers company reports for free; also earnings estimates, surprises, and alerts are offered.

APPENDIX F

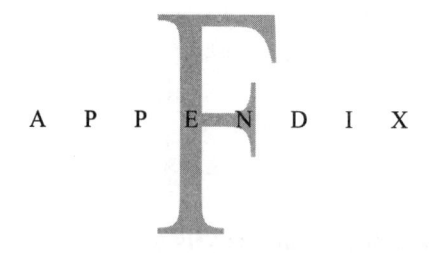

# NEW-ECONOMY TERMS

The following is a list of terms that might be helpful, not only for investing, but for everyday communication. The following sampling of e-speak can be used, among others, when shopping for a new computer or researching a B2B stock.

**Bandwidth:** This is the "brainpower" of transmitting data. The more bandwidth, the faster the rate of an electronic communications system.

**Bioinformatics:** The use of computer power to assist in uncovering the genetic code; this leads to developing new drugs in the biotech field.

**Bluetooth:** A computer chip that has been developed to be placed into minicomputers such as mobile phones.

**Broadband:** A communications network that works at high speeds; it responds to different kinds of signals, such as voice.

**DSL (Digital Subscriber Line):** Using this line transforms a phone line into a high-bandwidth network.

# Appendix F  New-Economy Terms

**ECN (Electronic Communications Network):** This system allows for certain and approved traders to trade into the Nasdaq markets.

**Financial Architecture:** A quantitative approach toward markets or world economies.

**GB:** Gigabytes of storage capacity on computer hard drives. A gigabyte is a billion bytes or characters.

**Genomics:** The study of genomes, which includes the mapping and sequencing of genes; this is spurring research in biotechnology.

**GM (Genetically Modified Goods):** This refers to foodstuffs, such as wheat, which has been genetically modified.

**HTML (Hypertext Markup Language):** A formatting language that is used in the creation of Web pages.

**HTTP (Hypertext Transfer Protocol):** Rules governing how Web pages are transferred over the Internet.

**JAVA:** A program language for software that can be run through the Internet; the program does not have to be loaded onto a hard drive.

**LEO (Low-Earth Orbiting Satellites):** It is planned that utilizing these satellites will take geography out of the communications equation.

**LINUX:** A computer operating system that is available to programmers at a low cost or for free.

**MPS:** A format that compresses sound, keeps quality, and sends it over the Internet in small files.

**Nano:** A billionth of something, such as a nanosecond or nanobreath. It can refer to anything small.

**Online:** On the Internet.

**PCS (Personal Communications Services):** A wireless phone service similar to cellular telephone service.

**Pharmacogenomics:** The science of tailoring drugs to a patient's genetic profile.

**PKI (Public Key Infrastructure):** An online version of a signature; this allows signing documents over the Internet.

**Server:** Hardware or software that serves users; it generally refers to the equipment used to go online.

**SMS (Short Message Service):** Short text messages that are sent through wireless phone services.

**SNP (Single Nucleotide Polymorphism):** The difference of a single unit in the genetic code.

**T-1:** A leased telephone line used for connecting to the Internet; it is much faster than a traditional modem.

**Transparency:** The trend toward open communication and commercial enterprise, which the Internet is spawning.

**URL (Uniform Resource Locator):** An Internet address. One is necessary to visit a Web site.

**USB (Universal Serial Bus):** Attached to a computer, it allows the user to plug in digital cameras, scanners, and other attachments.

# INDEX

A/D line, 28
ACMAT Corporation (ACMTA), 174
Actual spreads, 10
ADC Telecommunications, Inc. (ADCT), 85, 189
Adobe, Inc. (ADBE), 78
Advance/Decline line, 28
ADVANTA Corporation (ADVNA), 176
Advertising, 44, 70
Aerospace industry, 122
Affymetrix, Inc. (AFFX), 75
AFLAC, Inc. (AFL), 88
After-hours trading, 16
Akamai Technologies, Inc. (AKAM), 71
Allscripts (MDRX), 120
Altera Corporation (ALTR), 190
Amazon.com (AMZN), 70, 71, 190
America Online (AOL), 87
American International Group (AIG), 88
American Locker Group, Inc. (ALGI), 178
American National Insurance Company (ANAT), 173
American Pacific Corporation (APFC), 179
American Physicians Service Group, Inc. (AMPH), 183
Amgen, Inc. (AMGN), 75, 190
Amlicon, Inc. (AMPI), 168
Amtran, Inc. (AMTR), 171
Analogue transmission, 83
Andrew Corporation (ANDW), 79
Andrx Corporation (ADRX), 81

AOL–Time Warner merger, 44, 45, 87
Apple Computer, Inc. (AAPL), 79, 190
Application service providers (ASPs), 69
Applied Materials, Inc. (AMAT), 78, 191
Ariba, Inc. (ARBA), 121
Arkansas Best Corporation (ABFS), 170
Aspect Communications Corporation (ASPT), 85
ASPs, 69
At Home Corporation (ATHM), 191
AT&T Corporation (T), 88
Atlantic American Corporation (AAME), 172
Autodesk, Inc. (ADSK), 79
Automatic Data Processing (AUD), 88
Averaging down and up, 106, 107
Avery Dennison (AVY), 88

B2B commerce, 22, 24, 121, 122
Bales, William, 92
Baltek Corporation (BTEK), 178
Bancinsurance Corporation (BCIS), 174
Bando McGlocklin Capital Corporation (BMCC), 175
Banking industry, 176–178
Banner ads, 44, 70
Barber, Brad M., 149, 151–153
BCT International, Inc. (BCTI), 182
Bear spread, 131, 132
Behavioral finance, 146–164
    good trades, 164
    high-multiple/low-multiple stocks, 154–162

Behavioral finance (*Cont.*):
  market compulsion, 147, 148
  online trading, 149, 150, 152, 153
  overconfidence, 150, 151
  speculating to find safety, 151, 152
  what is it, 148, 149
Bell System breakup, 82
Benchmarking a stock, 17, 18
BF Enterprises, Inc. (BFEN), 175
Biogen, Inc. (BGEN), 75, 191
BioSource International, Inc. (BIOI), 75, 160
Biotech stocks, 72–76
Blue-sky laws, 25
BMCS Software (BMCS), 79
Bonds, 108, 109
Boyd Bros. Transportation, Inc. (BOYD), 171
Brand name, 48, 49
Broadband, 45, 46
BroadVision, Inc. (BVSN), 191
Broker/dealer, 7, 8
Buildout of Web sites, 46
Burn rate, 145
Business-to-business (B2B) commerce, 22, 24, 121, 122

Cadmus Communication Corp. (CDMS), 168
Callinan, Jim, 91
Capitalism, 110
Capsule reviews:
  biotech companies, 75, 76
  Internet companies, 71, 72
  listed stocks, 87, 88
  low-multiple stocks, 167–184
    (*See also* Low-multiple stocks)
  mutual funds, 90–102
  pharmaceuticals, 81, 82
  tech companies, 77–79
  telecom companies, 85, 86
  top 50 cap-weighted stocks, 189–198
Card dealers, 154
Cashflow, 144
Cashflow return on investment, 39
Casino Data Systems (CSDS), 169
CATS, 108

Cell Genesys, Inc. (CEGE), 76
Cellular Technical Services Company, Inc. (CTSC), 168
Century Bancorp, Inc. (CNBKA), 177
Cephalon, Inc. (CEPH), 76
Chattem, Inc. (CHTT), 178
Chesapeake, Inc. (CHK), 161, 162
Chiron Corporation (CHIR), 75, 191
CIENA Corporation (CIEN), 192
Cisco Systems, Inc. (CSCO), 45, 77, 192
Citizens Financial Corporation (CNFL), 174
Citrix Systems, Inc. (CTXS), 192
Click-through rate, 44
CMGI, Inc. (CMGI), 70, 72, 192
Comcast Corporation (CMCSK), 192
Comdisco (CDO), 86
Commerce One, Inc. (CMRC), 122
Commissions, 25
Company debt, 143, 145
Company information, 143–145
Company market caps, 86
Computer industry, 168, 169
Conexant Systems, Inc. (CNXT), 192
Conservative stocks, 108, 109
Consolidated Mercantile Corp. (CSLMF), 175
Corporate governance standards, 5
Corporate reports, 144, 145
Costco Wholesale Corporation (COST), 193
Coté, Douglas, 18
Covered calls, 135–138
Crescendo Pharmaceuticals Corporation (CNDO), 82
CSFB study, 47, 48

Day trading, 33, 34, 68, 116
Dealer spread, 10
Dealers, 3
Deb Shops, Inc. (DEBS), 183
Deep out-of-the-money puts, 134
Dell Computer Corporation (DELL), 21, 78, 193
Delphi International, Ltd. (DLTDF), 173
Dentist, 148
Digital Impact, Inc. (DIGI), 44

# Index

Digital transmission, 83
Discipline, 106
Doral Financial Corporation (DORL), 175
Dot-com companies (spin-offs), 27
Dura Pharmaceuticals, Inc. (DURA), 81

Earnings momentum, 31
eBay, Inc. (EBAY), 37, 193
ECNs, 7
Efficient market theory, 149
Egghead.com, 70
Electronic communications networks (ECNs), 7
Emons Transportation Group, Inc. (EMON), 170
Enhanced index fund, 20, 21
ePresence, Inc. (EPRE), 169
Escalade, Incorporated (ESCA), 179
ETFs, 142
Exchange shares, 124, 130, 132, 133
Exchange-traded funds (ETFs), 142
Excite@Home (ATHM), 71
Expiration date, 49

Federal Screw Works (FSCR), 179
Fidelity Bancorp, Inc. (FSBI), 176
Finance industry, 174–176
Financial Industries Corporation (FNIN), 172
First Citizens Bancshares, Inc. (FCNCA), 177
First Defiance Financial Corp. (FDEF), 178
Formula Systems (1985), Ltd. (FORTY), 169
Friction, 150
Funds (*see* Mutual funds)

GCPIP address, 69
Gemstar International Group, Inc. (GMST), 193
Genentech, Inc. (DNA), 87
General Electric (GE), 88
Genesee & Wyoming, Inc. (GNWR), 172
Genzyme Corporation (GENZ), 76
Gilead Sciences, Inc. (GILD), 75
Global Crossing, Ltd. (GBLX), 193

Global standard for mobile (GSM), 84
Go2Net, Inc. (GNET), 44
Good trades, 164
Goto.com (GOTO), 37
Great Lakes Aviation, Ltd. (GLUX), 171
GSM, 84
Guinness Flight Inter.com Index Fund (GFINX), 65

Hedging:
 different styles, 111
 gapping up and down, 133, 134
 options, 131, 132
 shorting QQQ, 134, 135
Helen of Troy Limited (HELE), 179
Herd mentality, 112, 113
HHH, 56, 57
High-multiple stocks, 154
HOLDRs, 56, 57, 130
Human Genome Sciences, Inc. (HGSI), 75, 120, 121
Human genomics projects, 81

i2 Technologies, Inc. (ITWO), 193
IDEC Pharmaceuticals Corporation (IDPH), 82
Immunex Corporation (IMNX), 193
Income tax (*see* Taxes)
Incyte Pharmaceuticals, Inc. (INCY), 76
Index funds, 20, 97
Indexes, 53–65
 Isdex Index, 62–65
 QQQ, 53–57, 185–188
 *Wired* Index, 58–62
Indications, 126, 127
Industrial sector, 178–184
InfoSpace.com, Inc. (INSP), 44, 72
Inside market, 125
Inside spread, 10
Insurance industry, 172–174
Insurance Management Solutions Group, Inc. (INMG), 173
Integral Vision, Inc. (INVI), 184
Intel Corporation (INTC), 21, 77, 194
Interactive TV, 40
Intercontinental Life Corporation (ILCO), 172

Interest-sensitive growth stocks, 109
Intermet Corporation (INMT), 184
International Data Corporation (IDC), 121
Internet:
 advertising, 44
 brokers and, 23
 component parts, 66–72
 investor Web sites, 214, 215
 new applications, 36
 perfect market, 37
 telecommunication link to, 83
 today's highway system, as, 24
Internet infrastructure, 45, 46
Internet jungle, 47, 48
Internet-related indexes, 58–65
Internet service providers (ISPs), 68, 69
Internet stocks/companies:
 broad analyst coverage, 71, 72
 core companies, 69–71
 haves vs. have-nots, 43
 infrastructure companies, 68, 69
 P/E ratio, 41, 42
 size, 47–49
 underlying value, 43–49
 valuation, 47–49
Intuit, Inc. (INTU), 194
Investment objectives, 105, 139, 140
Investor Web sites, 214, 215
Investors Title Company (ITIC), 173
Invitrogen Corporation (IVGN), 75
Ipswich Bancshares, Inc. (IPSW), 178
Isdex Index, 62–65
Isis Pharmaceuticals, Inc. (ISIP), 82
ISPs, 68, 69
Isramco, Inc. (ISRL), 183

Janus Venture Fund (JAVTX), 92–96
JB Oxford Holdings, Inc. (JBOH), 175
JDS Uniphase Corporation (JDSU), 45, 194
Jones Pharma, Inc. (JMED), 81

K-Tron International, Inc. (KTII), 180
Kahneman, Daniel, 152
Kawaja, Stephan, 47
Key stocks, 17–21
Kimball International, Inc. (KBALB), 179

King Pharmaceuticals (KG), 81
KLA-Tencor Corporation (KLAC), 79, 194
Knape & Vogt Manufacturing Company (KNAP), 180
Knowledge-based economy, 39
Korn-Ferry, International (KFY), 87
Kos Pharmaceuticals, Inc. (KOSP), 81

Level I, 125
Level II, 125–129
Level II quote source, 128
Level III, 126
Level 3 Communications, Inc. (LVLT), 194
Lindberg Corporation (LIND), 180
Linear Technology Corporation (LLTC), 194
Listed markets, 8–10
Listed stocks (broad analyst coverage), 88
Listing of stocks (*see* Capsule reviews)
LM Ericsson Telephone Company (ERICY), 195
Long-term investing, 115–124
 day trading, 116
 growth areas to watch, 120, 121
 investment timing/market events, 118
 market sentiment, 116, 117, 122, 123
 portfolio size, 123, 124
 sectors to watch, 117, 121, 122
 short-term pain, 118–120, 123
Low-multiple stocks, 155–162, 167–184
 attractiveness, 156–158
 author's winning trades, 158–162
 banking industry, 176–178
 computer industry, 168, 169
 finance industry, 174–176
 industrial sector, 178–184
 insurance industry, 172–174
 telecommunications industry, 169–172
Low-P/E stocks, 109
Lower-valued Nasdaq sectors, 140
LSI Logic Corporation (LSI), 87
Lucent Technologies, Inc. (LU), 87
Lycos, Inc. (LCOS), 72

Margins, 43, 44
Market cap, 12

# INDEX

Market cap-weighted index, 56
Market compulsion, 147, 148
Market makers, 3, 4, 6, 126
Market sentiment, 116, 117, 122, 123
Market volatility, 115, 116
Market volume, 86
Marsh Supermarkets, Inc. (MARSA), 182
Marten Transport, Ltd. (MRTN), 170
Mauboussin, Michael, 47
Maxim Integrated Products, Inc. (MXIM), 195
McClain Industries, Inc. (MCCL), 182
MCI WorldCom, Inc. (WCOM), 85, 195
McLeod USA (MCLD), 85
MedImmune, Inc. (MEDI), 195
Megamergers, 44, 45
Metro One Telecommunications, Inc. (MTON), 86
Metromedia Fiber Network, Inc. (MFNX), 195
Mexican stocks, 118
Microsoft Corporation (MSFT), 43, 77, 195
Millennium Pharmaceuticals, Inc. (MLNM), 81
Minntech Corporation (MNTX), 183
Mobile phones, 84
Modern Times Group MTGNY (ADR), 169
Momentum trading, 31, 110–112
Money transfer, 33
Moore, Gordon, 21
Moore's Law, 21, 77, 84
Motorola, Inc. (MOT), 87
Municipal zeros, 108, 109
Mutual funds, 89–102
   growth, 117
   Janus Venture Fund (JAVTX), 92–96
   RS Emerging Growth Fund (RSEGX), 90–92
   Rydex OTC Investor (RYOCX), 96–98
   taxes, 141
   Van Wagoner Emerging Growth (VWEGX), 98–102

Naked calls, 136
Napco Security Systems, Inc. (NSSC), 181
NASD, 5
Nasdaq:
   adding stocks for trading, 29
   corporate governance standards, 5
   democratization of market, 29
   growth, 11, 12, 25
   growth companies, 13–15
   industry breakdown, 13
   listing requirements, 15, 16
   low-valued sectors, 140
   negotiated market, as, 9
   non-U.S. companies, 14, 15
   nonstop world trading, 26
   two markets, 5
Nasdaq-100 Index, 14, 53–57, 185–188
Nasdaq Composite Index, 12, 13, 114
Nasdaq National Market, 5
Nasdaq SmallCap Market, 5
Nasdaq stocks in S&P indexes, 199–213
Nash-Finch Company (NAFC), 182
National Association of Securities Dealers (NASD), 5
National Mercantile Bancorp (MBLA), 176
National Security Group, Inc. (NSEC), 173
National Western Life Insurance Company (NWLIA), 173
NAV, 141
Negotiated market, 9
Net asset value (NAV), 141
Network Appliance, Inc. (NTAP), 195
Network Solutions, Inc. (NSOL), 69, 72
New-economy terms, 216–218
New market participants, 32, 33
New York Stock Exchange (see NYSE)
Nextel Communications, Inc. (NXTL), 79, 196
Non-Nasdaq stocks, 86–88
Non-U.S. companies, 14, 15
Novell, Inc. (NOVL), 196
Novellus Systems, Inc. (NVLS), 78
NPC International, Inc. (NPCI), 184
NTL Incorporated (NTLI), 85, 196
NYSE:
   A/D line, 28
   adding stocks for trading, 29

NYSE (*Cont.*):
    exclusivity, 28–30
    listing requirements, 8
    Rule 500, 28, 29

Odean, Terrance, 149, 151–153
Oil price increases, 34
Oil stock crash (1980s), 163
Old Dominion Freight Line, Inc. (ODFL), 170
Old economy stocks, 158
    (*See also* Low-multiple stocks)
"Online Investors: Do the Slow Die First?" (Odean/Barber), 149
Online trading, 147–153
Options, 49, 131, 134
    bear spread, 131, 132
    income, and, 135, 136
    out-of-the-money puts, 131, 134
    selling calls naked, 136
    selling covered calls/using margin, 137, 138
Oracle Corporation (ORCL), 78, 196
OTC bulletin board (OTCBB), 4, 5
Out-of-the-money put, 131, 134
Overconfidence, 150, 151
Overtrading, 150
Overweighting in a sector, 107

P&F Industries, Inc. (PFIN), 183
P.A.M. Transportation Services, Inc. (PTSI), 170
P/E multiples, 38–42, 67, 155, 156
P/GR ratio, 112
PACCAR, Inc. (PCAR), 181
PanAmSat Corporation (SPOT), 196
Parametric Technology Corporation (PMTC), 79
Park-Ohio Holdings Corporation (PKOH), 181
Paychex, Inc. (PAYX), 196
PEG ratio, 67
People's Bancshares, Inc. (PBKB), 177
PeopleSoft, Inc. (PSFT), 78
Perfect market, 37
Personal computer (PC), 77
Pharmaceuticals, 38, 79–82

Pink-sheet stocks, 4
Pioneer Railcorp. (PRRR), 172
PMC-Sierra, Inc. (PMCS), 197
Portfolio size, 123, 124
Price savaging, 40
Price-to-earnings growth ratio (PEG ratio), 67
Price to sales (P/S), 67
Price-weighted index, 56
Primus Telecommunications Group, Inc. (PRTL), 85
Prodigy Communications Corporation (PRGY), 72
Product cycle, 77
Professional Group, Inc. (PCIM), 174
Profit margins, 143
"Prospect Theory: An Analysis of Decision under Risk" (Kahneman/Tversky), 152
Put bear spread, 131, 132
PVF Capital Corp. (PVFC), 177

QQQ, 14, 53–57, 132–135, 185–188
Qualcomm, Incorporated (QCOM), 197
Quicken, 36
Quote, 10
Qwest, 84

Railworks Corporation (RWKS), 171
Ramsay Youth Services, Inc. (RYOU), 184
RCM Technologies, Inc. (RCMT), 182
Republic First Bancorp, Inc. (FRBK), 176
Research, 114, 158–160
Return on equity, 143
Risk profile, 106, 139, 140
Roanoke Electric Steel Corporation (RESC), 181
Royce Focus Trust, Inc. (FUND), 174
RS Emerging Growth Fund (RSEGX), 90–92
Rule 500, 28, 29
Rydex OTC Investor (RYOCX), 96–98

S&K Famous Brands, Inc. (SKFB), 183
S&P 500, 132
S-1 Corporation (SONE), 122

# Index

Santa Fe Financial Corporation (SFEF), 175
Schay, Alexander, 47
Scott Technologies, Inc. (SCTT), 179
Sector investing, 107
SEHK, 11, 12
Self-reliant investors, 33
Selling short, 110, 111, 134–138
Semantics, 30
Short interest, 155, 156
Short-term investing, 125–138
   charts, 129, 130
   covered calls, 135–138
   exchange shares, 130, 132, 133
   gapping up and down, 133, 134
   Level II trading, 125–129
   naked calls, 136
   options, 131, 132, 135–138
   shorting QQQ, 134, 135
Shorting, 110, 111, 137, 138
Shorting QQQ, 134, 135
Siebel Systems, Inc. (SEBL), 197
SmallCap Nasdaq, 5
Social Security, 151, 152
Sonesta International Hotels Corporation (SNSTA), 180
Source Capital Corporation (SOCC), 176
Specialist, 9
Speculating to find safety, 151, 152
Spending patterns, 42
Spinning off dot-com companies, 27
Spread, 10, 11
Star Telecommunications, Inc. (STRX), 85
Stealth short-term gains taxes, 141, 142
Steel Technologies, Inc. (STTX), 184
Sterling Financial Corporation (STSA), 177
Stock Exchange of Hong Kong (SEHK), 11, 12
Stock indexes (*see* Indexes)
Stock market, 110
Stocks (*see* Capsule reviews)
Stop orders, 68
Stop-loss order, 134
Strike price, 131
STV Group, Incorporated (STVI), 180

Sun Microsystems, Inc. (SUNW), 78, 197
Sycamore Networks, Inc. (SCMR), 46

Take-out value, 43
Talk.com, Inc. (TALK), 169
Taxes, 140–142
   ETFs, 142
   mutual funds, 141
   stealth short-term gains taxes, 141, 142
TBC Corporation (TBCC), 182
Tech companies of yesteryear, 40
Tech stocks, 76–79
   broad analyst coverage, 77–79
   impact of, 27
   Nasdaq, and, 15
   QQQ, and, 54
Telecom Deregulation Act, 82
Telecommunications industry, 82–86, 169–172
Tellabs, Inc. (TLAB), 78
10-K, 144
10-Q, 144
Terminology, 30, 216–218
3COM Corporation (COMS), 78
Time Warner–AOL merger, 44, 45, 87
Top 50 cap-weighted stocks, 189–198
Trading friction, 150
Trading on margin, 34
Trading volume, 86
Transaction cost, 18
Transport Corporation of America, Inc. (TCAM), 171
Trucking industry, 11
TSR, Inc. (TSRI), 168
Tversky, Amos, 152

Undervalued stocks, 158
Unwise spending, 42
USA Truck, Inc. (USAK), 170

Valuation tools, 67
Valuations, 48, 113, 114
   (*See also* P/E multiples)
Value investing, 156
   (*See also* Low-multiple stocks)
Van Wagoner Emerging Growth (VWEGX), 98–102

VERITAS Software Corporation (VRTS), 197
Village Super Market, Inc. (VLGEA), 181
Viropharma, Inc. (VPHM), 121
VoiceStream Wireless Corporation (VSTR), 197
Volatility, 68, 115, 116

WAP, 47
Waters Instruments, Inc. (WTRS), 181
Web sites, 214, 215

Wholesalers, 7
Wine industry, 11
*Wired* Index, 58–62
Wireless application protocol (WAP), 47
Wireless communications, 46, 47, 84

Xillinx (XLNX), 198

Yahoo! Inc. (YHOO), 42–44, 71, 198

Zero-coupon bond, 108, 109

# ABOUT THE AUTHOR

Max Isaacman is a registered investment advisor and the author of *How to Be an Index Investor*. A sought-after speaker and popular financial columnist for the *San Francisco Examiner* and other publications, he has appeared on *CBS MarketWatch* and *Bloomberg Television*. Isaacman has worked for a number of leading firms throughout his 35-year career: vice president with Lehman Brothers, investment officer with The Bank of California, account executive with Merrill Lynch, and partner and branch office manager with SG Cowen and Company. For more on Isaacman, visit his Web site: *www.xchangesec.com*.